Japan in Transformation, 1945–2010

2nd edition

Jeff Kingston

Longman
is an imprint of

PEARSON

Harlow, England • London • New York • Boston • San Francisco • Toronto
Sydney • Tokyo • Singapore • Hong Kong • Seoul • Taipei • New Delhi
Cape Town • Madrid • Mexico City • Amsterdam • Munich • Paris • Milan

PEARSON EDUCATION LIMITED

Edinburgh Gate
Harlow CM20 2JE
United Kingdom
Tel: +44 (0)1279 623623
Fax: +44 (0)1279 431059
Website: www.pearsoned.co.uk

First edition published in Great Britain in 2001
Second edition published in Great Britain in 2011

© Pearson Education Limited 2001, 2011

The right of Jeff Kingston to be identified as author of this work has been asserted by
him in accordance with the Copyright, Designs and Patents Act 1988.

Pearson Education is not responsible for the content of third party internet sites.

ISBN: 978-1-4082-3451-8

British Library Cataloguing in Publication Data
A CIP catalogue record for this book can be obtained from the British Library

Library of Congress Cataloging-in-Publication Data
Kingston, Jeff, 1957–
    Japan in transformation, 1945–2010 / Jeff Kingston. – 2nd ed.
        p. cm.
    Includes bibliographical references and index.
    ISBN 978-1-4082-3451-8 (pbk.)
    1. Japan–History–1945– I. Title.
    DS889.K546 2011
    952.04–dc22
                                2010028076

10 9 8 7 6 5 4 3 2 1
14 13 12 11 10

Set in 10/13.5pt Berkeley book by 35
Printed and bound in Malaysia (CTP-VVP)

Introduction to the Series

History is narrative constructed by historians from traces left by the past. Historical enquiry is often driven by contemporary issues and, in consequence, historical narratives are constantly reconsidered, reconstructed and reshaped. The fact that different historians have different perspectives on issues means that there is also often controversy and no universally agreed version of past events. *Seminar Studies in History* was designed to bridge the gap between current research and debate, and the broad, popular general surveys that often date rapidly.

The volumes in the series are written by historians who are not only familiar with the latest research and current debates concerning their topic, but who have themselves contributed to our understanding of the subject. The books are intended to provide the reader with a clear introduction to a major topic in history. They provide both a narrative of events and a critical analysis of contemporary interpretations. They include the kinds of tools generally omitted from specialist monographs: a chronology of events, a glossary of terms and brief biographies of 'who's who'. They also include bibliographical essays in order to guide students to the literature on various aspects of the subject. Students and teachers alike will find that the selection of documents will stimulate discussion and offer insight into the raw materials used by historians in their attempt to understand the past.

Clive Emsley and Gordon Martel
Series Editors

Contents

Author's Acknowledgements

I am especially indebted to my students and colleagues at Temple University Japan who provided the inspiration, support and time needed to revise, expand and update this edition, one that reflects significant changes in Japan and my perspectives over the past decade. I also want to thank my wife Machiko Osawa for her sustained patience and wise insights. Ochan, Rhubarb and Goro, a trio of dignified mutts, have been best friends during this project and also deserve credit for indulging and distracting me.

I am grateful for the comments, advice, inspiration, assistance and insights of the following people who are all duly absolved: Junko Akama, Mike and Marie Therese Barrett, Tom Boardman, Mary Brinton, Roger Buckley, David and Noriko Campbell, John Campbell, Kyle Cleveland, Gerald and Midori Curtis, Greg Davis, Phil Deans, George Deaux, Alexis Dudden, Bill Emmott, Philip Evanson, Philip Everson, Carol Gluck, Jon Gomon, Roger Goodman, Ivan Hall, Hiroshi Hamaya, Mariko Hashioka, Laura Hein, Andrew Horvat, TinTin Htun, Velisarios Kattoulas, Atsushi Maki, Gordon Martel, James Morley, Jack Mosher, Mariko Nagai, Akiko Okitsu, Robert Orr, Jr., David Pilling, Lawrence Repeta, Donald Richie, Richard Samuels, Murray and Jenny Sayle, Fritz Schmitz, Mark Selden, Emi Sumitomo, Stephen Talasnik, Kazuko Tanaka, Hisashi Urashima, Shinya Watanabe, Herschel Webb, Robert Whiting, Charles Worthen, Hyun Sook Yun and Dominic Ziegler.

At my publishers I would like to thank Josie O'Donoghue and Christina Wipf Perry especially for shepherding the manuscript through the process with patience, flexibility and efficiency.

Publisher's Acknowledgements

We are grateful to the following for permission to reproduce copyright material:

Text

Extract on page 43 from *The Emptiness of Japanese Affluence*, 1 ed., M. E. Sharpe (McCormack, G. 1996); Document.1 from *The Columbia Guide to Modern Japanese History*, 1 ed., Columbia University Press (Allenson, G. 1999) pp. 223–6. Copyright © 1999 Columbia University Press. Reprinted with permission of the publisher; Document.2 from *Embracing Defeat: Japan in the Wake of Defeat*, W. W. Norton & Co Ltd (Dower, J. 1999) pp. 211–12. Copyright 1999 by John W. Dower. Used by permission of W. W. Norton & Company, Inc. Reproduced by permission of Penguin Books Ltd.; Document.4 from *MITI and the Japanese Miracle: The Growth of Industrial Policy, 1925–1975*, 1 ed., Stanford University Press (Johnson, C. 1982) pp. 318–19; Document.5 from OECD Policy Brief, Economic Survey of Japan, 2006; Document.10 from Japanese Call '37 Massacre a War Myth, Stirring Storm, *New York Times*, 23/01/2000, 4 (French, H. W.); Document.12 adapted from Ministry of Finance Japan, www.mof.go.jp/english; Document.13 from *Japan: A Documentary History*, Vol. 2, M. E. Sharpe (Lu, D. J. 1997) pp. 520–4, From Japan: A Documentary History, ed. David J. Lu (Armonk, NY: M. E. Sharpe, 1997), pp. 520–524. Translation copyright © 1997 by David J. Lu. Reprinted with permission of M. E. Sharpe, Inc.; Document.14 from Panel: Secret Nuke Pact Hushed Up for Decades, http://backup.asahi.com/english/TKY201003090385.html, The Asahi Shimbun; Document.23 from OECD Economic Surveys: Japan, September 2009, p. 100; Document.26 from Asahi editorial 12/30/2010, http://www.asahi.com/english/; Document.28 from *The Straitjacket Society: An Insider's Irreverent View of Bureaucratic Japan*, 1 ed. Kodansha International Ltd (Miyamoto, M. 1994) pp. 20–4; Document.30 from Diet Officially

Declares Ainu Indigenous, *The Japan Times*, 07/06/2008 (Ito, M.); Document.31 from Japan in the Midst of a Third Great Transition, *The Japan Times*, 27/06/1999, p. 1 (Katz, R.); Document.34 from Law Schools Come Under Friendly Fire, *The Japan Times*, 28/01/2008 (Jones, C.)

In some instances we have been unable to trace the owners of copyright material, and we would appreciate any information that would enable us to do so.

Picture Credits

The publisher would like to thank the following for their kind permission to reproduce their photographs:

(Key: b-bottom; c-centre; l-left; r-right; t-top)

Aflo. Co. Ltd.: 1c, 2c, 4c; **Alamy Images**: 3c; **Gamma, Camera Press**: Sumiko Kurita 7c; **Press Association Images**: Press Association Images 5c, 6c, 9c; **Reuters**: 8c

All other images © Pearson Education

Every effort has been made to trace the copyright holders and we apologise in advance for any unintentional omissions. We would be pleased to insert the appropriate acknowledgement in any subsequent edition of this publication.

Chronology

1945   Japan surrenders, WWII ends and US Occupation of Japan begins

1946   Emperor Hirohito renounces divinity

Massive repatriation of Japanese scattered around Asia

International Military Tribunal for the Far East (IMFTE) is established to prosecute Class A war criminals

1947   Cold War begins and US occupation enters its second phase-the reverse course.

General strike banned by SCAP

New Constitution drafted by US and ratified by the Diet in 1946 comes into effect

Massive land reform commences

1948   IMFTE (Tokyo Tribunal) concludes proceedings

1949   Dodge Line of fiscal austerity targets hyperinflation

Communists prevail in China's civil war

1950   Korean war begins, providing stimulus to Japanese economy

US begins to pressure Japan to rearm

1951   San Francisco Peace Treaty signed, leading to end of occupation the following year

1952   US Occupation ends and San Francisco Peace Treaty comes into effect.

Yen is pegged at 360:$1.

1953   Japanese government begins to roll back and dilute Occupation reforms.

First outbreak of Minamata mercury poisoning.

Korean War ends.

1954   Self-Defense Forces (SDF) are established.

Reparations agreement is signed with Burma.

1955 Liberal Democratic Party (LDP) is formed.

Population is 89 million.

Japan joins the General Agreement on Trade and Tariffs (GATT). Era of high-speed growth begins.

1956 Japan joins the United Nations (UN).

Reparations agreement is signed with the Philippines.

1957 Nobusuke Kishi, once a suspected class 'A' war criminal, becomes prime minister.

1958 Popular protests against the revision of National Police Law.

Reparations agreement is signed with Indonesia.

1959 Democratic Socialist Party is established.

Reparations agreement is signed with South Vietnam.

1960 Massive street protests against the renewal of the Security Treaty with the United States forces the cancellation of President Eisenhower's visit and leads to the ousting of Prime Minister Kishi.

Hayato Ikeda becomes prime minister and announces the income doubling plan.

1961 Farmers constitute 29% of the workforce. Basic Agricultural Law is passed.

1962 First Japanese-made atomic reactor commences operating.

Active trade agenda is aimed at lowering tariffs on a mutual basis with key trading partners.

1963 Japan becomes a member of the Organization for Economic Co-operation and Development (OECD).

1964 Olympic Games are held in Tokyo.

Japan enters the International Monetary Fund (IMF).

These events symbolize Japan's rehabilitation and reintegration into the world community.

1965 Population reaches 98 million.

Japan–Korea Basic Treaty is signed, normalizing relations.

1966 Inaugural meeting of Asian Development Bank is held in Tokyo.

1967 Farmers constitute 19% of the workforce.

Basic Law on Environmental Pollution is passed, spurred by large anti-pollution citizens' movement.

1968 Japan's GNP ranks second in the world after the United States.

Beginning of trade disputes with the United States.

Consumers aspire to own the three Cs: car, air conditioner (cooler) and colour television. Japan becomes the world's leading producer of televisions.

Yasunari Kawabata receives the Nobel Prize in Literature.

1969   President Nixon pledges to return Okinawa to Japanese sovereignty in 1972.

Students and police clash on university campuses.

1970   Environmental Agency is established, responding to public anxiety over horrific pollution incidents.

Osaka hosts the first world fair held in Asia.

Yukio Mishima, noted author and flamboyant rightist, commits suicide.

1971   Emperor Hirohito tours Europe.

Nixon halts dollar/gold convertibility.

UN votes Peking in and Taipei out.

1972   Okinawa reverts to Japan.

United States normalizes ties with the People's Republic of China (PRC) without prior notification, stunning the Japanese government. Prime Minister Tanaka then normalizes relations with PRC amid strident criticism from within the LDP by party members loyal to Taiwan.

Winter Olympics held in Sapporo.

Yen rises to 272:$1.

Japanese terrorists strike in Tel Aviv.

1973   Organization of Petroleum Exporting Countries (OPEC) drives up oil prices and triggers global slowdown in economic growth. This sparks inflation and panic buying in Japan.

Anti-pollution legislation is incorporated into the Criminal Code.

1974   Prime Minister Tanaka is greeted by anti-Japanese riots in Bangkok and Jakarta.

Former Prime Minister Eisaku Sato wins the Nobel Peace Prize.

1975   Government sponsors recession cartels and unveils other programmes aimed at the 'sunset' industries, such as shipbuilding, steel, textiles, etc.

There is a record number of bankruptcies.

Population is 112 million.

1976   Lockheed scandal is exposed and former Prime Minister Tanaka is arrested on suspicion of taking bribes related to the purchase of planes by a domestic airline from Lockheed.

1977   Japanese average life expectancy rises to age 73, the highest in the world.

Prime Minister Fukuda initiates 'heart-to-heart' diplomacy with countries of the Association of Southeast Asian Nations (ASEAN), involving aid for industrialization and diplomacy aimed at promoting reconciliation with Indochina. Unemployment reaches 1.1 million.

1978   Government agrees to 'voluntary' restraints on car exports to the United States to cope with growing trade tensions. Yen rises to 185:$1.

1979   G-7 Summit is hosted by Tokyo. Textile trade dispute with the United States is resolved.

1980   Prime Minister Masayoshi Ohira dies in office on the eve of parliamentary elections, helping his LDP win a large victory from the sympathy vote.

1981   Government continues 'voluntary' restraints on car exports. Government establishes Commission on Administrative Reform aimed at privatizing state-owned enterprises.

1982   Korea and China protest about Japanese high school textbooks, complaining that atrocities and excesses are glossed over.

Six Japanese are arrested and another eleven are charged for industrial espionage in the United States (Silicon Valley).

1983   Former Prime Minister Tanaka is found guilty of corruption. Prime Minister Nakasone makes the first official postwar visit of a Japanese prime minister to South Korea.

1984   Trade agreements with the United States on citrus and meat imports.

The over-65 population reaches 10% of the total population.

President Chun Doo Hwan of Korea visits Japan and the Emperor expresses regret about the annexation of Korea in 1910.

1985   Agreement with the United States on steel trade.

Government telecommunication and railway monopolies are privatized.

520 Japanese die in a domestic plane crash.

The Plaza Accord paves the way for *endakka* (sharp appreciation of the yen).

1986   Takako Doi becomes the first woman to lead a political party, the Japan Socialist Party.

Retirement age is raised to 60 years from 55.

1987   Japan National Railway is broken up and privatized.

Rengo, an umbrella labour union federation, is formed.

The defence budget exceeds 1% of GNP.

The United States announces economic sanctions against Japan.

Diplomatic dispute erupts with South Korea over Japanese textbooks' treatment of their shared past.

1988   Trade surplus with the United States hits a record high. Japan's overseas foreign direct investment is the highest in world.

Trade negotiations with the United States focus on construction. With the completion of new tunnels and bridges, the four main islands are connected by rail services.

1989   Emperor Hirohito dies, ending the Showa Era (1926–89). The Heisei Emperor, Akihito, ascends the throne.

Recruit scandal engulfs political and bureaucratic elite.

Unpopular consumption tax (3%) is implemented.

1990   GDP grows by 7.5%, but economic bubble bursts with the implosion of prices for stocks and land. Prolonged recession begins.

1991   Gulf War debacle as Japan is embarrassed by the appearance of exercising chequebook diplomacy while letting other nations assume the risks and burdens.

1992   Severe economic downturn.

New political reform parties emerge in response to public disenchantment with corruption and the mismanagement of economic policies.

Government passes a controversial peace-keeping law that allows Japanese armed forces to participate in UN peace-keeping in Cambodia, their first return to the region since the Second World War and their first overseas duty since the re-establishment of the military in 1954.

1993   The LDP is defeated in the House of Representatives elections for first time since 1955 and a non-LDP coalition takes power.

Prime Minister Hosokawa makes a specific apology to South Korea about abuses during colonial rule.

Crown Prince Naruhito marries.

1994   Major electoral political reform legislation is enacted. Two non-LDP coalition governments fall and the LDP, in coalition with the Socialist Party, regains power.

Justice Minister resigns over denying the Nanking Massacre happened.

1995   Kobe earthquake, the nation's worst since the 1923 Tokyo earthquake, devastates the city.

Aum Shinrikyo unleashes nerve gas attacks on subways in Tokyo.

Spiritual leader Shoko Asahara and other members are arrested.

Yen reaches postwar peak at 79:$1.

Less than a majority of the Diet passes an equivocal apology resolution commemorating the fiftieth anniversary of the end of the Second World War.

Former comedians win gubernatorial elections in Tokyo and Osaka.

1996   Bureaucrats' reputation is sullied by a series of revelations about incompetence and corruption.

Japan and South Korea dispute sovereignty over a small island.

Rogue traders lose Daiwa Bank $1.1 billion and Sumitomo Corporation $2.4 billion.

Personal computer ownership per capita is less than half of the US figure.

1997   Prime Minister Hashimoto increases consumption tax and scales back stimulus spending, stifling nascent economic recovery. Financial 'Big Bang' initiated.

17 million Japanese travel overseas, doubling departures registered in 1988.

Japan leads the bailout of Southeast Asian economies felled by regional currency crisis.

Kyoto hosts global environmental summit.

1998   Banking crisis persists and the government mounts a $600 billion taxpayer-funded bailout despite the unpopularity of this program.

Long-Term Credit Bank bankruptcy leads to its temporary nationalization.

North Korea launches a missile over Japan's main island.

1999   Tokaimura nuclear accident shakes public confidence in nuclear power and government competence.

Japan–United States Defence Guidelines Bill is approved by the Diet.

Defence vice-minister resigns over remarks supporting nuclear rearmament.

Legislation conferring legal status on a national flag and national anthem is passed amid controversy over the conservative shift in national politics.

2000   Unemployment stands at 3 million. Prime Minister Obuchi dies in office.

His successor, Yoshiro Mori, stirs controversy with reference to Japan being a divine country centred on the Emperor.

2001   Prime Minister Junichiro Koizumi initiates sweeping economic reforms involving deregulation and privatization. After 9/11 he embraces a more robust security relationship with the United States, dispatching naval vessels for Afghansitan-related refuelling mission in the Indian Ocean. His first visit to Yasukuni Shrine provokes angry reactions within Japan and with China and South Korea.

First case of BSE (bovine spongiform encephalopathy) detected in Japanese cows.

Emperor Akihito acknowledges the Korean lineage of the Imperial family.

2002   Japan co-hosts the FIFA World Cup for soccer with South Korea.

Women account for 7.5% of Diet members.

Bilateral relations with China remain in deep freeze due to Prime Minister Koizumi's Yasukuni visits.

2003   Japanese whaling draws continuing international criticism while scientific report concludes that consumption of whale meat is dangerous because of high concentrations of methyl mercury.

Stringent testing for BSE introduced along with new food safety law.

2004   Prime Minister Koizumi dispatches troops to Iraq, the first time the SDF has been deployed overseas in a combat zone.

Ichiro Suzuki breaks US baseball record for hits in a season.

2005   Anti-Japanese protests intensify in China.

The LDP wins a landslide victory in the Lower House in support of postal privatization.

2006   Prime Minister Koizumi makes his sixth visit to the Yasukuni Shrine, worsening ties with China and South Korea.

Japan imposes sanctions on North Korea for ballistic missile and nuclear tests.

Prime Minister Shinzo Abe oversees passage of bill mandating Patriotic Education, turns spotlight on fate of Japanese abducted by North Korean agents while also engaging in fence-mending diplomacy with China and South Korea.

2007   Diet passes legislation on constitutional referendum and LDP pledges to revise the war-renouncing Article 9 of the Constitution.

Government reports losing tens of million pensions records.

LDP loses Upper House elections to the Democratic Party of Japan (DPJ). Prime Minister Abe is ousted from LDP leadership.

Series of domestic food scandals and false labelling lead to selection of 'deception' as kanji of the year.

2008   Media's frenzied coverage of tainted frozen gyoza from China reveals fragility of bilateral relations and trust.

Diet recognizes Ainu as indigenous people.

Prime Minister Yasuo Fukuda unable to break political impasse in divided Diet and abruptly resigns.

Government carries out fifteen executions of prisoners on death row.

2009   Non-profit organizations and unions establish a tent village in Tokyo for fired workers, focusing public discourse on social disparities and an inadequate safety net.

DPJ ousts LDP from Lower House in landslide victory, giving it control of both houses of the Diet, ending the LDP's long reign.

New York Yankees' Hideki Matsui is named Most Valuable Player of the baseball World Series.

2010 Japan Airlines, the flagship national carrier, files for bankruptcy.

Japan begins third decade of economic stagnation.

Asashoryu, a Mongolian grand champion (*yokozuna*) in sumo, is forced to resign after a series of incidents outside the ring.

Toyota's massive recall involving defective brakes and accelerators highlights problems in Japanese management and declining quality standards.

Prime Minister Yukio Hatoyama and DPJ Secretary General Ichiro Ozawa are engulfed in money scandals. Both are forced to resign, partly due to Hatoyama's mishandling of relations with the US and breaking promises to Okinawans over military base relocation. Naoto Kan becomes the fifth prime minister in four years, the first with background as a social activist.

Who's Who

This is a shortlist of some of the people who made history in Japan's post-Second World War era. It aims to provide brief biographical data for readers about key figures mentioned in the text or who were influential in their fields. By definition, such a list focuses on prominent figures, but this should not be construed as to exaggerate their importance or to minimize the importance of ordinary citizens. The lack of women on this list does not imply that they have not played a crucial part in contemporary Japan, but it is a telling absence that reflects prevailing realities. As is the custom in Japan, the family name comes first.

Abe Kobo (1924–93): One of the best-known Japanese literary figures in the postwar era, who focuses on themes of alienation and identity, often with Kafkaesque scenarios. *Women in the Dunes* (1962) is his most acclaimed novel.

Emperor Hirohito (1901–89): The Emperor reigned for 62 years, longer than any other Japanese Emperor, ascending to the throne in 1926. His era is known as *Showa* (Enlightened Peace). Debate over his role in and responsibility for the war persists. He died a popular figure, known to most Japanese for his keen interest in marine biology and for his self-effacing style. The outpouring of international condolences and the large attendance of foreign dignitaries at his funeral indicate how far Japan was rehabilitated and reintegrated into the community of nations following the Second World War.

Ienaga Saburo (1913–2002): Controversial historian who launched a series of lawsuits since 1965 that challenged the constitutionality and legality of the government's school textbook review system. He protested the government efforts to force him to modify his depiction of Japan's brutal wartime actions during the 1931–45 period and maintained that the textbook review system amounts to censorship, a view that the courts eventually vindicated.

Ikeda Hayato (1899–1965): Former elite bureaucrat in the Ministry of Finance turned politician, he served as prime minister as a member of the Liberal Democratic Party (LDP) from 1960 to 1964. He is remembered for his income doubling plan and his success in refocusing public attention towards economic growth rather than the controversial security ties with the United States that polarized politics in 1960. He sought to maximize Japan's growth potential by expanding public spending, lowering interest rates and cutting taxes.

Ishihara Shintaro (1932–): Three-term governor of Tokyo, novelist and outspoken conservative. He is famous for criticizing United States–Japan bilateral relations in his book, *The Japan That Can Say No* (1989), denying the Nanking Massacre happened and calling on the Self-Defense Forces (SDF) to be vigilant about foreigners in the event of an earthquake.

Kawabata Yasunari (1899–1972): The most famous and widely translated Japanese novelist, he was the first to win the Nobel Prize in Literature (1968). His novels are often termed quintessentially Japanese because of their conscious evocation of traditions, aesthetics and relationships that conjure up a world disappearing under the onslaught of modernization. Many of his masterpieces were written before the Second World War, but among his postwar novels *The Sound of the Mountain* and *Thousand Cranes* are notable. He committed suicide.

Koizumi Junichiro (1942–): Maverick LDP politician who served as prime minister 2001–06. He is known at home for privatization and deregulation initiatives, vowing to destroy the LDP, sharp cuts in public works spending and a charismatic presence. His dispatch of troops to Iraq, the first foreign deployment to a combat zone since the Second World War, was unpopular. He tried to normalize relations with North Korea but instead ignited controversy over the fate of Japanese nationals abducted by Pyongyang. His six visits to Yasukuni Shrine angered many at home and also damaged relations with China and South Korea. Some Japanese now blame his policies for widening disparities and shrinking the safety net.

Kurosawa Akira (1910–98): Japan's most internationally renowned film director and script writer won a lifetime achievement Oscar in 1990. His most famous movies are his samurai epics such as *Seven Samurai* (1954), *Throne of Blood* (1957), *Kagemusha* (1980) and *Ran* (1985), while film critics favour *Rashomon* (1950) and *Ikiru* (1952). *No Regrets for Our Youth* (1946) explores political oppression during wartime Japan while *The Bad Sleep Well* (1960) depicts collusion between big business, politicians and bureaucrats. Acclaimed overseas, he enjoyed less critical and commercial success at home.

Mishima Yukio (1925–70): Prolific author of fiction, drama and essays, his real name was Hiraoka Kimitake. His novels are some of the best post-Second World War literature in Japan, fusing Japanese traditions and Western influences. His homosexuality and ritual suicide, calling for a revival of militarism and the Emperor system, have overshadowed his literary accomplishments among a Japanese public that, in general, does not accord him the same stature he enjoys among international audiences.

Morita Akio (1921–99): Founder of Sony and Japan's most famous postwar businessman, he contributed to Japan's internationalization in many ways. Fluent in English, he served as an articulate and savvy spokesman for Japan. He made Sony the first Japanese company to list its shares on the New York Stock Exchange and its success translated into Japanese products becoming synonymous with high quality. He had a key role in trying to ease United States–Japan trade frictions.

Murakami Haruki (1949–): An important figure in postmodern literature, this popular novelist is known for works steeped in dreamlike fantasies incorporating magical elements, criticism of his generation's spiritual emptiness and the decline of human values in Japan. The *Wind-up Bird Chronicle* (1997) touches on war crimes while his non-fiction *Underground* (2000) explores the consequences of Aum Shinrikyo's sarin gas attack on the Tokyo subway.

Murayama Tomoiichi (1924–): Entering a historic coalition government with the LDP, this chairman of the Japan Socialist Party became the first Socialist prime minister (1994–96) in the post-Occupation era. His ascendancy to power also marked the decline of the Socialists because his tie-up with the LDP alienated the party faithful. During his administration, the twin tragedies of the Kobe earthquake and the Aum Shinrikyo subway gas attacks rocked Japan. On the fiftieth anniversary of the end of the Second World War, he apologized to the victims of Japanese aggression.

Nakasone Yasuhiro (1918–): Conservative LDP politician who served as prime minister (1982–87) under the aegis of Kakuei Tanaka, his most important supporter. His cabinets were referred to as the Tanakasone governments in recognition of his mentor's power behind the scenes. A personable statesman, he enjoyed close relations with President Ronald Reagan and Prime Minister Margaret Thatcher. A hawk on security issues, he played a significant part in expanding Japan's defence profile. He oversaw ambitious fiscal and administrative reforms and the privatization of government-operated monopolies in telecommunications and the railways.

Ozu Yasujiro (1903–63): Film director noted for his depictions of contemporary family life and the corrupting influence of postwar modernization.

Tokyo Story (1953) is his most famous film, evoking a timeless melancholy about what was fading quickly in a transforming Japan. The elegant simplicity of his films is evident in laconic dialogue and the everyday situations with which ordinary Japanese could identify.

Takeshita Noboru (1924–2000): Leading protégé of Kakuei Tanaka who served as prime minister (1987–89) and held numerous cabinet portfolios in a Diet career that began in 1958. Like his mentor, he resigned from office under the cloud of corruption. During the 1990s, his control of what had been the Tanaka faction, the largest in the LDP, gave him unrivalled political influence as the party's kingmaker.

Tanaka Kakuei (1918–93): Kingpin of the LDP during the 1970s and 1980s, he served as prime minister (1972–74) but resigned in the Lockheed corruption scandal, was arrested in 1976, sentenced to jail in 1983 and died while appealing his sentence in 1993, eight years after he suffered a debilitating stroke. He personified money politics in Japan and was the fixers' fixer. His protégés, Noboru Takeshita, Shin Kanemaru and Ichiro Ozawa, dominated national politics in the 1990s.

Yoshida Shigeru (1878–1967): The second most influential postwar politician after Kakuei Tanaka, he twice served as prime minister (1946–47, 1948–54). He grudgingly enacted liberal Occupation era reforms and resisted US pressures to rearm, arguing that Japan's precarious economic situation precluded reviving military forces.

Prime Ministers Since 1952

(Family name first as is custom in Japan)

Yoshida Shigeru (1948–54)
Hatoyama Ichiro (1954–56)
Ishibashi Tanzan (1957)
Kishi Nobusuke (1957–60)
Ikeda Hayato (1960–64)
Sato Eisaku (1964–72)
Tanaka Kakuei (1972–74)
Miki Takeo (1974–76)
Fukuda Takeo (1976–78)
Ohira Masayoshi (1978–80)
Suzuki Zenko (1980–82)
Nakasone Yasuhiro (1982–87)
Takeshita Noboru (1987–89)
Uno Sosuke (1989)
Kaifu Toshiki (1989–91)
Miyazawa Kiichi (1991–93)
Hosokawa Morihiro (1993–94)
Hata Tsutomu (1994)
Murayama Tomoiichi (1994–96)
Hashimoto Ryutaro (1996–98)
Obuchi Keizo (1998–2000)
Mori Yoshiro (2000)
Koizumi Junichiro (2001–06)
Abe Shinzo (2006–07)
Fukuda Yasuo (2007–08)
Aso Taro (2008–09)
Hatoyama Yukio (2009–10)
Kan Naoto (2010–)

Glossary

Amakudari: Descent from Heaven. A reference to the common practice of retired senior bureaucrats moving to well-paid, sinecure positions in firms that they dealt with in the course of their government duties. Often criticized as a source of collusive relations between bureaucrats and the firms they hope to join upon retiring.

Article 9: The article in the Japanese Constitution that bans maintaining of military forces and the resort to war to settle international disputes.

ASEAN Regional Forum (ARF): This forum focuses on security issues in the Asia-Pacific area.

Asia-Pacific Economic Cooperation (APEC): APEC was established in 1989 as an informal dialogue group in response to the dynamism, growth and accelerating integration among member economies. Over the years APEC has developed into the primary regional vehicle for promoting open trade and investment and regional economic cooperation. APEC's twenty-one members include Australia, Brunei, Canada, Chile, People's Republic of China, Hong Kong (China), Indonesia, Japan, Republic of Korea, Malaysia, Mexico, New Zealand, Papua New Guinea, Peru, the Philippines, Russia, Singapore, Chinese Taipei, Thailand, the United States and Vietnam. The combined economies account for approximately 45% of world trade. The Association of Southeast Asian Nations (ASEAN), the Pacific Economic Cooperation Council (PECC) and the South Pacific Forum (SPF) have observer status. The APEC Secretariat was established in 1993 and is located in Singapore.

Asian values: A thesis popularized in the early 1990s that the traditional family and community-centred values of Asian societies explain their superior economic performance and social cohesion. Critics point out the rich variety of traditions and values in Asia and suggest that the assertion of Asian values by governments was motivated by a reluctance to accommodate the political consequences of economic development. Proponents of Asian values often criticize advocates of democracy and human rights for embracing values alien to Asia, while these advocates counter by pointing out that Asian religions and philosophies are consistent with democracy and human rights. The economic crisis that hit Asian economies in 1997 was interpreted as discrediting some of the major assertions of proponents of Asian values.

Association of Southeast Asian Nations (ASEAN): A regional organization established in 1967, including ten nations of Southeast Asia – Brunei, Cambodia, Indonesia, Laos, Malaysia, Myanmar (Burma), the Philippines, Singapore, Thailand and Vietnam.

Aum Shinrikyo (Supreme Truth Sect): A new religious cult centred on the teachings of Shoko Asahara. It staged an attack on Tokyo subways in 1995 using sarin gas.

Big Bang: Financial deregulation programme initiated by the government of Prime Minister Ryutaro Hashimoto in 1996 often characterized by the media as the 'little whimper' for failing to meet expectations for sweeping liberalization.

Burakumin: 'Hamlet people' is the term used to refer to some 1 million Japanese today. Visually indistinguishable from other Japanese, 'hamlet people' suffer discrimination in jobs, housing, marriage, etc. because they are identified as being members of this class. During the Tokugawa era (1603–1868) this class became hereditary and was linked to 'polluting' activities such as slaughtering animals.

Diet: The parliament in Japan which is composed of an elected Upper and Lower House.

Doken kokka: Construction state. A reference to the vast spending on public works projects with implications of environmental devastation and political corruption.

Enjo kosai: Compensated dating, usually between junior or high school girls and middle-aged men, often involving sex.

Fukoku kyohei: Literally 'rich nation, strong military'. This was the rallying slogan of the Meiji era government (1868–1911).

Gaiatsu: Foreign pressure. This term refers to the pressures put on the Japanese government by other governments to modify various policies. In some cases, such pressures are actually welcomed as a way to overcome a domestic political impasse that is preventing necessary reforms desired by the government. However, inviting or staging *gaiatsu* as a means of overcoming political inertia has nurtured public resentments about what is portrayed in the mass media as high-handed tactics by other nations, notably the United States.

Gaijin: Foreigner(s).

GNPism: Focus on economic growth.

Gyosei shido: Administrative guidance. A reference to the informal manner in which bureaucrats wield their broad regulatory and discretionary powers to ensure corporate compliance with government goals and policies. Implicit is the threat to use those powers in a manner harmful to those who do not comply.

Habatsu: Factions within the Liberal Democratic Party (LDP).

Heisei: Era of 'achieving of peace' (1990–present) under the reign of Emperor Akihito.

Hinomaru: The national flag with a red circle in the middle of a white background.

Honne: Inner feelings, usually unexpressed to maintain decorum and because they may not conform to social norms and expectations.

Ie: The patriarchal family system that denied women independence and legal rights. The Constitution sought to correct this bias with decidedly mixed results. Many Japanese women today still bridle under what they see as the legacy of this male-oriented system in the home, in society and at work. Conservatives often blame current social problems on the decline of the *ie* system.

Ijime: Bullying is a pervasive practice in society that is aimed at imposing conformity within a specific group and ostracizing those who do not conform or meet expectations. High-profile suicides among students show this problem to be especially evident in schools.

Iron Triangle: The nexus of power involving big business, the bureaucracy and the LDP that is said to control Japan in the post-Second World War era.

Japan, Inc.: A term coined to characterize the close relationship between the government and big business in Japan and the government's focus on economic issues.

Joho kokkai: Information disclosure permitting citizens access to official documents, thus promoting transparency and accountability.

Jusen: Real estate lending subsidiaries of banks that incurred massive unrecoverable loans in the wake of the bubble, threatening the collapse of the Japanese financial system in the mid-1990s and forcing a government bailout despite strong public criticism.

Kakusa shakai: Unequal society, a term symbolizing growing discontent with neo-liberal economic reforms that have widened disparities in society and created 'winners' and 'losers'.

Kankan settai: Lavish wining and dining of central government bureaucrats by prefectural officials as part of lobbying efforts for budget allocations.

Kanson mimpi: Bureaucratic arrogance towards the public.

Kara shucho: Claiming expenses for fictional business trips became standard operating procedure for bureaucrats throughout the nation.

Keiretsu: Bank-centred, industrial conglomerates that dominate the Japanese economy, many of which have strong links with the pre-Second World War *zaibatsu*. The exclusionary business practices and conflicts of interest within the *keiretsu* have come under scrutiny as a source of trade friction.

Kimigayo: Your Majesty's Reign. The national anthem is controversial because of its apparent reference to the days when the Emperor was an absolute monarch, making it a divisive political issue between conservatives and progressives.

Koenkai: Local political support organizations that mobilize voters and funds for politicians.

Kokusaika: Internationalization. A concept that is frequently invoked with mixed results to broaden horizons among Japanese and inculcate a positive value for interaction with foreigners and their cultures.

Koseki: A family register, maintained over the generations with information about births, deaths, marriages, etc.

Kozo oshoku: Structural corruption in Japan's political system.

Liberal Democratic Party (LDP): Formed by a merger of the Liberal Party and the Democratic Party in 1955. It is the conservative political party that dominated Japanese politics until 2009.

Messhi hoko: Self-sacrifice.

Mura hachibu: Village ostracization imposed on those who do not meet social expectations in rural Japan.

Narikin: The nouveau riche who emerged during the bubble at the end of the 1980s who engaged in conspicuous and often garish consumption fuelled by wealth generated by spiralling land and stock prices.

Nenko: The seniority employment system that has determined wages and promotions, but is now no longer sacrosanct as firms shift towards a more merit-oriented system.

Nopan shabushabu: Notorious restaurants featuring beef, mirrored floors and waitresses wearing short skirts and no panties. The wining and dining of Ministry of Finance bureaucrats at such establishments by businessmen under their jurisdiction provoked public outrage in the late 1990s and became symbolic of the collusion between corporate Japan and the government, and the special favours involved.

Omoiyari yosan: Literally 'sympathy budget'. A reference to the money the Japanese government pays to base US troops in Japan. This amounted to over $3.5 billion in 2008.

On: A personal sense of social debt or obligation created in a relationship by a benevolent act.

Red Purge: The Supreme Commander of the Allied Powers (SCAP) and the conservative Japanese government initiated a crackdown beginning in 1947 on left-wing activists, radicals, unions, etc. as a consequence of the Cold War-inspired reverse course. The purge was a response to shared concerns that prevailing socio-economic conditions left Japan vulnerable to the appeal of communism, a prospect feared by the United States and their conservative allies in the Japanese government.

Reverse course: After 1947, the US Occupation in Japan became influenced by the Cold War between the United States and the USSR. Punitive policies were replaced by an emphasis on rebuilding Japan into a showcase for American-style democracy and capitalism. The progressive New Deal policies implemented between 1945 and 1947 were in many cases 'reversed' by more conservative policies. Prior to 1947, SCAP and the Japanese government sought to prosecute right-wing militarists, but after 1947 the government engaged in what is known as the Red Purge, cracking down on left-wing unions and activists.

Salarymen (sararimen): Salaried white-collar workers who are often the subject or object of both mockery and respect. Their image is of hard working, extremely loyal company employees who place greater emphasis on work than on the family and personal desires.

Supreme Commander of the Allied Powers (SCAP): General Douglas MacArthur served in this capacity during the US Occupation of Japan (1945–52) and as the de facto leader of what was nominally a multilateral institution that governed the country and sought to realize the goals of demilitarization, democratization and decentralization. SCAP also refers to the institutions of the Occupation and is often used interchangeably with general headquarters (GHQ).

Self-Defense Forces (SDF) (*Jietai* in Japanese): The military forces of Japan.

Seiken Kotai: Political change referring to the snowballing disaffection among voters with the LDP during the 2009 election campaign that gave the Democratic Party of Japan (DPJ) a landslide victory.

Shinjinrui: New species. A negative reference by older people used when criticizing the various presumed failings of the younger generation.

Showa: Era of 'enlightened peace' (1926–89) under the reign of Emperor Hirohito.

Soapland: An establishment where men pay for sexual services.

Tatemae: Public behaviour conforming to acceptable norms.

Yakuza: Organized crime syndicates in Japan.

Yoshida Doctrine: The policy of Prime Minister Shigeru Yoshida (1946–47, 1949–54), emphasizing the need of Japan to concentrate resources on economic recovery as a way to deflect US demands that it rearm in the early 1950s.

Zaibatsu: Family-owned industrial conglomerates that dominated the pre-Second World War Japanese economy. Initially, these were targeted for dissolution by SCAP because they were held to be responsible for supporting and abetting the 1931–45 military rampage through Asia. However, after the reverse course, SCAP did not aggressively proceed with the dissolution. During the Occupation the ownership and structure of these conglomerates was transformed and the pre-Second World War *zaibatsu* became the post-Second World War *keiretsu*.

Zainichi: Ethnic Koreans born in Japan who are descendants of Koreans brought to Japan during the colonial period (1910–45) as Japanese subjects, many as forced labourers. In many respects younger generations have been raised as Japanese, but face considerable discrimination and live in Japan as special permanent residents. In recent years there has been a rise in naturalization.

Zaitech: The speculative activities by corporations in land and stock unrelated to core business activities.

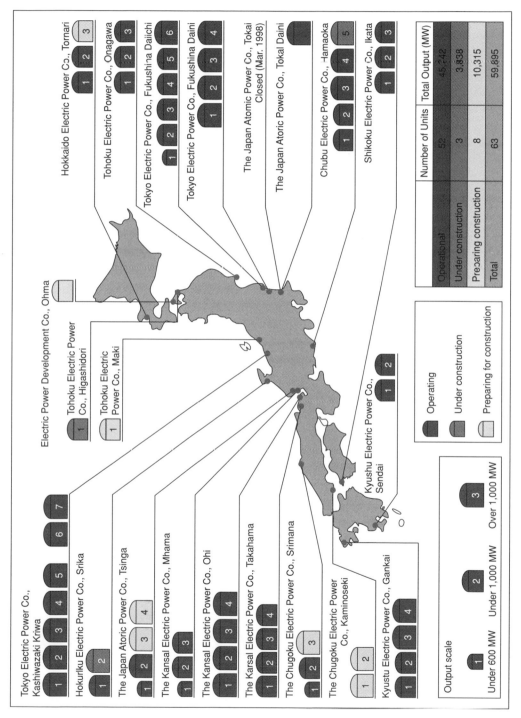

Map 1 Nuclear Power Plants in Japan

Tokyo Electric Power Co., Kashiwazaki Kriwa
1 2 3 4 5 6 7

Hokuriku Electric Power Co., Srika
1 2

The Japan Atoric Power Co., Tsinga
1 2 3 4

The Kansal Electric Power Co., Mhama
1 2 3

The Kansal Electric Power Co., Ohi
1 2 3 4

The Karsal Electric Power Co., Takahama
1 2 3 4

The Chugoku Electric Power Co., Srimana
1 2 3

The Chugoku Electric Power Co., Kaminoseki
1 2

Kyustu Electric Power Co., Gankai
1 2 3 4

Electric Power Development Co., Ohma
1

Tohoku Electric Power Co., Higashidori
1

Tohoku Electric Power Co., Maki
1

Hokkaido Electric Power Co., Tornari
1 2 3

Tohoku Electric Power Co., Onagawa
1 2 3

Tokyo Electric Power Co., Fukushina Daiichi
1 2 3 4 5 6

Tokyo Electric Power Co., Fukushina Daini
1 2 3 4

The Japan Atomic Power Co., Tokai
Closed (Mar. 1998)

The Japan Atoric Power Co., Tokal Daini
1

Chubu Electric Power Co., Hamaoka
1 2 3 4 5

Shikoku Electric Power Co., Ikata
1 2 3

Kyushu Electric Power Co., Sendai
1 2

Operating
Under construction
Preparing for construction

	Number of Units	Total Output (MW)
Operational	52	45,142
Under construction	3	3,838
Preparing construction	8	10,315
Total	63	59,895

Output scale

Under 600 MW	Under 1,000 MW	Over 1,000 MW
1	2	3

Part 1

BACKGROUND

1

Introduction

This book provides an overview of Japan from the end of the Second World War in 1945 until 2010, a period of tumultuous change that has transformed the way Japanese view their world and act in it. This ideological transformation has been driven and reinforced by institutional changes, rapid economic development, political ferment and the dynamic tension between prevailing norms and shifting realities. Transformation has been experienced, rejected, embraced and reviled, leaving no corner of the archipelago, nor any sector in society, unaffected. This does not mean that there are not substantial elements of continuity; change is incremental, cumulative and always includes considerable overlap between old and new. The past continues to resonate powerfully in the present and old verities linger, influencing attitudes, inclinations and patterns of behaviour. And yet, the past and these verities are fading as Japan enters the second decade of the twenty-first century.

The period covered in this book has been a time when Japan was reinventing itself and trying to overcome the horrors of war that it suffered, while doing little until the 1990s to acknowledge or address those it inflicted. For much of this period, **GNPism** was the driving force of Japan's revival, nurturing a collective identity based on economic growth. Overcoming the devastation of war provided a singularity of purpose and shared goal as Japan sought to regain a place in the community of nations. A people who had collectively peered into the abyss were haunted by wartime privations and sought security above all in rebuilding a robust economy and embracing peaceful means to attaining desired ends. The relatively egalitarian distribution of the fruits of growth strengthened social cohesion in a society where collective values remain resilient. Stable employment provided a sense of security, nurturing loyalty and a work-centred identity.

Students of history can learn much from examining and comparing the intended and unintended consequences of choices and policies made by people and how these are affected by the given institutional arrangements,

GNPism: Focus on economic growth.

and political and economic conditions. The complex interweave of historical forces and factors does not lend itself to easy assessments. Students of history need to train their senses to analyse not only what happened, but also to grasp what did not happen and why. Historians are acutely aware that History with a capital H does not exist. Those who chronicle and interpret the past are all guilty of selectivity in what they focus on and what they push to the side. Omissions, emphasis and interpretations reflect an inherent subjectivity. Students of history need to hone their critical thinking skills to engage and question the material presented, reading between the lines and in the margins, and considering the sources used, ignored and those that do not even exist. As Graham Swift points out, history 'is that impossible thing: the attempt to give an account, with incomplete knowledge, of actions themselves undertaken with incomplete knowledge' (in *Waterland* (London: Picador), 1992: 93–4 [originally published in 1983]). Good history will stimulate thinking and raise as many questions as it answers. Why is history important? Cicero perhaps best summed it up as an exercise in self-cultivation and maturity by suggesting, 'Not to know what happened before you were born is always to remain a child.' At a minimum, history is the basis for being an informed and judicious observer of the world in which one lives.

Understanding contemporary Japan is important because of its global reach and the closer and sustained interactions between countries and people that characterize the world in the twenty-first century. It is a leading nation economically, technologically, strategically and in terms of its cultural influence. Explaining Japan is especially difficult because, perhaps more than with other countries, knowledge of Japan too often relies on, and remains blinkered by, misleading stereotypes. There is a rich history of orientalism among foreign observers that has fostered a tendency to focus on what is exotic, mysterious, surreal or odd. Images of Japan around the world frequently remain fixed in time and it is not rare to see magazine cover stories on modern Japan depicting a *geisha*, a *sumo* wrestler, a *samurai* or a militaristic rising-sun flag. These are aspects of Japan that have become familiar by repetition, but they tend to obscure and ignore how much change has occurred in modern Japan. For example, one frequently hears how conformist the Japanese are, but one needs to question such trite characterizations. As elsewhere, many Japanese are conformist and in many cases groups dictate individual behaviour to a great extent. However, conformity is not unique to Japan and group or peer pressure remains powerful in most societies. One also needs to distinguish between public behaviour (**tatemae**) and private feelings and attitudes (**honne**). For many Japanese, *tatemae* is essentially common sense, doing what is proper and expected, but this should not be confused with *honne*. Here too, Japanese behaviour differs little from people elsewhere who also do what is expected of them in public. Paradoxically,

Tatemae: Public behaviour conforming to acceptable norms.

Honne: Inner feelings, usually unexpressed because they do not conform to social norms and expectations.

it is possible for Japanese to express their individuality and assert themselves within their conformity. If one plays by the rules sufficiently, one can get away with quite a bit of individualism and society will look the other way.

Similarly, the tired trope about Japanese being excessively deferential to authority is misleading and overlooks significant changes in public attitudes and the relationship between citizens and the state. People are challenging the government and holding it accountable by supporting greater transparency through information disclosure laws, with non-profit organizations often playing a critical role in this process. The media may remain more beholden than is becoming, but it is also feistier in shining a light on unscrupulous practices and keeping people better informed about how government and the private sector are betraying their good faith. Japan is also experiencing a gradual shift from the *rule by law* to the *rule of law*, meaning less discretionary regulatory powers for bureaucrats and a more even playing field where established rules apply more equitably in a more accessible judiciary. The pace and scope of judicial reforms in the twenty-first century have been remarkable. Moreover, subjects such as increasing income inequality, domestic violence, political and corporate cover-ups, divorce, cancer, abortion, shotgun marriages, discrimination, unseemly relationships between politicians, the financial sector and **yakuza**, systemic corruption, spreading drug use, suicides, mental depression and dissent within the Imperial family are no longer taboo. In reading Japan, it is essential for the observer to look beyond the first impression, to remain sceptical about what one thinks one knows about it and always recall that sweeping generalizations are a lazy way out in a diverse and changing nation of 126 million people. This is a dynamic society in flux with a tremendous capacity for change and a sense of urgency about the need to do so that is not always fully reflected in policy outcomes. The tension between what is needed and what is happening is frustrating for many Japanese, but also gives impetus to reform.

Yakuza: Organized crime syndicates in Japan.

The postwar era has been a time of miraculous economic success for Japan and has seen a vast improvement in the lives of most Japanese people. At the time Japan lay in smouldering ruins in 1945, who would have guessed the rapid recovery from war devastation, and the material progress that ensued? Japan at the outset of the twenty-first century certainly has its share of problems, but these do not diminish how much has been accomplished in improving living and working conditions in such a brief period of time. As in other industrialized societies, the costs of progress have been high, taking a toll on the environment, the family and the sense of community. The repercussions of progress have challenged society in many ways and in doing so have stoked a healthy introspection and a relatively high level of self-criticism. Over the years, the troubles of society have been the impetus for citizens to challenge the status quo. One of the great changes between Japan in the 1950s and 2010 is the attitude and sense of mission held by growing numbers of ordinary citizens who are now engaged in non-governmental, non-profit and other organizations trying to increase accountability, transparency and myriad other reforms. The radical activism of the 1950s and 1960s has given way to a more centrist, pragmatic and popular activism, working through the status quo rather than trying to topple it, meaning that the agenda of change is more incremental and less dramatic and polarizing.

Since the oil shocks of the 1970s, there has been more concern about the fragility of what has been achieved and concerns about balancing the need to change in order to survive and the desire to protect those who would be the losers from such changes. The political economy of Japan has thus featured a dynamic tension between the forces of transformation and the beneficiaries of the status quo. Japan's material success has transformed expectations, aspirations and inclinations that have gradually eroded this status quo of **Japan, Inc**. There is greater economic, political and cultural space for the expression of diversity and this is having an impact on the pace and nature of transformation. Intensified interaction with the outside world is also reinforcing this trend. Japan is thus becoming a far more complex society with more options and choices and less certainty. This is a troubled time as people try to cope with the destabilizing and disconcerting ramifications of change as it ripples through society. It is also a time when the currents of change are welcomed by those who have been stifled by a relatively rigid system. The system that has brought so much prosperity to so many since the Second World War is now blamed for many contemporary problems. Despite the emerging consensus favouring a wide-ranging set of reforms to address evident problems, there is much less certainty on how to navigate these uncharted waters. People know that reform is needed but remain ambivalent because of the potentially harmful consequences.

Suddenly in 2009, in the wake of the global economic crisis sparked by the sub-prime loan debacle in the United States, the Japanese came to understand the dangers of deregulation affecting the labour market. Deregulation of the employment system was one of many neo-liberal reforms adopted by the government aimed at reviving an economy that has remained mired in recession since the early 1990s. When Japan's export markets collapsed in 2008–09, however, many non-regular workers lost their jobs, highlighting growing risk and disparities in a society that has emphasized minimizing both. The growing ranks of the **working poor** in 2009 (some 10 million) and unemployed (about 3.5 million) drew heightened media scrutiny, holding up a mirror for society. This is not the Japan most Japanese wanted to see and they blamed the ruling **Liberal Democratic Party (LDP)** for recklessly raising risk while at the same time paring back the safety net needed to mitigate the consequences. Growing anxieties and anger, coupled with a sense that

Japan, Inc.: A term coined to characterize the close relationship between the government and big business in Japan and the government's focus on economic issues.

Working poor: refers to people who work, but earn less than ¥2 million a year, often with little job security. These people and their households often live in poverty and have few prospects for improvement. Their lack of resources discourages many from marrying and also disadvantages their children's life chances.

Liberal Democratic Party (LDP): Formed by a merger of the Liberal Party and the Democratic Party in 1955. It is the conservative political party that dominated Japanese politics until 2009.

the LDP had run out of ideas, handed a landslide election victory to the Democratic Party of Japan (DPJ) in 2009, ending a prolonged period of one party dominance, the so-called 1955 system. This represents a tectonic change in Japanese politics, one that is part of a much larger and ongoing transformation.

In focusing on transformation, this book emphasizes the consequences and outcomes of trends, choices, policies and actions in the initial decades of the period under study relevant to selected themes. Here we consider the influence of the US Occupation (Chapter 2), postwar political changes (Chapter 3), factors favouring the economic miracle (Chapter 4), Japan's relations with Asia (Chapter 5), security (Chapter 6), the changing situation of women (Chapter 7), the implications of a rapidly ageing society (Chapter 8), the 'Lost Decade' of the 1990s (Chapter 9) and the ongoing paradigm shift in the twenty-first century (Chapter 10) which help define what kind of society Japan is becoming.

The US Occupation of Japan, 1945–52

ENEMIES TO ALLIES

An important story of the Occupation concerns how the United States and Japan were able to transform their bitter rivalry into a close alliance. During the Pacific War (1941–45), the propaganda machines of both nations demonized and dehumanized the enemy to an extraordinary extent. Each side committed atrocities, but focused only on those committed by the other, and citizens on both sides of the Pacific were conditioned to expect the worst from each other (Dower, 1986b). The Japanese had seen sixty-six of their major cities reduced to ashes by extensive conventional bombing and firebombing. The twin tragedies of **Hiroshima and Nagasaki** in August 1945 brought an abrupt end to what has been called a 'war without mercy', but the decision to surrender was opposed by military leaders until the Emperor intervened and broke a deadlock among his senior advisors. Japan's nearly 15 year rampage through Asia (1931–45) was finished, in the end claiming the lives of an estimated 3 million Japanese and over 15 million Asians, mostly in China. Japanese brutality in war, including mistreatment of prisoners-of-war (POWs), generated sentiments favouring retribution and punishment. It was in this inhospitable climate that **US troops** landed in Japan and began the Occupation.

The Occupation was aimed at demilitarizing and democratizing Japan. The United States arranged for the repatriation of some 7 million Japanese scattered around the rubble of empire throughout the Asian theatre, an operation that taxed the logistical capacity of the US military and added to the already large problems of unemployment and food and housing shortages. Upon returning home, the troops were demobilized and sent home with a train ticket and a bag of rice.

The demilitarization of Japan meant the elimination of the armed forces. This was seen to be a guarantee that Japan would not again embark on military adventurism. In the first 2 years of the Occupation purges of thousands of

Hiroshima and Nakasaki: A nuclear weapon was dropped on Hiroshima 6 August 1945, killing a total of 140,000 people, including many Koreans working in the city's factories, while another nuclear weapon was dropped on Nagasaki on 9 August 1945 killing a total of 80,000 people. The victims were mostly civilians.

US troops: There is an apocryphal tale that merchants in the Ginza understood that there was a Christian holiday that involved someone called Santa Claus and hoped to welcome the US soldiers. This may explain why GIs reported seeing a giant Santa Claus hanging on the side of a store – nailed to a cross.

officers, bureaucrats and industrialists blamed for the war were a further hedge against a revanchist threat. Democratization was also seen to guarantee Japanese pacifism by eliminating the concentration of power exercised by a small elite prior to and during the war. By spreading power within the government and among all citizens, including voting rights for women, and by supporting a robust press and unions, the **Supreme Commander of the Allied Powers (SCAP)** was attempting to inoculate Japan from the scourge of militarism. US policies in the Occupation are best understood in the context of what people at that time thought had been the sources of Japan's descent into militarism.

WHAT WENT WRONG?

There are competing schools of thought when it comes to explaining what went wrong in Japan during the 1930s and 1940s. Some scholars trace the problem to the Meiji Constitution of 1889. They argue that the absence of checks and balances within the government and the concentration of broad discretionary powers in the office of the Emperor created a distorted system. The advisors of the Emperor could wield power and authority to promote their agenda without having to accommodate the usual debate and compromise characteristic of a parliamentary system of democracy. During the Meiji period (1869–1911), these powers were used to transform Japan and promote modernization under the slogan *fukoku kyohei*. Scholars generally credit the Meiji Emperor's advisors with using these powers wisely, but given the unchecked discretionary powers of government concentrated in the potential for the abuse of power, authoritarianism and radical swings in policy carried ominous potential. In this system, the military exercised de facto veto power because it could block the formation of a cabinet. The rising fortunes of the military based on victory over China in 1895 and Russia in 1905, combined with its decisive political power in forming cabinets, facilitated the emergence of military-dominated governments in the 1930s.

The Great Depression that started in 1929 in the United States and soon spread around the world became a catalyst for Japanese militarism. The sharp decline in world trade caused by protectionist policies had a devastating impact on the Japanese economy, hitting the majority of Japanese still living in the countryside especially hard. The dislocation in rural areas dependent on the export of silk involved the familiar cycle of indebtedness, loss of land, growing class disparities and often the selling of daughters into prostitution. Many of Japan's military officers were farm boys who were angered at the ineffectiveness of the government in bringing relief to their country brethren.

Supreme Commander of the Allied Powers (SCAP): General Douglas MacArthur served in this capacity during the US Occupation of Japan (1945–52) and as the de facto leader of what was nominally a multilateral institution that governed the country and sought to realize the goals of demilitarization, democratization and decentralization. SCAP also refers to the institutions of the Occupation and is often used interchangeably with general headquarters (GHQ).

Fukoku kyohei: Literally 'rich nation, strong military'. This was the rallying slogan of the Meiji era government (1868–1911).

In addition, they were disenchanted with the corruption and excess displayed by leading industrialists and politicians. In this turbulent time of socio-economic upheaval, the military engaged in assassinations and other acts of intimidation against government officials, often in the name of the Emperor. Young military officers were committed to purifying Japan by imposing greater discipline and rooting out the corrupt excesses of capitalism and party politics. Some scholars have described this as fascism, but there were significant differences from developments in Germany and Italy where Hitler and Mussolini rose to power.

The Taisho era (1912–25) was a heady period for Japanese internationalism and democracy. There is general agreement that Japan became disenchanted with the post-First World War international system because it seemed weighted to the advantage of the Western-directed status quo and relegated Japan to the second tier of nations. The roots of Japan's alienation from the international system are long and complex, but clearly Western racism and double standards played a key part. Japan's moderates had little to show for their efforts at working within the international system, prompting criticism of those efforts and highlighting the insults and sacrifices Japan was seen to be enduring at the hands of the Western powers. The Japanese invasion of Manchuria in 1931 and its withdrawal from the League of Nations in 1933 marked the end of Japan's support for the international system. The militarist hardliners succeeded in taking over Japan's foreign policy, steering it on a collision course with the United States as they escalated expansion into China, especially after 1937, and later targeted Southeast Asia's natural resources.

Reischauer (1977) has suggested that Taisho democracy was going well until it was hijacked by the militarists in the 1930s, arguing that Japan was on a trajectory of modernization until this process was derailed by a relatively small group of ultra-nationalists. Those sympathetic to his view argue that the Occupation was an effort to revive democracy and return Japan to the modernization trajectory. Others argue that Taisho democracy was an illusion doomed to fail because of the structural flaws of the Meiji Constitution that favoured the emergence of authoritarianism. Proponents of this view dismiss the 'hijacking' theory and point out that the shift towards ultra-nationalism and imperial expansionism enjoyed broad media and popular support (Young, 1998). Blaming a small group of fanatics, they argue, tends to exonerate the Japanese people from responsibility for Japan's expansionist rampage in Asia and overlooks sustained public enthusiasm for such policies. These differing interpretations of what went wrong are connected to the ongoing debate over continuity and transformation between contemporary and wartime Japan. Did SCAP remake wartime Japan or, in making common cause with the existing conservative elite, did it accommodate a certain degree of continuity unimaginable in occupied Germany?

DEMOCRATIZATION

MacArthur and his advisors exercised a decisive influence on the nature of democracy in Japan. Confident in victory and:

> With a minimum of rumination about the legality or propriety of such an undertaking, the Americans set about doing what no other occupation force had done before: remaking the political, social, cultural, and economic fabric of a defeated nation, and in the process changing the very way of thinking of its populace. (Dower, 1999: 78)

Perhaps the boldest initiative was in writing the new Constitution in 1946 and compelling its acceptance by the Japanese **Diet**. It is often considered the greatest achievement of the Occupation and has never been amended since being promulgated in 1947. The Emperor was forced to renounce his divinity and was stripped of all political power. Interestingly, his support for the new Constitution proved critical in winning its acceptance among the public. Sovereignty was vested in the people and the prewar aristocracy lost its privileged status. Women were given the right to vote and, indeed, the **rights of women** as specified in the Constitution are perhaps some of the most progressive in the world. In reality, these ideals have remained elusive. The new Constitution specifies and guarantees a total of thirty-one civil and human rights, clearly responding to the widespread trampling of these rights under the Meiji Constitution.

The new Constitution is based on the British system of parliamentary supremacy rather than the US system of checks and balances between the respective branches of government. The Constitution promotes the autonomy of the judiciary and a Supreme Court was established with the power of determining the constitutionality of laws, although it has demonstrated little enthusiasm for exercising this power of review.

Article 9 of the postwar Constitution aimed to impose pacifism by prohibiting Japan from maintaining armed forces and obliging it to renounce the right of belligerency [**Doc. 1, pp. 118–21**]. Although the language is clear and the intentions of the legislation were spelled out in Diet interpellations in 1946, since the early 1950s the **Self-Defense Force (SDF)** has existed and Japan now has one of the five largest defence budgets in the world. The constitutionality of the SDF has been challenged, and some lower court decisions have determined the SDF to be unconstitutional, but the higher courts have consistently affirmed the constitutionality of the SDF. **Article 9** remains prominent in political discourse, and some in the conservative elite seek to revise it to give Japan greater leeway on security, but it remains highly valued by the Japanese people (see Chapter 6).

Diet: The parliament in Japan which is composed of an elected Upper and Lower House.

Rights of women: Beate Sirota Gordon, author of *The Only Woman in the Room* (1998), recounts her role in driving around Tokyo in early 1946, gathering all the books she could find on various constitutions and participating in drafting the new Constitution. It was she who advocated inclusion of progressive provisions for women.

Article 9: The article in the Japanese Constitution that bans the development of military forces and the resort to war to settle international disputes.

Self-Defense Forces (SDF) (*Jietai* in Japanese): The military forces of Japan.

Article 9: More than 7,000 Article 9 Associations aimed at preserving this war renouncing article were established in Japan during the first decade of the twenty-first century in response to moves by conservative politicians to revise the Constitution.

Land reform: In 1946 land reform was aimed at reducing tenant farming (66% of all farms in 1943) where farmers paid nearly half of their production to landlords as rent, ensuring their poverty. Nearly 6 million farming households were affected by this land redistribution policy, rural incomes became more equal and the political power of the rural elite was reduced significantly.

Zaibatsu: Family-owned industrial conglomerates that dominated the pre-Second World War Japanese economy. Initially, these were targeted for dissolution by SCAP because they were held to be responsible for supporting and abetting the 1931–45 military rampage through Asia. However, after the reverse course, SCAP did not aggressively proceed with the dissolution. During the Occupation the ownership and structure of these conglomerates was transformed and the pre-Second World War *zaibatsu* became the post-Second World War *keiretsu*.

Reverse course: After 1947, the US Occupation in Japan became influenced by the Cold War between the United States and the USSR. Punitive policies were replaced by an emphasis on re-building Japan into a showcase for American-style democracy and capitalism. The progressive New Deal policies

SCAP also promoted democracy by promoting **land reform** in the countryside and a strong union movement that drew inspiration from the New Deal reforms under the Roosevelt administration during the 1930s. Union organizers, including many communists, were released from jail and legislation protected their right to establish unions. Given the miserable working and living conditions prevailing in the aftermath of war, the unions grew rapidly and became more radical in their demands and tactics.

The first year and a half of the Occupation were a time of grand efforts at socio-economic reforms based on the belief that Japan needed to be transformed in order to exorcise the demons of militarism. Right-wing militarists and alleged sympathizers were purged from government service and banned from elected office. The powers of the police were restricted and centralized police authority was abolished. The educational curriculum was modified to eliminate vestiges of imperial ideology and central government control over the educational system, including textbooks, was curtailed. The conservative landlord class was targeted, with land reform aimed at redistributing land in favour of the farmers actually working the land. The rural gentry was considered a bastion of conservatism and thus a barrier to democratization; removing their economic clout based on large landholdings and onerous sharecropping arrangements was a strategy to eliminate their political influence.

MacArthur also promoted trust-busting tactics at the expense of the *zaibatsu*, the large family-owned industrial conglomerates that dominated the Japanese economy since the Meiji era. Reports about large-scale pilfering by the *zaibatsu* of public stockpiles of commodities soon after the surrender on 15 August 1945, at a time when ordinary citizens were at the brink of starvation, made a deep impression on MacArthur. In addition, analysts suggested that the *zaibatsu* were willing accomplices of the military and had benefited handsomely from military expansionism and war-related procurements. Breaking up the *zaibatsu* was intended to promote the general policy of deconcentrating power as that was seen to be the major flaw of the Japanese prewar system. The excessive concentration of power, political and economic, was thought to have made it easier for a small coterie of conspirators to hijack national policy for their own ends.

THE REVERSE COURSE

The record of SCAP on democracy after 1947 left much to be desired. The 'reverse course' is the term often used to describe the sudden conservative shift in US Occupation policies. The reverse course was one of the early consequences of the Cold War that was just heating up between the United States and the Soviet Union (Schaller, 1985). The first salvo involved MacArthur banning a general strike that had been called for 1 February 1947. This signalled the beginning of the end for the radical union movement as SCAP withdrew its support and encouraged the union-busting tactics of Japanese corporations and the government. For the United States, in waging a worldwide ideological war, it became imperative that Japan be a success story. Japan was to be a showcase for the superiority of capitalism and the American way. Thus, retribution and any reforms that might impede Japan's rapid recovery were shoved to the side in favour of policies that would transform Japan into a 'bulwark of the free world' in Asia. This was also a time when political attitudes in the United States were rapidly shifting to the right, meaning that the New Deal-inspired reforms that had initially animated the Occupation were out of favour. It is perhaps difficult to appreciate the sudden swing in the mood of the country, but the rise of McCarthyism and communist witch-hunts were soon central features of the US political landscape and were echoed in US policy in Japan.

The anti-*zaibatsu* efforts of SCAP had little impact because there were very few trustbusters and there were many opponents skilful at defending big business. The Japanese conservative political elite repeatedly warned SCAP that over-zealous reforms of the *zaibatsu* would play into the hands of the communists by slowing economic recovery and prolonging the suffering of workers. Since the Occupation was indirect, meaning that SCAP depended on the Japanese government for implementing its ambitious agenda of reforms, there was ample opportunity for modifying, vitiating and slowing the pace and extent of reform initiatives. They quickly teamed up with American allies, including some large, influential US corporations that had prewar ties with the *zaibatsu* and were concerned that their business interests might be adversely affected (Davis, 1997). They lobbied Congress for support, lamenting the 'left-wing' inclinations of SCAP and pointing out that busting the *zaibatsu* would prolong Japan's dependence on US aid. Thus, the domestic political fallout of the Cold War in the United States resonated strongly in Japan. In the end, the *zaibatsu* emerged from the Occupation in modified form as **keiretsu**.

THE LEGACIES OF OCCUPATION

From 1947, the Japanese government, supported by MacArthur, unleashed a **Red Purge** that targeted those Japanese considered to have left-wing views. Union activists, members of the Communist Party, writers and government

implemented between 1945 and 1947 were in many cases 'reversed' by more conservative policies. Prior to 1947, SCAP and the Japanese government sought to prosecute right-wing militarists, but after 1947 the government engaged in what is known as the Red Purge, cracking down on left-wing unions and activists.

Keiretsu: Bank-centered, industrial conglomerates that dominate the Japanese economy, many of which have strong links with the pre-Second World War *zaibatsu*. The exclusionary business practices and conflicts of interest within the *keiretsu* have come under scrutiny as a source of trade friction.

Red Purge: The Supreme Commander of the Allied Powers (SCAP) and the conservative Japanese government initiated a crackdown beginning in 1947 on left-wing activists, radicals, unions, etc. as a consequence of the Cold War-inspired reverse course. The purge was a response to shared concerns that prevailing socio-economic conditions left Japan vulnerable to the appeal of communism, a prospect feared by the United States and their conservative allies in the Japanese government.

officials were affected by the purge. The success of the Japanese Communist Party in the 1949 elections, continued labour unrest and Mao's victory in China had hardened attitudes. The resulting infringement on the civil liberties enshrined in the new Constitution certainly reflects badly on the US commitment to the democratic ideals it was espousing and reminded not a few Japanese of the authoritarian system they had endured before and during the war. Certainly, most Japanese enjoyed far more freedoms and rights during the Occupation than they had under the militarists, but the use of tactics inimical to democracy cast a cloud over US ethics and leadership. Censorship was also prevalent as SCAP prohibited negative commentary about the Occupation and discussion of the atomic bombings. Ironically, SCAP was nurturing democracy, but was itself unaccountable and could and did act arbitrarily, claiming rights and privileges that put its staff above the law. Moreover, the virtual imposition of a democratic constitution on Japan with little consultation or compromise generates doubts about the nature of Japanese democracy that still resonate today. In order to achieve its goals, SCAP sometimes acted outside the law or issued what amounted to edicts in an effort to create a semblance of legality. The suppression of democracy for the sake of democracy proved to be a lasting paradox of the American interregnum [**Doc. 2, pp. 121–2**].

Dower, the pre-eminent historian of the Occupation, argues that SCAP's neo-colonial revolution from above pursued an agenda of both progressive change and reaffirmation of authoritarian structures of government. It is a telling commentary that, 'while the victors preached democracy they ruled by fiat; while they espoused equality, they themselves constituted an inviolate privileged caste . . . almost every interaction between victor and vanquished was infused with intimations of white supremacism' (Dower, 1999: 211). While the embrace of peace and democracy may well be the talismanic legacy of the Occupation, the gutting of the union movement, suppression of dissent and ruthless repression during the Cold War-inspired Red Purge left a bitter taste and did little to promote tolerance. The American embrace of the conservative elite in Japan during the reverse course enabled the latter to slow the pace of reform, shift it to the right and consolidate their power; once the Occupation ended in 1952 they were in a position to roll back or dilute many of the reforms.

The US decision not to prosecute **Emperor Hirohito** for war crimes was controversial at the time because allies and leftists in Japan believed that he should be held accountable for the excesses committed by the Imperial armed forces (see Bix, 2000, for a detailed account of the Showa Emperor's active involvement in waging war and US complicity in covering up that role in the postwar era.) The Americans believed that Hirohito was more valuable to their reform efforts alive and free than dead or incarcerated and feared

Emperor Hirohito (1901–89): The Emperor reigned for 62 years, longer than any other Japanese Emperor, ascending to the throne in 1926. His era is known as *Showa* (Enlightened Peace). Debate over his role in and responsibility for the war persists. He died a popular figure, known to most Japanese for his keen interest in marine biology and for his self-effacing style. The outpouring of international condolences and the large attendance of foreign dignitaries at his funeral indicate how far Japan was rehabilitated and reintegrated into the community of nations following the Second World War.

creating a martyr for the nationalist movement. The **Showa** Emperor went on to become a symbol of Japan's postwar renaissance and is widely credited with having a constructive role during and after the Occupation. However, the decision to absolve the Emperor of war responsibility cast a cloud over the Tokyo War Crimes Tribunal and muddied the entire issue of war responsibility. If the national leader could not be held accountable, others felt justified in also evading their responsibility for what happened because they believed they were acting in his name. Significantly, this meant that few Japanese really confronted their support of Japan's military violence in Asia or the prevailing racist attitudes that had condoned it.

Japanese remain ambivalent about the Occupation. The policies of democratization and demilitarization were generally welcomed at the time and there is still a substantial residue of goodwill emanating from the positive legacies of that period. Older Japanese, who lived during the Occupation, recall the hardships and some unfortunate incidents, but express generally positive impressions about the process of transformation unleashed by SCAP. Certainly, the Occupation went better than anyone had anticipated at the time of surrender and the United States is credited with enacting policies that laid the foundations for subsequent economic success. In addition, many Japanese were relieved that the American Occupation bore no resemblance to Japan's often brutal occupation of China and Southeast Asia during the war. It is perhaps one of the most benign and non-punitive occupations in history, an extraordinary achievement given the level of hostility between the United States and Japan at the end of the war.

The Occupation helps explain why American influence is so strong in Japan and why Washington looms so large in the mindset of Tokyo. The patterns of relationships developed during the Occupation have lingered too long; many Japanese slide easily between resentment and respect for the US because they chafe at the **unequal relationship**. More than a half-century after the Occupation ended, established patterns persist, reflecting Japan's sense of vulnerability and dependence on the US security umbrella.

Conservative Japanese frequently trace many of Japan's current social problems back to the Occupation. They see women's legal equality, the end of the patriarchal *ie* system, educational reforms, the new Emperor system, demilitarization, etc., and a vague process of Americanization as harmful to the Japanese social fabric. In 1998, one of the largest grossing films produced in Japan was *Pride*, an epic hagiography focusing on Prime Minister Hideki Tojo and the injustice of the Tokyo War Crimes Tribunal that led to his death by hanging. Certainly, the proceedings of the tribunal ignored due process and they serve as compelling evidence of American hypocrisy and victor's justice. However, the popular press and right-wing writers tend to portray the Japanese defendants solely as victims of biased legal proceedings without

Showa: Era of 'enlightened peace' (1926–89) under the reign of Emperor Hirohito.

Unequal relationship: Prime Minister Yukio Hatoyama (2009–2010) has called for ending the unequal relationship and developing a partnership among equals, meeting stiff resistance from Washington where the patterns of the past persist and an ally that does what it is told is valued.

Ie: The patriarchal family system that denied women independence and legal rights. The Constitution' sought to correct this bias with decidedly mixed results. Many Japanese women today still bridle under what they see as the legacy of this male-oriented system in the home, in society and at work. Conservatives often blame current social problems on the decline of the *ie* system.

Yushukan Museum: Renovated in 2002, the Yushukan Museum is Ground Zero for an unrepentant perspective on Japan's shared history with Asia and a shifting of blame for Japanese aggression. The exhibits emphasize Japan's sacrifices and victimization while glossing over the considerable devastation and violence inflicted by Japanese colonialism in Korea (1910–45) and Japan's Imperial Armed Forces waging aggression 1931–45, especially in China but also through much of the rest of Asia. Under US pressure, suggestions that President Franklin Roosevelt deliberately provoked the Japanese attack on Pearl Harbor were modified in 2006.

examining the question of whether they in fact committed war crimes. Such an exonerating narrative is also evident at the **Yushukan Museum** adjacent to Yasukuni Shrine in central Tokyo. In Japan as elsewhere, the present is usually projected on to the past in ways that tend to do history little service.

HIROSHIMA AND PEARL HARBOR

Japanese and Americans look back at their shared past through the images conjured up by two catastrophic events. Pearl Harbor, what President Roosevelt described as the 'Day of Infamy', remains shorthand for sneaky treachery. Many Americans draw on this memory of victimization to vindicate their subsequent actions and to ascribe undesirable national characteristics to the Japanese. By focusing on the single event, there is no need to examine the preceding process of polarization between the two nations that began back in 1853 when Commodore Perry arrived in Japan with an armada and demanded that Japan sign an unfavourable treaty of commerce with the United States. In the subsequent nine decades, there are numerous instances of American actions that were provocative, insensitive and punitive. So it is folly to examine Pearl Harbor in a historical vacuum and to portray the United States as an innocent victim of an inexplicable outrage. There is plenty of blame to share on both sides of the Pacific for the outbreak of war.

Similarly, when Japanese recall the war it is usually to dwell on their own suffering. Hiroshima has become a symbol of Japan's victimization during the war. Unfortunately, the lure of victimization has tended to obscure Japan's role as victimizer and how its own suffering was a consequence of its actions and choices. The victims of Japanese aggression remain faint images in the official history. There are signs of improvement, however. The haunting exhibits displayed at the Peace Memorial Museum in Hiroshima previously presented the atomic bombing in a historical vacuum, with no attempt to explain how or why this tragedy occurred. Now, dioramas provide enough historical background for visitors to realize that this was not some inexplicable natural disaster. These efforts to provide a more balanced view have not been replicated throughout Japan. Balance has also been elusive in the United States. For example, in 1995 the Smithsonian Museum in Washington, DC, facing Congressional pressure, staged a watered-down exhibit about the atomic bombings that averted eyes from the horrific consequences (Hein and Selden, 1997). Clearly, the past still lingers in the present and both nations have only begun to come to terms with the tragedies of their shared past. The consequences remain an undercurrent in dealing with current frictions that flare up between these allies.

Part 2

ANALYSIS

3

Postwar Politics

Postwar politics in Japan has been marked by the dominance of the conservative Liberal Democratic Party (LDP) since its formation in 1955. Scholars often refer to the **Iron Triangle** or Japan, Inc. to describe the nexus of political power involving big business, the LDP and the bureaucracy. The bureaucracy has had a dominant role in forging the policy agenda, but politicians and business lobbies also exercise influence. The strong state model suggested by Johnson (1982) has been challenged in recent years by those who argue that the bureaucracy is not as autonomous and dominant as his analysis suggests (see Richardson, 1997, for a comprehensive critique). Calder (1991) suggests a model of 'crisis and compensation' in which the LDP initiates policy reforms in response to critical political pressures. Ramsayer and Rosenbluth (1993) argue that the LDP has a key mediating role in balancing competing interests and agendas in a manner that allows the LDP to influence outcomes. Broadbent (1998) argues that big business has been dominant in the postwar period, supporting various measures and compromises that sustained LDP hegemony and thus its own interests. Journalists such as von Wolferen (1989) argue that Japan is characterized by an absence of a locus of power, explaining why there is so much evident policy drift on the important issues. Fallows (1994), another influential journalist, portrays a powerful and predatory neo-mercantilist state using trade as a weapon of domination.

The 1955 system of prolonged one-party rule was dismantled with the LDP's ouster from power following a landslide victory by the **Democratic Party of Japan (DPJ)** in 2009. This historic victory drew on voter impatience with the LDP's failure to mitigate the consequences of economic crisis and the widening of social disparities.

The Lost Decade of the 1990s led to economic hardship and a loss of confidence in the powers that be. The '**Lehman Shock**', as the global economic crisis that began in 2008 is called, forced Japanese to face the new realities of a riskier employment model supported by the LDP and embraced by

Iron Triangle: The nexus of power involving big business, the bureaucracy and the LDP that is said to control Japan in the post-Second World War era.

Democratic Party of Japan (DPJ): A rainbow coalition spanning the political spectrum, led by former LDP renegades such as Ichiro Ozawa Yukio Hatoyama and Seiji Maehara, but, with strong roots in progressive organizations such as the former Socialist Party and Rengo, the umbrella union confederation. The appeal of this broad constituency helps in elections, but sometimes makes it difficult to forge a common policy agenda. The DPJ was established in 1998 by the merger of four parties opposed to the LDP. In 2003, the DPJ merged with Ichiro Ozawa's centre-right Liberal Party.

Lehman Shock: The collapse of Lehman Brothers investment bank in September 2008 revealed the vulnerability and interdependence of the global financial system. Initially, because Japan's banks had strong balance sheets and relatively little exposure to the sub-prime mortgage market, there was a misplaced confidence that the crisis would not affect Japan. However, as the crisis deepened and depressed global economic activity, Japan's exports plummeted and the economy went into a deep recession. People were unhappy that they were paying for the consequences of reckless Wall Street 'cowboys', and grew disenchanted with the ruling LDP's handling of the crisis. The Lehman Shock had a key role in the LDP's ouster from power in 2009.

Seiken kotai: Political change referring to the snowballing disaffection among voters with the LDP during the 2009 election campaign that gave the Democratic Party of Japan (DPJ) a landslide victory.

employers. Deregulation and liberalization of the labour market led to one-third of workers being hired on a contingent basis on fixed contracts, one of the factors that contributed to widening income disparities and a surge in the number of working poor. Suddenly, employers responded to the global downturn by firing or not renewing the contracts of nearly one-quarter of a million workers from the end of 2008 to the summer of 2009. As unemployment spiked to 5.7% in July, just as election campaigning was in full swing, so too did voter discontent. Angry voters decided political change (*seiken kotai*) was their best hope, repudiating the political forces that have dominated since the US Occupation. To understand the significance of this tectonic shift it is crucial to understand the historical context.

THE 1955 SYSTEM

The 1955 system is a reference to the conservative, one-party-dominated political system that prevailed in Japan from 1955 to 2009 with a brief hiatus spanning 1993–94. It was a system that mainstreamed conservative politics and emphasized economic growth, political stability and close ties with the United States. In 1955, two conservative parties merged to create the LDP. This party held power continuously until 1993 before being ousted by a fragile coalition of small political parties even though the LDP had won more seats in the Diet than any other party. However, in 1994 the LDP returned to power in a coalition government and remained the dominant party in Japan until it was routed in the 2009 elections.

The tension between conservative and progressive political forces was a defining feature of the 1955 system, at least until the LDP and Japan Socialist Party (JSP) joined in a coalition government in 1994. Progressive in this context meant the Marxist and radical left political culture that prevailed in trade unions and among the members of the JSP, the largest opposition party in Japan until its demise in the mid-1990s. The LDP was formed in 1955 in response to the growing unity and strength of the left and efforts to pursue a 'class struggle' supported by Sohyo (General Council of Trade Unions of Japan), Japan's largest union organization at that time.

The 1950s and 1960s witnessed bitter ideological battles in Japan between supporters of the progressive agenda, led by the JSP, and conservative forces rallying around the LDP. The LDP stood for overturning many of the reforms initiated during the American Occupation, including an overhaul of the Constitution. These efforts to roll back the American reforms were opposed by progressive forces, provoking widespread strikes, media protests and periodic Socialist boycotts of the Diet. The LDP also stood for close security ties with the United States and supported the presence of US bases in Japan, a stance opposed by the JSP.

The LDP enjoyed the support of business, the bureaucracy and the middle classes, represented by farmers, merchants, owners and employees of family businesses and small manufacturing concerns. The JSP represented the modern sectors of rapidly developing Japan, attracting unionized blue-collar workers, some white-collar 'salarymen' and generally younger, well-educated urban voters. Back in the late 1950s the LDP seemed to represent a shrinking, backward-looking, tradition-bound constituency, but one of the interesting stories of Japanese politics is how the LDP managed to reinvent itself to become a party with broader appeal. The JSP, meanwhile, pursued policies and promoted an ideological agenda that became increasingly irrelevant and unattractive to Japanese voters. Perhaps the highpoint of the Socialists' political fortunes came with the mass street protests in 1960, opposing the renewal of the **United States–Japan Security Treaty** [**Doc. 3, pp. 122–5**]. The JSP evolved from this position of relative strength as the vanguard of progressive forces and the leading opposition party to a pale shadow of itself in the mid-1990s. The end of the Cold War, the tempering of ideological disputes within Japan and the JSP's controversial decision to form a coalition government with the rival LDP in 1994 proved its undoing.

The LDP is composed of factions (*habatsu*) that date back to its establishment in 1955. The factions are made up of varying numbers of LDP Diet politicians and coordinate distribution of party and ministerial posts. Factions are not necessarily issue-focused – most serve to enhance the status and bargaining power of individual members and to provide access to pork-barrel projects and campaign funds. The LDP leadership needs to balance factional rivalries, ensuring that the fruits of power are fairly distributed. Managing intra-factional politics is ultimately the job of the party president who has also served concurrently as prime minister through much of the past half century.

In the wake of the divisive political battles over the revision of the United States–Japan Security Treaty and the ousting of Prime Minister Nobusuke Kishi (1957–60), Prime Minister **Hayato Ikeda** (1960–64) redirected party efforts and public attention to his ambitious economic agenda, the income doubling plan (see Packard, 1966, for a full discussion of this dramatic period). This was a programme aimed at fostering rapid economic growth based on regional infrastructural development initiatives, low interest rates and reconciliation with unions. Aside from the enormous success of this programme, the flow of central government money to regional and local authorities created a distribution apparatus that enabled the LDP to expand its power base via lucrative pork-barrel projects. LDP members maintained

Salarymen (sararimen): Salaried white-collar workers who are often the subject or object of both mockery and respect. Their image is of hard working, extremely loyal company employees who place greater emphasis on work than on the family and personal desires.

United States–Japan Security Treaty: Revised and extended in 1960 by Prime Minister Nobusuke Kishi (1957–60), a suspected Class-A war criminal who had had a decisive role in establishing the LDP in 1955. Kishi secured Diet approval of the security treaty despite an opposition boycott, but was forced to resign as a result of the ensuing popular backlash. Demonstrators were worried that the alliance would put Japan in danger and violated the Peace Constitution. Many were also appalled that a discredited wartime leader had become prime minister only a dozen years after the disastrous and devastating war had ended.

Habatsu: Factions within the Liberal Democratic Party (LDP).

Ikeda Hayato (1899–1965): Former elite bureaucrat in the Ministry of Finance turned politician, he served as prime minister representing the Liberal Democratic Party (LDP) from 1960 to 1964. He is remembered for his income doubling plan and his success in refocusing public attention towards economic growth rather than the controversial security ties with the United States that polarized politics in 1960. He sought to maximize Japan's growth potential by expanding public spending, lowering interest rates and cutting taxes.

Koenkai: Local political support organizations that mobilize voters and funds for politicians.

Doken kokka: Construction state. A reference to the vast spending on public works projects with implications of environmental devastation and political corruption.

Koizumi Junichiro (1942–): Maverick LDP politician who served as prime minister 2001–06. He is known at home for privatization and deregulation initiatives, vowing to destroy the LDP, sharp cuts in public works spending and a charismatic presence. His dispatch of troops to Iraq, the first foreign deployment to a combat zone since the Second World War, was unpopular. He tried to normalize relations with North Korea but instead ignited controversy over the fate of Japanese nationals abducted by Pyongyang. His six visits to Yasukuni Shrine angered many at home and also damaged relations with China and South Korea. Some Japanese now blame his policies for widening disparities and shrinking the safety net.

koenkai (personal support associations in their electoral district) which became mechanisms for channelling massive public works projects and industrialization initiatives to the local electoral districts and thus a key factor in election campaigns. Politicians who delivered were returned, making them dependent on their factions and the access to project funding they provided (Curtis, 1999).

This focus on pork-barrel politics has had a devastating impact on the environment, as wetlands were paved over, rivers and coastlines were concreted, unnecessary dams were built, and roads and bridges to nowhere became much criticized staples of the *doken kokka*. As a result, Japan has the highest per capita cement consumption in the world. With 12% of the nation's workforce engaged in construction by the late 1990s, and given the opportunities for raising campaign funds due to the nature of *dango* (rigged bidding system for public works contracts), it is not surprising that the government lavishes a considerable budget on this sector. Corruption is rife and collusion involves politicians, bureaucrats, businessmen and the underworld. The LDP long-championed the *doken kokka*, boosting public works spending to counter economic recessions, but in doing so it contributed to massive increases in Japan's public debt by issuing deficit bonds to cover the massive outlays.

This huge burden of public works-related debt means that future generations will be paying off mega-projects that they neither need nor desire. Lamenting these construction boondoggles, McCormack asserts that, 'too much of the energy, capital, and skills of the Japanese people had been appropriated, mobilized, and focused in a political economy of exploitation, both human and material, that ultimately exhausted both the people and their environment' (McCormack, 1996: 64). But for the LDP, these pork-barrel infrastructure projects solidified the foundations of its power.

This was the distorted logic of the *doken kokka*, one that has been abandoned in the twenty-first century. Prime Minister **Junichiro Koizumi** (2001–06) cut public works spending by 30% during his tenure and subsequent governments have not returned to the former spendthrift ways, but there is still much fat to trim in the yet massive public works budget. The DPJ is targeting such wasteful spending, announcing cancellation and postponement of numerous projects as its shifts budget priorities from public works to expanded social services.

During the 1970s, the LDP reinvented itself as a catch-all party that was able to offer a vision that had broad appeal beyond its traditional constituencies. Ideology was downplayed in an effort to retain power. The LDP has been identified as the party of the status quo and has had enormous success in convincing voters from all social strata that their interests were tied to that status quo. Rather than emphasizing the policy issues that divided society, the LDP promoted economic recovery and growth, reviving the Meiji era quest for catching up with and overtaking the West. This emphasis on economic progress has been dubbed 'GNPism', an ideology that brought disparate groups together to work for the common goal of development. Overtaking the West had an appeal for a nation still reeling psychologically from the catastrophic defeat in war and humbling Occupation.

The LDP was also adept at embracing opposition issues and integrating them into its own party platform. As the public and media grew concerned about the environmental costs of rapid industrialization, the LDP took the lead in promoting policies aimed at addressing these concerns. The 1970 'Pollution Diet' passed tough environmental laws in response to growing public outrage over the environmental and health costs of economic growth. According to Broadbent (1998), big business and the LDP cooperated on cleaning up water and air pollution as a means of shoring up the legitimacy of the LDP and preserving a political order favourable to business interests. As popular agitation spread, the costs of not responding outweighed the costs of neutralizing critics by taking meaningful action. He describes the rapid improvement in air and water in the 1970s, far surpassing similar efforts in other industrialized nations, as the second 'miracle' in postwar Japan and gives much of the credit to the 'voluntary' compliance of the business community. Yet, it was not until 2009 that the government finalized a 'comprehensive' settlement to compensate the victims of mercury poisoning by Chisso Corporation in the fishing port of **Minamata**, more than 50 years after it was first discovered.

By selectively embracing progressive issues, the LDP significantly broadened its base of support beyond its traditional strongholds and in so doing undermined the opposition. By virtue of its political monopoly in Japan's one-party democracy, the LDP could claim to be the only party with solutions, making small adjustments and demonstrating enough flexibility on the issues to preserve the essential interests and features of the status quo.

THE DECLINE OF RADICALISM

The decline of radical political activity in Japan since the 1970s mirrors the demise of the Socialist Party. It is ironic that a society known for harmony (*wa*) and consensus (*goi*) has a rich tradition of postwar protest. Labour agitation in the late 1940s and 1950s belies contemporary assertions about a benevolent, patron–client tradition of management–labour relations (Garon, 1987; Gordon, 1998). In addition to student protests in the 1960s and 1970s

Minamata: Minamata has become a symbol of the environmental consequences of rapid economic growth and dilatory efforts to stop the pollution, punish the polluting company and compensate the victims. Chisso Corporation dumped methyl mercury into the waters off Minamata from the pre-Second World War era, but the amounts vastly increased during the 1950s. Minamata disease refers to the neurological damage suffered by people who ingested fish contaminated by the industrial effluent. The disease was first discovered in 1956, but the pollution continued until 1968. A similar outbreak in Niigata was discovered in 1965. Advocates strongly criticize the 2009 compensation deal as too small and limited in scope, and forcing victims to abandon further legal action.

targeting the US alliance and the Vietnam War, the environmental movement also marked a period of often exuberant assertion of the democratic
rights bestowed on the Japanese people in the new Constitution. Since then,
through isolation, marginalization, cooptation and classic divide-and-rule
tactics, the government has succeeded in dampening radical political movements. The violent street protests over the United States–Japan alliance of the
1960s have given way to a resigned acceptance. The **Chukaku-ha** (Middle
Core Faction) that led campus protests in the late 1960s amidst the Vietnam
War and carried out terrorist attacks both in and outside Japan while spear-
heading opposition to Narita International Airport has disappeared from
the political landscape. Campus politics are quiescent and in 1999 the final
parcel of land needed to build Narita's long-awaited second runway was
finally sold by a farmer who had held out for a quarter of a century. Most
Japanese seem unaware now that Narita had once served as a powerful political
symbol of the left's opposition to the government's heavy-handed ways.

Chukaku-ha: This faction grew out of the inter-necine struggles within the communist move-ment. It was a militant leftist group that organ-ized demonstrations opposing the presence of US bases in Japan and the United States–Japan Security Treaty, the Japanese Imperial system and global imperialism. It also advocated return of Okinawa to Japanese sovereignty and opposed construction of Narita Airport due to forced eviction of farmers from the land used to build the facility.

Kozo oshoku: Structural corruption in Japan's political system.

CORRUPTION

In all societies political corruption has been a blot on democratic development and Japan is no exception. A vast majority of postwar prime ministers
have been implicated in corruption scandals and shady practices are systemic
(Samuels, 2005). This ***kozo oshoku*** persists despite fitful efforts at political
reform (Bowen, 2003). In the 1980s and 1990s, the scandals grew more
blatant and the press played a more aggressive part in exposing the grubby
venality of politicians and bureaucrats. The economic bubble in the late
1980s raised the stakes and led to widespread corruption involving astronomical sums. The Recruit (1988) and Sagawa Kyubin (1992) scandals
were a sign of the times, confronting the public with the dirty facts of their
dysfunctional political system. The existence of corruption among politicians
left few people surprised, but the extent of the problem was stunning and
unexpected. The extensive involvement of bureaucrats in a variety of
influence-buying scandals also challenged public perceptions of their civil
servants. The mandarins had always been seen as the best and brightest
and as such beyond reproach and untainted by malfeasance. However, once
their indiscretions were reported, the public mood turned ugly and the
media delighted in revealing the dirty laundry, pettiness, incompetence and
other shortcomings of government officials. Public disenchantment with
this sordid state of affairs became a significant factor in ending one-party rule
and creating momentum for political reform.

THE SHADOW SHOGUN

Prime Minister **Kakuei Tanaka** (1972–74) has been perhaps the most influential Japanese politician in the post-1952 era, playing a dominant part in the national political scene from the early 1970s until he lost control of his faction in 1985 (Schlesinger, 1997; Samuels, 2005). His legacy is synonymous with money politics because his name is always linked with the Lockheed bribery scandal first exposed in Congressional hearings in Washington, DC. He developed the art of raising funds, selling access and delivering contracts and in the process cobbled together the most powerful faction in the LDP. He tapped the construction industry for funds and rewarded them with generous public works contracts doled out at his bidding. He was the architect of the 'construction state' and made it his business to determine who would benefit from the largesse (McCormack, 1996). Even after he was indicted (1974), prosecuted on corruption charges (1977) and later found guilty (1983), he continued to control the LDP because he had the largest faction and wielded considerable influence over the bureaucrats who made key decisions affecting his 'clients'. His constituents remained loyal, re-electing him to office despite the scandals.

The Recruit scandal first came to public attention in June 1988. Recruit was a relatively new up-and-coming company with a range of ventures connected with the information industry. It was best known for its job information services, but the scandal involved an as yet unlisted real estate affiliate called Recruit Cosmos. In 1986, unlisted shares of the company were offered at favourable prices to various influential government officials and politicians, many of whom bought the shares with money lent by Recruit. Public anger mounted as it became apparent that the beneficiaries included a who's who of Japanese politicians, even including figures from the opposition parties. In addition, Recruit purchased millions of dollars of tickets to fund-raising parties for virtually all key political figures.

Hiromasu Ezoe, the founder and head of Recruit, was trying to purchase influence, connections and favourable decisions on projects or regulations that affected his business ventures. His extensive efforts to rig the system also extended to the bureaucrats whose once high reputation rapidly declined over the ensuing years. The endless exposés and scandals made it glaringly apparent that government officials could be bought. It is further damning that only one government official was convicted for his part in the Recruit scandal and not until 1999. The politicians who were implicated in the scandal never were indicted and continued to dominate Japanese politics.

Tanaka Kakuei (1918–93): Kingpin of the LDP during the 1970s and 1980s, he served as prime minister (1972–74) but resigned in the Lockheed corruption scandal, was arrested in 1976, sentenced to jail in 1983 and died while appealing his sentence in 1993, eight years after he suffered a debilitating stroke. He personified money politics in Japan and was the fixers' fixer. His protégés, Noboru Takeshita, Shin Kanemaru and Ichiro Ozawa, dominated national politics in the 1990s.

SAGAWA KYUBIN

Sagawa Kyubin, a major parcel delivery company, was implicated in an even more massive scandal that broke in the summer of 1992. Over a period of 20 years Sagawa Kyubin had made vast illicit payoffs to politicians that dwarfed the Recruit 'donations'. Even a public inured to venality took notice of press reports about a cart piled high with ¥500 million (about $4 million) in ten-thousand yen notes being wheeled into the office of the LDP's chief fixer, **Shin Kanemaru**. Later it emerged that Kanemaru had also used Sagawa Kyubin to request the assistance of the *yakuza* to silence some right-wing political activists who were harassing **Noboru Takeshita**, faction leader, kingmaker and former prime minister (1987–89) in the LDP. The press highlighted a dinner he hosted to express his gratitude to a ranking *yakuza*, also arranged by the trucking firm, to illustrate the confluence of power in contemporary Japan. Kanemaru, a gruff, old-school politician who had teamed up with Takeshita in 1987 to gain control of the Tanaka faction, later was forced to resign from politics as the Sagawa Kyubin scandal triggered a wider investigation into his finances. A raid on his home uncovered a horde of 100 kilograms of gold, ¥3 billion in bond certificates and stacks of cash – the booty from decades of politics and the largesse of construction firms thankful for the contracts he had arranged, all duly noted in his files.

The Tanaka machine had been taken over by his lieutenants and run with the same brash cash-and-carry approach to politics. The Tanaka machine's influence was so pervasive, even involving the opposition, that there seemed to be no viable, untainted alternative. In 1993, however, five months after Kanemaru's conviction for tax evasion, the public decided to 'vote the bums out of office', ending the LDP's stranglehold on power. Even though it remained the single largest party, a fragile coalition of small parties took power for less than a year.

Shin Kanemura: The man who met with Kanemaru and helped quiet the sound trucks effusively praising Takeshita in a form of humiliating harassment known as *homegoroshi* (excessive flattery) was the notorious Susumu Ishii, head of the Inagawa-kai, one of Japan's three largest *yakuza* syndicates.

Takeshita Noboru (1924–2000): Leading protégé of Tanaka Kakuei who served as prime minister (1987–89) and held numerous cabinet portfolios in a Diet career that began in 1958. Like his mentor, he resigned from office under the cloud of corruption. During the 1990s, his control of what had been the Tanaka faction, the largest in the LDP, gave him unrivalled political influence as the party's kingmaker.

POLITICAL REFORM

In 1994 the Diet passed electoral-reform legislation. Under the new system, there is a complicated mix of single-seat constituencies and proportional representation in the Diet. The old system featured multiple-seat constituencies, meaning that a number of top vote-getters would be elected from a district. Now, under the new system, voters directly elect only one member from their district and also vote separately for a party in the regional bloc for proportional representation.

Electoral reform was propelled by the need of politicians to appear to be responding to public outrage about the extent of corruption scandals. It was the most significant legislation passed by the first non-LDP government for four decades. In addition, the success of the government in delivering economic prosperity had long been its source of legitimacy, but as the recession persisted, public patience with the usual practices wore thin. In the wake of the Recruit and Sagawa Kyubin scandals, politicians of all political stripes sought to reinvent themselves as crusading reformers. Suddenly everyone called for political reform and the existing electoral system proved a handy target. Many of the ills of the political system were attributed to the electoral system and thus changing it was portrayed as a means of taming corruption, refocusing political debate on the real issues facing society and creating the basis for a two-party system. However, the new electoral system could not meet such lofty expectations and an issues-oriented, corruption-free system remains an elusive goal, although the rise of the DPJ in 2009 may herald the advent of a stable two-party system of alternating government. Ironically, the new mixed system of single-seat constituencies and proportional representation, one that favours larger parties such as the LDP, was passed by a governing coalition of smaller parties that had fared reasonably well under the prevailing multiple-seat constituency system.

The electoral reform did not address the unequal representation of urban and rural voters (nor systemic corruption). The Supreme Court has ruled that the current system is unconstitutional because urban voters are systematically underrepresented while sparsely populated rural districts are significantly overrepresented. The votes of rural voters count, on average, over twice as much as urban voters in terms of national political representation, and in some places more than four times as much, but despite the court ruling no election results have been overturned. In general, the LDP has gained from this disparity in voting power because it enjoys the support of rural voters owing to generous agricultural subsidies and pork-barrel public works projects.

THE CHANGING LOGIC OF JAPANESE POLITICS

To understand the changing logic of Japanese politics it is useful to consider the pillars of the 1955 system. As Curtis argues:

There were four crucial pillars supporting the '55 system. One was a pervasive public consensus in support of policies to achieve the catch-up-with-the-West goal. A second was the presence of large integrative interest groups with close links to political parties. The third was a bureaucracy of immense prestige and power. And the fourth was a system of one-party dominance. Just to list these features of the '55 system is to indicate how profoundly Japan changed in the 1990s. All of these pillars of policy making had either weakened or crumbled. (Curtis, 1999: 39)

By the 1990s Japan had caught up with the West, the large integrative interest groups (such as unions) were no longer so unified or close to the parties, the bureaucracy's reputation was in tatters due to a series of widely publicized corruption scandals and one-party dominance had given way to LDP-led coalition governments. In addition, policy issues that animated the 1955 system were no longer compelling or divisive. When the Socialists joined the LDP in a coalition government in 1994, it was clear that the ideological divide no longer mattered. As a price for gaining a taste of power, the Socialist Party abandoned its opposition to the existence of the Self-Defense Forces, the United States–Japan Security Treaty, nuclear power, the national anthem and the national flag – issues that had once been emotive and defining. The principles that instilled loyalty in the party faithful through years of opposition had been discarded, a watershed that spelled the end of the JSP as a significant political force.

The sharp cleavages that marked Japan in the 1950s and 1960s became muted and the class-based appeals of the JSP no longer resonated in an increasingly affluent polity. The LDP oversaw a period of rapid economic growth combined with a relatively equal distribution of the fruits of that growth. The LDP derived its legitimacy from its economic stewardship and growing numbers of Japanese identified their interests with those of the status quo.

As a result of the Lost Decade of the 1990s, the ways and means of Japan, Inc. have been discredited, leaving voters primed for reforms as long as they are minimally disruptive to their lives. What is fascinating about Japan since the mid-1990s is the strong appeal of reform in political discourse and deep-seated ambivalence about the associated risks and consequences. In this context, a new leader emerged who set in motion substantive reforms that have shaken Japan's fusty political establishment.

Until Prime Minister Junichiro Koizumi (2001–06) came along pledging to destroy the LDP, his own party, and warning, 'No pain, no gain', voters were reluctant to accept the uncertainties and risks associated with navigating the uncharted waters of reform. This political maverick pressed ahead with an ambitious array of reforms while forcing banks to clear up the bad loans that left many virtually bankrupt during the Lost Decade of the 1990s. Privatization and deregulation became his neo-liberal mantra, one that attracted popular support because he offered hope for recovery from the doldrums of the 1990s recession. He was to be Japan's answer to Thatcher and Reagan in adopting market-oriented solutions to jump-start economic recovery and boost sagging productivity. In the 2005 elections he defined the campaign as a referendum on reform in general, and postal privatization in particular, winning a massive mandate. He convinced voters that the LDP was not only the party of reform, but also one that was cool and modern, reaching out to urban voters with his celebrity-rich, media-savvy campaign. He demonstrated that he was the most gifted campaigner of his generation, combining charisma, snappy sound-bites and bold gestures that conveyed a sense of a leader with vision. Following his departure the LDP reverted to its old ways, but found that it no longer measured up to public expectations. His LDP successors were never able to convince the public they offered reform and hope and when the economy nose-dived in 2008–09, voters turned against the conservatives and the deregulation measures they blamed for growing disparities and greater risk.

Seiken kotai (political change)

The landslide victory of the DPJ in the 2009 Lower House elections, following a similar repudiation of the LDP in the 2007 Upper House elections, ended the 1955 system and Japan's half-century of one-party rule. From the end of 2008 until the elections in August 2009, the national mood favouring *seiken kotai* gained increasing momentum, driven by an imploding economy and despair over the LDP's failure to provide leadership or policies people could believe in. Unlike the hiatus of power in 1993–94, the LDP has been replaced by a large party with staying power. This momentous change drew on various factors: the LDP's inability to promote sustainable recovery from the Lost Decade; a cascade of scandals implicating the ruling political and bureaucratic elite; growing income disparities; and the consequences of greater risk caused by deregulation of the labour market. Voters repudiated the LDP and its agenda of reform because it had brought considerable pain with little tangible gain. The DPJ offered fresh thinking about Japan's considerable problems and challenges. Voters warmed to its promise of exerting political control over the unpopular and privileged bureaucrats and curbing *amakudari*, a system that allocates high-paying sinecures to retiring bureaucrats, which is notorious as a hotbed of corruption, bid-rigging and waste of taxpayer funds. The DPJ's shifting spending away from public works towards expanded social services also enjoys public support, especially given Japan's rapidly ageing society and the urgent need for an expanded safety net for the 10 million working poor, 3.5 million unemployed and 1 million single

Amakudari: Descent from Heaven. A reference to the common practice of retired senior bureaucrats moving to well-paid, sinecure positions in firms that they dealt with in the course of their government duties. Often criticized as a source of collusive relations between bureaucrats and the firms they hope to join upon retiring.

mother households. The DPJ is also providing relief to families by increasing child-rearing subsidies and providing free public schooling through high school. Voters remain sceptical, however, that the rise of the DPJ will bring improvement and remain anxious about the government's ability to address issues such as growing disparities and the demographic time bomb. They are also concerned that two of the DPJ's top leaders, Ichiro Ozawa and Prime Minister Yukio Hatoyama (2009–2010), had to step down in part due to political fund scandals that cast doubt that the change of parties means a change in political practices. Whether or not the DPJ offers change Japanese voters can believe in, Japan stands to benefit from the emergence of party competition. Having held the LDP accountable, voters in twenty-first century Japan are now feeling feisty, and are impatient for positive results. This marks a significant change from the 1955 system when constituents remained loyal party followers even when the LDP faltered because it was the default option and there were no credible alternatives.

4

The Economic Miracle

The economic miracle refers to the spectacular economic growth recorded by Japan during the 1950s and 1960s. Japan rose phoenix-like out of the ashes of war to build a world-class economy. This was certainly not an anticipated or likely outcome. Most of Japan's large cities had been reduced to rubble and its industrial capacity had been decimated by sustained aerial bombing. Adequate housing was in short supply, food was scarce and these problems were aggravated by the return of some 7 million Japanese troops and civilians scattered around Asia. Japan was a nation without capital, raw materials or friends. What went right?

THE DEVELOPMENT STATE

Johnson (1982) argues that the key factor in explaining Japan's economic miracle was the not-so-invisible hands of state-sponsored development [**Doc. 4, pp. 125–6**]. According to Johnson, the Ministry for International Trade and Industry (MITI) played the main part in orchestrating economic growth by channelling low-cost loans and other support to targeted sectors of the economy. This process of picking winners was not infallible, but was often very effective in nurturing the growth of industries in promising areas. At a time when capital was scarce and foreign exchange was strictly controlled, MITI sponsorship had a significant impact. In addition, MITI had a key role in brokering technology licensing deals with US corporations on attractive terms, thus sparing Japanese firms the time and cost of research and development. The government also helped by encouraging cartels to avoid excessive competition and by supporting a variety of protectionist practices that helped reserve the domestic market for domestic producers. MITI and other ministries often exercised control through **gyosei shido**. This informal approach amounted to strong suggestions about desired actions,

Gyosei shido: Administrative guidance. A reference to the informal manner in which bureaucrats wield their broad regulatory and discretionary powers to ensure corporate compliance with government goals and policies. Implicit is the threat to use those powers in a manner harmful to those who do not comply.

policies or results and it was in the best interests of the recipient of such advice to comply or risk facing the troubles that powerful bureaucrats could cause.

FAVOURABLE FACTORS

The media dubbed Japan's rapid recovery from the war and high growth between 1955 and 1973 as the 'economic miracle', but scholars have taken issue with this characterization. This is not to diminish the success, but rather to place that success in historical context. In examining the factors favouring postwar economic growth in Japan it is important to bear in mind that Japan was an industrialized nation before the war and already possessed advanced technological knowledge. Thus, even though the nation was devastated by the war, Japan's economic recovery was relatively quick because it had a reservoir of experienced policy-makers, businessmen and scientific experts to draw on.

Institutions and policies mattered a great deal because Japan had little margin for error in its straitened circumstances. During the war the bureaucracy gained extraordinary powers to mobilize the nation's scarce resources in order to deploy them most effectively. Under what is known as the 1940 system, the Japanese economy was tightly managed and planned by the bureaucrats who wielded their powers to maximize Japan's industrial capacity. Under the American Occupation, many of these same bureaucrats continued to exercise power because the Americans ruled indirectly through the Japanese bureaucracy. Johnson argues that the Supreme Commander of the Allied Powers (SCAP) kept this wartime economic system largely intact, conferring extensive regulatory powers on the economic ministries. Through this power over the allocation of resources, the government directed the course and pace of national economic recovery. The men who had maximized Japan's scarce resources during the war were well prepared for their role in orchestrating the 'miracle'. Bureaucratic continuity favoured rapid growth because of the accumulated institutional expertise in implementing economic policies under adverse conditions. It also helped that corporate Japan had also worked within this system and knew the ropes.

In addition, SCAP had a critical and positive role in creating favourable conditions for growth. Japanese reparations were minimized and early plans to strip Japan of its remaining industrial plant and equipment were scrapped in favour of promoting Japanese growth in accordance with Cold War aims. There was no equivalent to the Marshall Plan that had jump-started economic recovery in Europe because there was little support for using

American taxpayers' money to support Japan. Instead, the United States stabilized Japanese government finances and fixed the exchange rate at a low level (360 ¥ = $1) favourable for exports. The land reform played a critical part in boosting food production and creating a growing middle class of consumers for the products of Japanese industry (Cohen, 1987). The Americans also succeeded in loosening the dominance of the *zaibatsu*, permitting the emergence of some of Japan's leading companies, such as Sony and Honda.

The war procurements by the American military during the Korean War (1950–53) are often credited with pulling Japan out of a dire postwar recession and putting the economy on a steep growth trajectory. Prime Minister **Shigeru Yoshida** referred to this estimated $3 billion windfall as a 'gift from the gods' because austerity measures imposed by the United States in 1949, known as the **Dodge Line**, had drastically shrunk domestic demand and threatened to stifle recovery. War on the peninsula provided a much-needed stimulus.

Unhindered access to the US market and technology also played a key part in Japan's growth spurt. The US market provided the crucial economies of scale while licensing of US technology on favourable terms saved Japanese companies enormous research and development expenses. US companies were inclined to license their technology because the business operating environment in Japan was not favourable for foreign firms. Restrictions on land ownership, foreign exchange and profit repatriation, in addition to low consumer demand, discouraged most foreign firms from establishing operations in Japan, an outcome that was consistent with the government's protectionist inclinations. In addition, the US government was eager to promote Japan's economic success in order to further its Cold War aims and had a role in expediting the flow of technology to its protégé in the Pacific. It is also true that Japanese firms were quicker to adopt recent technological innovations than their foreign counterparts. Technology that was developed abroad was rapidly disseminated on the plant floor in Japan's factories as they pursued their goal of becoming competitive and overtaking the West.

In this respect, the war devastation proved an opportunity as Japan had to rebuild most of its industrial plant and equipment from scratch. Thus, Japanese industrial plants were, on average, more modern and had more advanced technology than was the case in the United States where there was no urgency in renovating or replacing ageing facilities or production lines. The war thus inadvertently had a key role in modernizing Japan's factories.

High levels of literacy among the Japanese and a good educational system helped make this possible. The rapid pace of change and dissemination of new technologies in factories necessitated constant job training and upgrading of skills, a task made easier by widespread literacy among Japan's

Yoshida Shigeru (1878–1967): The second most influential postwar politician after Kakuei Tanaka, he twice served as prime minister (1946–47, 1948–54). He grudgingly enacted liberal Occupation era reforms and resisted US pressures to rearm, arguing that Japan's precarious economic situation precluded reviving military forces.

Dodge Line: Joseph Dodge, a Detroit-based banker, was brought in by SCAP and recommended tight fiscal discipline and monetary contraction in 1949 to rein in hyperinflation. He called for a balanced national budget, more efficient tax collection and job cuts in the public sector. His policies tamed inflation, but sent the economy into a recessionary tailspin.

blue-collar workers. It also helped that workers came to enjoy relatively secure employment and did not feel threatened by the introduction of new technologies. The spread of an implicit lifetime employment system after the Second World War facilitated worker acceptance of labour-saving technologies that were resisted and became a focal point of unrest in other industrialized nations.

Japan also benefited from having new frontiers at home and abroad. Rebuilding the economy and developing the hinterland of Japan proved a powerful stimulus, as did the massive migration of young Japanese from those hinterlands to urban areas. This migration sparked demand for housing, transportation and consumer goods. Overseas, suddenly, by the 1960s, Japanese consumer electronics began to take world markets by storm. These markets represented a new frontier that Japanese exporters, most notably in autos and electronics, have been successfully tapping ever since.

Corporate Japan also benefited from the high savings rate of the Japanese people. In the mid-1950s the savings rate of families was about 13%. As incomes rose over the course of the miracle so did their savings, averaging 25% of disposable income by 1974, more than quadruple the American rate (Allinson, 1997: 101). People saved because they were accustomed to frugality and until 1961 there was no mandatory medical insurance or social security system and social welfare programmes were limited. In addition, land and housing was relatively expensive and in pursuit of the ubiquitous 'My Home Dream' (owning one's own house) there has been a strong tendency to save. There are other reasons why Japanese tend to have a high savings rate, but the consequence is a large pool of capital that is almost all saved in bank or postal savings accounts. Even in the late 1990s, less than 10% of Japanese owned stocks or bonds. Government policy kept interest rates on bank accounts low, meaning that corporate borrowers could also borrow at low rates. Thus, the high savings rate and a government decision to favour producers over consumers by keeping interest rates low gave Japanese firms a competitive edge in terms of the cost of capital. In expanding and modernizing production facilities and adopting new technologies, this proved an important factor in the success of Japan, Inc.

The so-called three jewels of the Japanese employment system – lifetime employment, seniority wages and enterprise unions – are often cited as important factors in propelling economic growth. Lifetime employment and the **nenko** wage system worked to the mutual advantage of workers and employers. Workers gained job security and steady wage increases while employers cultivated the loyalty, commitment and skills of their workers. In-house training programmes only made economic sense if firms could count on keeping their skilled employees, and in this regard the lifetime

Nenko: The seniority system that has determined wages and promotions, but is now no longer sacrosanct as firms shift towards a more merit-oriented system.

employment system succeeded. Job security also facilitated the introduction of new labour-saving, productivity-enhancing technologies because unions and workers did not feel threatened by innovation.

The seniority wage system also was based on economic logic. Under this system young workers are paid relatively little in exchange for the promise that once they reach a certain level of seniority they will be rewarded for their loyalty with relatively high wages. Thus, initial wages are usually pegged below worker productivity, but eventually rise to exceed worker productivity. This system is also seen to suit the life-cycle income needs of workers, boosting wages when they reach their forties at a time when various family-related expenses usually rise. For employers, this system made sense because in the aftermath of war, when capital was scarce, the prevalence of new workers meant that wage outlays were kept low. This conferred a competitive advantage on Japanese firms, at least until the age pyramid of the workforce in the late 1980s shifted towards older, more expensive and less productive workers who were also relatively less adept with the proliferating new technologies.

Enterprise unions helped ensure a minimum of labour turmoil. In the late 1940s and early 1950s Japan experienced a period of intense labour conflict that is difficult to reconcile with perceptions that harmony is a traditional characteristic of employment relations in Japan. Radical unions frequently engaged in work stoppages, strikes and factory takeovers while employers struck back with the normal array of union-busting measures, often with the complicity of government officials and the help of gangsters (Hein, 1990; Whiting, 1999; Takemae, 2002). In the end, the firms prevailed, weeding out activists and taming the labour movement by establishing in-house unions. This created a forum for dialogue, compromise, input, information sharing and confidence-building measures that helped forge close bonds between workers and managers. The relative absence of bitter labour disputes and the cooperative spirit engendered in the workplace have contributed to Japan's economic success.

It is also clear that low spending on social security and defence favoured recovery because there was little diversion of scarce funds into such programmes. The government relied on the United States to provide military security and on companies to offer job security. There was an inclination to place the burden of social security on the family, tapping into Confucian values of filial piety and traditions that placed great importance on the family unit. The needs of the retired, aged and infirm were considered the duty of the family with minimal government assistance. It was only in the late 1970s that Japan initiated extensive social welfare policies.

Japan was also fortunate in enjoying favourable external economic conditions. The price of **oil** remained extremely low until 1973, an important consideration for a resource-dependent nation like Japan. This meant that the burgeoning energy requirements of Japanese industry did not have much of an impact on the costs of production. In addition, the world economy in general experienced relatively robust growth, creating good markets for Japanese exports. It was important that Japan enjoyed free access to the US market and that there was an improving global trading environment in which levels of protectionism were declining significantly and extensively under the auspices of the General Agreement on Trades and Tariffs (GATT) which was launched in 1948. With US support, Japan gained membership to GATT in 1955.

ADVERSARIAL TRADE

Some commentators argue that as Japan tapped into export markets, it kept its own market tightly protected. This unreciprocal pattern of trade did not become an international issue immediately, mostly because the United States chose to overlook such problems (Lincoln, 1990; Prestowitz, 1990). It was not until the late 1970s that Japan first began to run significant trade surpluses with the United States; before that the American government was inclined to sacrifice what many considered negligible commercial interests in Japan for the sake of the security alliance (Forsberg, 2000). In addition to maintaining cordial bilateral relations, the United States sought to further its Cold War-inspired objective of transforming Japan into the bulwark of the 'free world' in Asia (Schaller, 1985). Initially through tariffs and the strict control of the foreign exchange that was needed to purchase imports (the yen was not accepted for settlement of international transactions), the government was able to reserve the domestic market for domestic producers. Foreign producers were given limited access until domestic producers could produce competitive substitutes. Industrial cartels and price fixing were condoned by the government, creating markets closed to foreign enterprise. Cosy procurement relationships among the businesses grouped together in the large industrial conglomerates – keiretsu – and by the government also served to limit foreign penetration. As Japan bowed to international pressures to lower tariff barriers, critics argue that it fell back on non-tariff barriers that had the same stifling impact on imports. These predatory trading practices proved successful in protecting the domestic market and spurring exports (Prestowitz, 1990). Japanese exporters could subsidize exports from profits generated in the domestic market where prices were generally higher than those charged overseas. The home market thus became an export platform subsidized by Japanese consumers.

Protectionism benefited corporate Japan at the expense of consumers who faced high prices. This is thought by some observers to be representative of a larger pattern in which producers have been systematically favoured over consumers in Japan. In terms of various regulations, low interest rates (savers receive small returns, corporations borrow cheaply), price fixing, cartels, product liability, land use, infrastructure development, etc., it is argued that the government has routinely sided with Japan, Inc. In return for the benefits bestowed on corporate Japan, Japanese workers received job security, a steadily improving standard of living and a shared sense of national success.

A DUAL ECONOMY

One of the great achievements of rapid economic growth in Japan has been in limiting income disparities, but it has been uneven, particularly in terms of the employment conditions, job security and wages offered by small and medium-sized businesses and subcontractors. Japan's top corporations, such as Sony, Honda, Toyota and Toshiba, represent the most modern and advanced firms. The system of implicit lifetime employment and the other perquisites of full-time employment are generally limited to such modern, large corporations and cover less than 30% of the workforce. The majority of Japanese workers are not employed at these corporations and do not enjoy the same level of security and wages as their counterparts in the dominant corporations. During business downturns, small and medium-sized firms, many of which are subcontractors of globally renowned firms, lay off workers, cut back on overtime, trim bonuses (which can reach some five months of annual salary) and make other such adjustments. When assessing the success of large companies like Toyota, it is important to bear in mind that the parts-producing subcontractors are dependent and vulnerable. They are often asked to shoulder many of the cutbacks and costs necessitated by slack business, in effect insulating the core workforce from the vicissitudes of the business cycle.

Since the 1990s, the percentage of **non-regular workers**, those working on fixed term contracts without job security, seniority wage increases or other benefits, has increased dramatically. As of 2008, non-regular workers account for 34.1% of the workforce, up from 20% in 1992 and 16.4% in 1985. Between 1992 and 2002, the number of full-time workers declined by 3.5 million while the number of non-regular workers increased by 5.67 million. These marginalized workers played a peripheral role in the economic miracle and over time have become a more significant segment of Japan's labour market that helps explain widening disparities.

Non-regular workers: Various categories of workers who are not regular, full-time workers. This includes part-time, contract, temporary and dispatched workers. Many of these workers work long hours, sometimes more than forty hours a week, but by hiring them under these different conditions the firm can save money by not contributing to social insurance benefits, paying low wages and no bonuses; bonuses can equal five months of salary for full-time workers. These workers are all contingent workers, meaning they can be fired if the firm decides it does not need their services. Job protection for regular workers is relatively strong in Japan. Younger workers and women are disproportionately represented in the ranks of non-regular workers.

GROWTH AS IDEOLOGY

The income doubling plan announced by Prime Minister Ikeda in 1960 symbolizes the commitment of the government to growth at all costs. This ideology of GNPism became the mobilizing and unifying ideology of the dominant LDP. It was an enormously popular programme that generated a unified vision and was made possible by sustained government intervention. The stimulus of massive public works associated with the 1964 Tokyo Olympic Games spurred growth beyond ambitious targets while the success of those Games was taken as confirmation that Japan had recovered from the war and re-entered the community of nations. However, as discussed in Chapter 9, the heady years of double-digit growth brought Japan both the benefits and costs of a mature economy, providing a reminder that the sun also sets.

THE SETTING SUN

During the 1970s the fortunes of the Japanese economy dimmed for a variety of reasons. The ideology of growth was no longer as compelling and the environmental costs of the 'miracle' stirred a popular backlash against unfettered development. More importantly, Japan was rocked by the rapid surge in oil prices orchestrated by OPEC in 1973. The oil-price rise fuelled inflation, raised production costs, sparked industrial cutbacks and caused recession in the economies of Japan's trading partners. This jolt to the Japanese economy was preceded by the decision of the United States to abandon the 1944 Bretton Woods system of fixed exchange rates in 1971 which led to an appreciation in the value of the yen. The yen had been pegged at 360 to the US dollar since the Occupation and this relatively low value helped stimulate demand for Japan's exports. As a result of the US decision, the value of the yen rose to 310 to the dollar in 1971 and since then there has been an extended rise in the value of the yen. For Japan, the results were mixed. Imported natural resources became cheaper in yen terms, thus helping firms lower production costs and therefore export prices. However, the yen's appreciation raised the cost of Japanese products in overseas markets.

Oil shock: The Organization of Petroleum Exporting Countries (OPEC) instituted an oil embargo in 1973 in protest of US support for Israel in the Yom Kippur War. This led to substantial increases in global oil prices from $3 a barrel to $12 a barrel. Aside from the Israel angle, OPEC sought to offset the decline in their real income due to the devaluation of the US dollar after 1971 (oil prices are pegged to the US dollar).

As a consequence of rapid growth in the 1950s and 1960s, Japan in the 1970s had become a mature economy. It had already tapped into the dynamism of the domestic and overseas 'new frontiers' mentioned above and in the absence of fresh frontiers was unable to sustain such high levels of growth. In addition to confronting the limits of growth, Japan was experiencing heightened competition in export markets for heavy industrial products such as steel and shipbuilding. Regional rivals such as Korea and Taiwan had an edge on labour costs and were quickly climbing the technological ladder, closing the gap with Japan. The government sponsored a political solution to this economic problem by switching from a policy of picking winners to a policy favouring recession cartels with subsidies and tax breaks for 'sunset' industries (Katz, 1998). This approach protected jobs, but postponed the restructuring of the economy and made Japan a high-cost economy, forcing domestic exporters to rely on relatively expensive domestic inputs. This meant that Japan's leading companies carried its lagging companies. In the wake of the sharp appreciation of the yen in 1985, this situation became even less viable, forcing exporting companies to lower production costs by relocating production facilities offshore. In 1989, amid the hubris of the bubble economy, when the Japanese economic juggernaut seemed unstoppable and commentators spoke of a Pax Nipponica, Emmott's *The Sun Also Sets: Why Japan Will Not Be Number One* (1989) seemed poorly timed. Since then, his analysis has proved prescient about the woes that have beleaguered Japan since the 1990s [**Doc. 5, pp. 126–7**].

5

Japan and Asia: Past and Present

A LINGERING LEGACY

Many Japanese people and their government have not yet come to terms with the consequences of the Imperial Army's fifteen-year rampage and occupation of Asia between 1931 and 1945 when over 15 million Asians perished due to Japan's expansionist policies. The government has encouraged a selective amnesia regarding Japan's shared past with Asia through its powers of textbook censorship (Hein and Selden, 2000). Many Japanese regard themselves as victims of the Second World War and few recall the sustained victimization of neighbouring countries. Within Japan, debate over the war continues and there are some Japanese who defend their nation's actions, arguing that the excesses have been invented or exaggerated and that Japan's actions in Asia at that time were justified. Political leaders have sent mixed messages over the years, generating uncertainty in the region about whether Japan has taken responsibility for its past actions and is sincerely contrite about the devastating consequences of its aggression (Yamazaki, 2005; Dudden, 2008). As a result, generally good relations between Japan and other Asian nations remain troubled by the ghosts of the past (Wakamiya, 1999; Hasegawa and Togo, 2008).

The past resonates powerfully in contemporary Japan, especially regarding the unresolved and controversial legacy of its wartime actions. Many Japanese politicians continue to argue that Japan was motivated by a desire to liberate Asian nations from Western colonialism (Seaton, 2007). They point out that following the Pacific War, the process of decolonization brought freedom and independence to former colonies in Asia, suggesting that Japan deserves credit for promoting this process by challenging the colonial powers and nurturing Asian nationalist movements. In 1995, the Diet conducted considerable debate over a resolution marking the fiftieth anniversary since the end of the war. What began as an effort to put the past behind Japan by issuing an unambiguous apology became the focus of intense political debate. Finally, the Diet passed a compromise resolution that did little to convince other Asians that Japan was apologizing or taking responsibility for its past conduct [**Doc. 6, pp. 127–8**]. The final wording watered down the apology and tried to justify Japan's actions in the context of world history. Prime Minister **Tomoiichi Murayama** (1994–96) later added his own less ambiguous apology on the anniversary of Japan's surrender [**Doc. 7, pp. 128–9**].

What is it that other Asian nations want Japan to take responsibility for? Wherever the Japanese military operated in Asia it committed serious and extensive war crimes. Massacres of civilians, gruesome medical experiments on prisoners-of-war (POWs), random rape, systematic rape of tens of thousands of young women forced into sexual slavery, looting, famines, ethnic cleansing and forced labour claimed countless victims (Tanaka, 1998). The arrogant and often cruelly violent behaviour of the Japanese troops made a mockery of the **Pan-Asian ideology** espoused by the government at that time, leaving a lasting impression (Chang, 1997; Sato, 1997; Honda, 1999; Toer, 1999; Kratoska, 2005). While claiming to be engaged in building an Asia run by and for Asians, Japan was seeking to replace the Western colonial powers as the regional hegemon. Japan's invasion of Southeast Asia from 1941 was motivated by the search for the natural resources needed to continue its ongoing war in China, which began with its takeover of Manchuria in 1931 and escalated significantly after 1937 (Barnhardt, 1988; Marshall, 1995; Goto, 1997, 2003). The impending threat of an economic boycott by the United States in protest against Japanese aggression in China left two choices: withdrawal and negotiations over the future of China or expansion of the war so that Japan would not be vulnerable to such economic pressures. For a variety of reasons, the Japanese government opted to widen the war, spreading the catastrophe it started in China to the rest of the region. As Goto (2003) argues, the ideology of Pan-Asianism and the liberation of Asia that was used to justify invasion was merely a cover for Japan's self-interests and desire to feed its war machine with the abundant raw materials available in the region.

The liberation argument also has a China-sized hole. There was a consensus in Japan that in order for it to catch up with the Western powers it also needed to engage in imperialism, especially because it was poorly endowed with the natural resources needed for its industrial development. Because of proximity, rich reserves of natural resources and a potentially huge market, China was the obvious target for Japan to realize its ambitions. China was an independent nation in 1931 when Japan invaded and took over the Chinese province of Manchuria, and in 1937 when it escalated the conflict and sought to subjugate all of China. Since the end of the First World War, Japan had become the leading imperial power in China and had the largest

Murayama Tomoiichi (1924–): Entering a historic coalition government with the LDP, this chairman of the Japan Socialist Party became the first Socialist prime minister (1994–96) in the post-Occupation era. His ascendancy to power also marked the decline of the Socialists because his tie-up with the LDP alienated the party faithful. During his administration, the twin tragedies of the Kobe earthquake and the Aum Shinrikyo subway gas attacks rocked Japan. On the fiftieth anniversary of the end of the Second World War, he apologized to the victims of Japanese aggression.

Pan Asianism: An ideology dating back to the late nineteenth century that was invoked by Japanese intellectuals and leaders to justify Japan's colonial expansion and the invasion and occupation of Asian territories by the Imperial Armed Forces. Nominally, Japan was acting to liberate Asia from Western imperialism and as the only Asian nation to successfully industrialize, build a strong military and conduct diplomacy with Western nations on an equal basis, it claimed a special leadership role in Asia. Japan's victory over Russia in the Russo-Japanese War 1904–05 was inspirational to many Asian nationalists who did look to Japan's example as a model for their own nations. Many nationalists, however, were also skeptical about Japan's real intentions.

economic stake in the country. The rising tide of Chinese nationalism, how-ever, threatened Japan's substantial continental interests and the consequent political turmoil undermined its economic ambitions in China. The decision to subjugate China, still a sovereign nation at the time, was aimed at safe-guarding Japan's interests and helping it achieve its ambitions. Thus, where Japanese military actions were concentrated and most destructive it is hard to sustain the thesis that Japan came as a liberator looking out for the interests of fellow Asians.

Pan-Asianism also fails to explain Japanese colonialism in Korea or Taiwan. Resentment against Japan remains most vibrant in Korea because there the depredations of Japanese rule were experienced longest and Koreans remain very bitter and emotional about Japan's perceived failure to admit and take responsibility for what happened during the colonial era (1910–45). Japanese colonialism did facilitate significant economic development but, as else-where around the world, colonial rule was based on racism, inequality and violence, provoking a nationalistic backlash that remains surprisingly power-ful today (Dudden, 2006, 2008). In addition, the Korean minority is the largest non-Japanese ethnic group resident in Japan and still suffers from discri-minatory treatment, fuelling contemporary Korean anger towards Japan.

ATONEMENT AND WAR GUILT

The Japanese government maintains that all claims arising from the war have already been settled in the San Francisco Peace Treaty. Suits by groups of Asians who press various claims against the Japanese government are routinely rejected because they are seen to have no legal foundation. Thus, colonial subjects who fought with or otherwise assisted the Imperial forces (but were later denied pensions because they lost Japanese citizenship after the war), women who served their sexual needs, people forcibly brought to Japan as workers and POWs have had their claims rejected in the Japanese court system. Favourable rulings in lower courts have been overturned on appeal. The official line is that these issues have been resolved even though the steady stream of court cases suggests otherwise. In the first decade of the twenty-first century, Kajima, Nishimatsu and other implicated companies, however, have agreed to compensate former forced labourers even though under no legal compulsion to do so (for more on forced labour see Kratoska, 2005; Underwood, 2008; Kang, et al., 2009).

Inevitably, the manner in which Germany and Japan, allies during the war, have coped with the burdens of history invites comparison (Buruma, 1994). As McCormack argues:

In the scales of the twentieth century, the misery, suffering, destruction, and dislocation caused by Japanese expansion and war in mid-century was of a magnitude comparable to the German, and the contrast between the two countries in terms of how they face their own history at century's end is striking. The contrast between Japan and Germany in respect to the payment of war compensation is stark. In reparations, compensation, and pensions, by 1991, the German government had paid out the sum of 86.4 billion marks (6.9 trillion yen), and the German Treasury estimated that payments of a further 33.6 billion marks (2.7 trillion yen) would continue until the year 2030, for a total of around 10 trillion yen (roughly one hundred billion dollars) . . . By comparison, Japan had paid out a paltry 250 billion yen, forty times less, and less than is paid in a single year in pensions and benefits to Japanese veterans and their families. (McCormack, 1996: 245)

In addition, unlike in Japan, neither the government nor prominent politicians in Germany deny or try to justify their nation's actions during the Second World War.

Japan has been unable to overcome its shared history with Asia because government leaders have consistently failed to convey a sense of sincere remorse or contrition remotely comparable to that displayed by postwar Germany (Seaton, 2007). Carefully calibrated gestures and hedged admissions of wrongdoing have instead generated perceptions of a nation eager to bury the past before taking its measure. Prime Minister Koizumi visited Yasukuni Shrine, a locus of an unrepentant view of the war, six times while in office, derailing bilateral relations with Beijing and Seoul. In doing so, he convinced many neighbours that Japan is not contrite about its shared past and wants to put this unexamined history behind it.

Hein and Selden (2000) argue that this is because the Japanese do not believe that the rewards justify the costs, unlike the Germans who desperately want to be accepted by other Europeans as part of Europe. Kingston (2008) argues that this logic is changing given the rise of China as Japan's leading trading partner and the need to improve bilateral relations. After Koizumi, Japanese leaders have refrained from visiting **Yasukuni Shrine** and the Democratic Party of Japan (DPJ) has emphasized the need to take responsibility for the past.

TEXTBOOKS AND MASOCHISTIC HISTORY

Some historians in Japan argue that it has been excessively self-critical in appraising its wartime conduct. They assert that the '**victor's history**'

Yasukuni Shrine: Soon after taking power in September 2009, Prime Minister Hatoyama reassured Beijing that he and his cabinet members would not visit Yasukuni Shrine, stating he was interested in establishing a secular alternative for paying respect to the war dead and said that Japan must be more forthright in assuming responsibility for its past misdeeds.

Victor's history: Invoked by Japanese conservatives to divert attention away from the crimes and atrocities committed by the Imperial Armed Forces. The deeply flawed proceedings of the Tokyo Trial and the preordained convictions undermine the legitimacy of the court and the convictions of Japan's war criminals, but do not mean that they were innocent of the charges. In his lengthy dissent, Justice Pal eloquently dismisses the court, arguing it lacked standing in international law and was also critical that laws were retroactively applied to convict the defendants. He further argues that the Allies should also have been on trial for committing crimes against humanity, citing the atomic bombings. However, Justice Pal also agreed that the defendants did commit atrocities and war crimes.

Ienaga Saburo (1913–2002): Controversial historian who launched a series of lawsuits since 1965 that challenged the constitutionality and legality of the government's school textbook review system. He protested the government efforts to force him to modify his depiction of Japan's brutal wartime actions during the 1931–45 period and maintained that the textbook review system amounts to censorship, a view that the courts eventually vindicated.

generated at the Tokyo War Crimes Tribunal is biased and unfairly critical of Japan's actions. In their view, in order for Japanese to regain pride in their nation they need to develop a more sympathetic understanding of Japan's war record. The decision of the government to permit revisions to secondary school textbooks in 1996 that take a more critical view of this record has been harshly opposed by conservative pundits, historians and politicians. The conservative Japan Society for History Textbook Reform responded by sponsoring publication of a textbook in 2001 that portrays Japan's shared history with Asia in a favourable light, although less than 1% of schools adopted it (McNeill, 2005; Saaler, 2005).

In contrast, critics of Japanese textbooks both in Japan and abroad assert that for too long the government has whitewashed the national record in Asia. Since 1982, the governments in China and Korea have made Japanese textbooks an issue in their foreign relations by denouncing the watered-down history taught to Japanese students. The government has censored textbooks and downplayed incidents, employing circumlocutions and euphemisms that tend to minimize the negative consequences and shift responsibility away from the Imperial forces. Rather than masochistic history, they argue that the government has embraced a self-exonerating narrative that fails to impart to students a balanced understanding of what Japan did in the region and why this continues to complicate contemporary relations with Asia.

The case of **Ienaga Saburo**, a prominent Japanese historian, illustrates how the government has constructed an evasive version of history. Censorship by the government of his history textbook for high school students has been the focus of several lawsuits since 1965. The government argued that his views on Japan's actions in Asia were too negative and would not approve them for use in the school system without significant revisions. The government required him to delete certain sections regarding the medical experiments of Unit 731 and widespread rape, arguing that the facts had not been fully researched (on Unit 731 see Gold, 1996; Harris, 2001). The government has toned down descriptions of the massacre known as the Rape of Nanking, settling on vague references to the number of casualties and enigmatically suggesting that they died in the chaos (Yoshida, 2006).

Time and good research have vindicated Ienaga as all of the disputed interpretations and facts censored by the government have been proven by younger Japanese historians. In 1993 the Tokyo High Court ruled that the government exceeded its powers in censoring the textbooks he had written, but even now the debate over how the past should be taught is bitterly contested. Right-wing historians argue that young Japanese need to develop more pride in their nation while proponents of a full accounting of the past see more honour in forthright apology and gestures of atonement as a basis for improving future relations with Asia [**Doc. 8, p. 130**].

COMFORT WOMEN

Perhaps no single issue is as emotive and bitterly disputed as is the case of the comfort women. There is considerable proof that tens of thousands of young women, mostly from Korea, were forced into serving as sex slaves for the Japanese troops between 1932 and 1945. These are the so-called comfort women. Responsibility for this sordid system, and even its very existence, was denied by the Japanese government until a Japanese researcher found archival documents in 1992 that indicated official complicity at the highest levels in the military and bureaucracy (International Public Hearing Report, 1993; Yoshimi, 2001; Tanaka, 2001). Subsequent research and the testimony of comfort women and former soldiers have verified the reliance on coercion in recruiting these girls to staff what are euphemistically known as 'comfort stations' supervised by military officials. These girls report that they were raped and beaten at the outset before having to serve as many as thirty soldiers a day (Hicks, 1995).

Comfort women were a priority because the military authorities wanted to minimize sexually transmitted diseases by closely monitoring their health. For this reason, recruiters sought out virgins. Military leaders believed that the provision of sex slaves was preferable to soldiers roaming the countryside and ravishing local women; in China such actions had stoked anti-Japanese resistance. It is a measure of how important the comfort women were considered that they would frequently arrive at newly conquered territories or battlefronts along with provisions and ammunition.

The Japanese government's manner of dealing with this sordid story of sexual slavery is revealing. Despite persistent rumours and allegations, the government denied that such a system even existed. Confronted with damning archival evidence, the government then denied that it was involved, shifting responsibility on to private entrepreneurs. When this was shown also to be untrue, the government then argued that the comfort women were not coerced into service. Finally, under the weight of mounting evidence and widespread denunciations of its position of grudging and qualified admission of wrongdoing and responsibility, in 1993 the government accepted responsibility for the comfort women and expressed remorse in the Kono statement [**Doc. 9, pp. 130–2**]. Subsequently, in 1995 the government sponsored a non-governmental organization, the Asia Women's Fund (AWF), to compensate former comfort women. Only 364 women accepted offers of compensation, totalling $19 million, belying accusations by some Japanese that they have only come forward in order to extort money from Japan now that it has become a wealthy nation. Most former comfort women and their advocates refused offers from the AWF because they argue that this organization was set up solely for the purpose of allowing the Japanese government to evade accepting direct responsibility. In addition, advocacy groups in Korea actively discouraged women from accepting the solatium and subjected those that did to public indignities (Soh, 2009). In March 2007, shortly before the AWF was disbanded, conservative Prime Minister Shinzo Abe (2006–07) quibbled about the degree of coercion used in recruiting the comfort women, sparking a firestorm of criticism at home and abroad that forced him to retract his remarks.

Right-wing historians have sought to deny, minimize and mitigate this grim chapter in Japan's history. They argue that the women willingly signed up and that the government bears no responsibility because private entrepreneurs ran the comfort stations. They argue that the numbers of women involved have been vastly inflated. In addition, they argue that since the women were paid it is a simple case of prostitution and in this regard the story of the comfort women is essentially similar to that of other women everywhere war has been waged. This perspective is increasingly difficult to defend as more evidence and eyewitness accounts emerge that contradict the conservative version.

THE NANKING MASSACRE

Ishihara Shintaro (1932–): Three-term governor of Tokyo, novelist and outspoken conservative. He is famous for criticizing United States–Japan bilateral relations in his book, *The Japan That Can Say No* (1989), denying the Nanking Massacre happened and calling on the Self-Defense Forces (SDF) to be vigilant about foreigners in the event of an earthquake.

Did the 1937 Nanking Massacre really happen [**Doc. 10, pp. 132–4**]? This might seem like an absurd question, but **Shintaro Ishihara**, elected governor of Tokyo since 1999, is on record as having denied that the looting, rape and assembly-line murder reported by eyewitnesses ever took place. Chang, the author of *The Rape of Nanking* (1997), has been the target of vitriolic attacks by the Atarashii Rekishi Kyokasho o Tsukuru Kai (Japanese Society for New History Education) and other ultra-nationalist groups. Even the Japanese Ambassador to the United States took the unprecedented action of publicly denouncing her book. Chang's scholarship was careless regarding certain details, but her basic points are similar to those of many Japanese writers who have published works concerning what happened in Nanking, based on their careful research and solid documentation (Yoshida, 2006; Wakabayashi, 2007). Their reports about the atrocities draw on the testimony of soldiers and Chinese eyewitnesses (Honda, 1999). Yet, prominent conservative historians continue to dispute that the Japanese forces committed atrocities against Chinese civilians. As in other areas of history concerning Japanese wartime excesses, they argue that research is inconclusive and thus it is not appropriate to discuss these issues in textbooks (Kitamura, 2007).

This would not be important except for the fact that in contemporary Japan, conservative historians are enormously popular and very influential (Seaton, 2007). These right-wing efforts to sanitize history have an obvious appeal to those eager to shed the burdens of the past. Perhaps the national psyche has been affected by the prolonged recession at a time when China has surged ahead. In addition, suppression of the shameful incidents of history for so long meant that the public was unprepared for the deluge of critical commentary at home and abroad during the 1990s. It is not surprising people found it difficult to reconcile this narrative with what they had learned at school. Accepting the new revelations about the dark past meant putting the older generation on trial and taking on the thankless task of atoning for the sins of past generations. Some Japanese are also concerned about potential compensation claims at a time when Japan's economy has stagnated.

Honda, a respected journalist for the *Asahi Newspaper*, counters such views by arguing that the past cannot be denied and that the orchestrated amnesia adds to Japan's shame. In his view, Japan:

> Unlike Germany and Italy, has not followed up on the war crimes of its own people. By not acknowledging these crimes, we fail to grasp the complete picture of our own national character. Lacking this under-standing, we keep appealing to the world, talking about Hiroshima and Nagasaki and the nuclear situation. We, therefore, gain a reputation for emphasizing our role as a victim without ever reflecting upon our own violent aspect. (Honda, 1999: 139)

CONTEMPORARY TIES

It would be misleading to suggest that contemporary ties between Japan and Asia are dominated by arguments over history. Leaders in China and Japan now understand that bilateral relations are too important to hold hostage to history. Regional economic ties are strong and generally mutually beneficial. Japan is one of the world's leading donors of foreign aid and approximately two-thirds of its Official Development Assistance (ODA) is funnelled to Asian recipients [**Doc. 11, pp. 134–5**]. In addition, the Japanese government lends substantial sums of money at concessionary rates to Asian governments, mostly for large infrastructure projects. Some observers view the concentra-tion of ODA and concessionary lending in Asia as a form of war reparations, especially in the case of China. It also makes sense to focus on Asia because it represents a significant market for Japanese producers and increasingly is a platform for offshore production by Japanese producers driven from the high costs in Japan (Hatch and Yamamura, 1996; Katz, 1998). Thus, it is in Japan's self-interest to stimulate development and nurture stability in a dynamic region that is closely tied to Japan's future economic prospects. Japan's private sector has invested in and lent heavily to Asia and has thus also played a constructive part in promoting regional development.

Japan's relations in Asia have steadily improved since 1974 when Prime Minister Tanaka was greeted in the region by riots protesting against Japanese economic dominance. In response to this unexpected outbreak of anti-Japanese sentiments, the government re-evaluated its regional profile and crafted a policy aimed at winning the hearts and minds of its fellow Asians by projecting soft power. In 1977 Prime Minister Fukuda committed Japan to assist the **Association of Southeast Asian Nations (ASEAN)** in large-scale industrialization projects and ODA was increased. Morrison argues that Japan's nurturing of stability and development in Southeast Asia during the late 1970s marked a watershed in Japan's post-Second World War foreign policy (Curtis, 1994: 146).

In 1997 a chain of events, initially linked to foreign currency speculation, led to a region-wide severe economic crisis that had consequences eerily reminiscent of Japan's burst bubble (Ries, 2000). Asset prices and currency values tumbled, scores of banks and other firms went bankrupt, huge sums of money evaporated and the human misery index sky-rocketed. Speculative investments in stock and land deals, fuelled partly by Japanese capital, pumped up the Asian asset bubble during the 1990s. In 1997, when Japanese banks refused to roll over loans and retreated from further lending, the resulting credit crunch led to an economic débâcle of immense proportions. In response to the crisis, however, Japan mounted a generous financial bailout and earned considerable goodwill for doing so [**Doc. 12, pp. 136–8**].

Association of Southeast Asian Nations (ASEAN): A regional organization established in 1967, including ten nations of Southeast Asia – Brunei, Cambodia, Indonesia, Laos, Malaysia, Myanmar (Burma), the Philippines, Singapore, Thailand and Vietnam.

MULTILATERAL PARTICIPATION

Japan's political and security roles in the region are focused on multilateral organizations. The most important of these is ASEAN, which has ten members from Southeast Asia. Japan is a dialogue partner with ASEAN and participates in annual summits with leaders from China and South Korea under the auspices of ASEAN Plus Three. Cambodia served as the site of Japan's first major postwar diplomatic initiative. In 1993, with the cooperation of ASEAN, Japan sponsored and led United Nations Transitional Authority in Cambodia (UNTAC) to facilitate democratic elections and deliver that nation from the trauma of prolonged violence. This was the first time that Japanese troops had returned to Asia in the postwar era and the experience has gone a long way in reassuring Asian neighbours that they do not need to fear a resurgence of Japanese militarism. Thus, this humanitarian endeavour enabled Japan to make considerable progress in burying the ghosts of its shared past with Asian nations. The non-confrontational, consensus-building approach to diplomacy of ASEAN is shared by Japan and provides it with an opportunity to broaden and deepen its regional posture in a non-threatening manner.

Since 1994, the **ASEAN Regional Forum (ARF)** has served as the focus of regional security dialogue, involving the ASEAN 10 and other nations in the region, including China, Russia and the United States. In the post-Cold War era, Asia is a region with many sources of friction and a number of smouldering conflicts. In this context, the relative paucity of regional fora and webs of organizational relationships is considered a major vulnerability. Japan is credited with urging ASEAN to create the ARF as a forum to exchange views and information about perceived security threats while engaging in confidence-building measures. Japan views North Korea and China as the major threats to continued regional peace. **Asian Pacific Economic Cooperation (APEC)**, established in 1989, is the leading Pan-Pacific economic organization with 21 members, including Japan, and has taken the lead in promoting free trade, investment and economic cooperation. As with ASEAN and ARF, Japan values the multilateral, consultative approach in APEC.

THE FUTURE

The ongoing and vigorous public debate over the past is revealing about society. Japan is certainly not the only nation in the world with skeletons rattling around its historical closet. There is a powerful temptation to forget and inter that history, but it is hard to bury the past once it has been exhumed. Following the death of Emperor Hirohito in 1989, there has been an outpouring of troubling revelations in Japan. Until he died, many people held back out of respect for what he symbolized. And, as Dower argues, since he was never held accountable for his conduct during the war, nor ever accepted responsibility for the devastation his nation unleashed in Asia, many Japanese felt that there was no point in their doing so (Dower, 1999). What is clear is that diaries were suddenly 'discovered', archives yielded their secrets and the past that had been hastily buried suddenly returned with a vengeance. Public opinion polls are encouraging that this history is not

ASEAN Regional Forum (ARF): This forum focuses on security issues in the Asia-Pacific area.

Asia-Pacific Economic Cooperation (APEC): APEC was established in 1989 as an informal dialogue group in response to the dynamism, growth and accelerating integration among member economies. Over the years APEC has developed into the primary regional vehicle for promoting open trade and investment and regional economic cooperation. APEC's twenty-one members include Australia, Brunei, Canada, Chile, People's Republic of China, Hong Kong (China), Indonesia, Japan, Republic of Korea, Malaysia, Mexico, New Zealand, Papua New Guinea, Peru, the Philippines, Russia, Singapore, Chinese Taipei, Thailand, the United States and Vietnam. The combined economies account for approximately 45% of world trade. The Association of Southeast Asian Nations (ASEAN), the Pacific Economic Cooperation Council (PECC) and the South Pacific Forum (SPF) have observer status. The APEC Secretariat was established in 1993 and is located in Singapore.

North Korea: The admission by North Korea leader Kim Jong-il in 2002 that his government abducted thirteen Japanese nationals, eight of whom died under mysterious circumstances, thwarted plans by Prime Minister Koizumi to normalize relations. The immediate public outcry among Japanese was intense and since then the fate of missing abductees has become the focus of sustained media coverage. The Japanese government insists that their fates must be accounted for before it agrees to participate in initiatives aimed at getting Pyongyang to abandon its nuclear weapons programme under the auspices of the 6-Party talks (China, United States, Russia, South Korea, North Korea and Japan) launched in 2003.

being denied as Japanese want the government to acknowledge more forthrightly the nation's war responsibility and do more to atone for that past (Saaler, 2005).

In Asia, Japan is now cool and there is an infatuation with Japanese pop culture throughout the region. Young Asians are avid consumers of Japanese fashion, music, cartoons, games, dramas, fads and food. In much of Asia, and especially among the younger generation, the wartime and colonial past with Japan is not a major issue. In Korea and China, the past is fading more slowly and resentments linger more prominently than in the rest of Asia, but in these nations too there is a mania over Japanese pop culture.

Throughout Asia, Japan is more a source of inspiration than suspicion and worries about a revival of Japanese militarism are shared by few. Japan is seen as a powerful engine of growth and development. Numerous disputes and conflicts over territory and resources, and the uncertainties generated by **North Korea**'s nuclear weapons programme cast a cloud over the relative peace and stability that prevails in Asia. Japan is also worried about the rise of China as regional hegemon and is anxious about the evolving relationship between Washington and Bejing, fearing that its special relationship with the United States may decline in importance.

6

Japanese Security

THE UNITED STATES–JAPAN ALLIANCE

The close alliance between the United States and Japan remains the centrepiece of Japan's foreign policy and the foundation of its security. During the nearly 7-year Occupation (1945–52), the US government was able to impose and develop relationships that have kept the nations bound together despite the inevitable bilateral strains. As a result of the Cold War bargain between the United States and Japan, hammered out in the waning days of the Occupation, the United States gained rights to base its troops in Japan and in exchange agreed to provide security for Japan. The United States sought to have forward-based troops mostly as a deterrent against Soviet adventurism in Asia, although the communist 'menace' became more broadly defined to include China, North Korea and, later, North Vietnam. The original 1951 Security Treaty was modified in 1960 amid considerable public criticism [**Doc. 13, pp. 138–9**]. From the beginning it has been a lopsided arrangement in that the United States is obliged to defend Japan, but not vice versa. It is also lopsided in that the Japanese government has, in reality, little influence over what the US military does on the bases, nor does it have control over the overseas deployment of troops based in Japan. Revelations that the United States regularly ignored Japanese prohibitions on the presence of nuclear weapons in its territory, apparently with the government's acquiescence, highlights the fundamental imbalance in the alliance [**Doc. 14, pp. 139–41**]. The presence of 47,000 American troops in Japan coexists uneasily with the pacifist Constitution and has been a critical issue in domestic political debate throughout the Cold War era (1947–89) and since [**Docs 1 and 3, pp. 118–21 and 122–5**].

The United States–Japan Security Treaty has been a source of both friction and strength in the overall bilateral relationship. The bases are often an

Battle of Okinawa: In 2007, Prime Minister Shinzo Abe's government provoked outrage among Okinawans by suggesting that textbooks revise sections covering the Battle of Okinawa (April-June 1945). The government wanted to delete passages that implicated the Japanese Imperial Armed Forces in compelling and instigating mass suicides by Okinawans despite testimony by eyewitnesses. This attempt to whitewash Japanese responsibility provoked mass demonstrations and under the weight of contrary evidence the government backed down. This incident reveals ongoing efforts by Japanese conservatives to forge a less damning history and the lingering resentments among Okinawans regarding the huge sacrifices they were compelled to bear; more than 100,000 non-combatants or about one-quarter of the total civilian population died in the battle, as Tokyo used their island as a pawn to buy time for the defence of the main islands.

Omoiyari yosan: Literally 'sympathy budget'. A reference to the money the Japanese government pays to base US troops in Japan. This amounted to over $3 billion in 2008.

Relocation of bases: Activists in Okinawa oppose a plan to relocate the US Marine Corps Futenma Airbase, located in a heavily populated

irritant for the Japanese who live in the surrounding areas because of the noise and dangers of training missions and the criminal activities of soldiers. The concentration of the bases in Okinawa has meant that this island prefecture has suffered more than its fair share of the burden (Johnson, 1999). It was not until 1972, in response to strong Japanese pressure, that the United States agreed to return Okinawa to full Japanese sovereignty. Prior to that the United States had made this island group a de facto US militarized territory. Okinawans harbour resentment towards both the Japanese and US governments because they have not been consulted over bilateral defence agreements that affect them. Okinawans still hold the Japanese government responsible for the devastating **Battle of Okinawa** in April–June 1945, and feel a psychological distance from Japanese. Due to lingering anti-Japanese sentiments, it was the only prefecture in Japan that Emperor Hirohito never visited.

The brutal rape of a 12-year-old girl in 1995 by US marines brought anti-base resentments to a head and in 2006 the United States and Japan agreed to a plan for reducing and relocating US bases. About 75% of the land allocated for US bases in Japan is in Okinawa and more than 60% of the 47,000 troops are stationed there. Host nation support for the bases and troops, known in Japan as the *omoiyari yosan*, began in 1978 and has grown to over $3 billion a year.

On the other hand, the US security presence is unobtrusive to most Japanese and some see the US military presence as a reassuring safeguard. In addition, the bilateral alliance reassures Japan's neighbours in Asia, easing concerns that still linger about Japanese militarism and signalling that the United States will remain engaged in the region. Other Japanese across the political spectrum worry, however, that the US security presence might involve Japan in some conflict against its wishes and that it symbolizes a diminution of Japanese sovereignty.

Japan's reliance on the United States for its defence and the benefits of close economic relations have meant that Japan in practice has a foreign policy that more often than not is subservient to the US foreign policy agenda [**Doc. 15, p. 141**]. As the relationship has matured over the decades, the Occupation-era mentality on both sides of the Pacific has faded only slowly; thus, the patterns of interaction sometimes appear frozen in time and at others demonstrate a great deal of change. Prime Minister Hatoyama came into office in 2009 calling for a more equal partnership, implicitly questioning the Liberal Democratic Party's (LDP) more acquiescent stance since 1955. Subsequently, disputes have flared over plans to **relocate bases** and downsize the US military presence, highlighting ongoing tensions that test alliance management skills. By breaking his promise to the Okinawans on base relocation, preceded by prolonged waffling over alternatives, Hatoyama lost the confidence of the public, forcing his resignation.

THE REACTIVE STATE

Japan has often been criticized for having a weak and vacillating foreign policy. Blaker characterizes Japanese diplomacy as reactive and minimalist (Curtis, 1993). Rather than taking the initiative or articulating a strategic vision, he sees Japan merely coping with issues and problems as they crop up. Blaker defines minimalism as the practice of grudgingly making the least possible concessions required to avoid provoking a crisis, usually in United States–Japan relations. During the 1980s and 1990s, more often than not these concessions were related to persistent bilateral trade frictions and involved opening Japan's market. However, in relying on the United States (or other nations) to engage in *gaiatsu* to force such concessions, principally as a means of overcoming domestic pressure groups, the government has soured Japanese perceptions about its trading partners (Schoppa, 1997). Orchestrated foreign bullying can be effective, but it is a poor substitute for domestic political leadership and risks provoking a nationalistic backlash.

Japan's low key diplomacy often means that other nations do not fully appreciate what Japan is contributing, thus breeding resentments in Japan because its efforts and sacrifices are overlooked and minimized. Japan often appears selfish, parochial and cipher-like on the international stage and it has not wielded diplomatic clout commensurate with its economic strength.

During the 1997 Asian currency crisis Japan advocated a stabilization fund, but this was initially opposed by the United States. Since then, Japan's criticisms of International Monetary Fund (IMF) orthodoxy and its proposal for a stabilization fund have quietly drawn support. Such examples suggest that an inclination for a low-profile, behind-the-scenes role has denied Japan the credit it deserves in resolving international problems and advocating an alternative vision to that propounded by the United States.

In 2007 Japan proposed an Arc of Freedom and Prosperity encompassing Asian democracies. It was a rare instance of assertive regional diplomacy that went nowhere. Prime Minister Abe's tour through Asia aimed at drumming up support for the initiative drew lukewarm responses as leaders were wary that the underlying agenda was aimed at containing China. It was also curious that South Korea, a vibrant Asian democracy, was not included, a revealing absence that speaks volumes about the constraints the past yet imposes on Japanese aspirations. Indeed, in 2005 an Internet petition in China opposing Japan's bid to join the UN Security Council attracted more than 30 million supporters as public opinion was inflamed by Prime Minister Koizumi's visits to Yasukuni Shrine, symbol of an unrepentant stance about Japanese aggression against China.

urban location, to the fishing village of Henoko where there is an agreement to build a floating runway just off the coast adjacent to Camp Schwab. The Okinawan dugong, an endangered sea mammal inhabiting this area, was the plaintiff in a lawsuit filed in San Francisco seeking an injunction blocking the project. The floating helipads have also aroused local ire because they will severely damage the local coral reef. Anti-base sentiments among Okinawans reached a feverish pitch in 2010.

Gaiatsu: Foreign pressure. This term refers to the pressures put on the Japanese government by other governments to modify various policies. In some cases, such pressures are actually welcomed as a way to overcome a domestic political impasse that is preventing necessary reforms desired by the government. However, inviting or staging *gaiatsu* as a means of overcoming political inertia has nurtured public resentments about what is portrayed in the mass media as high-handed tactics by other nations, notably the United States.

TRANSFORMING JAPAN'S SECURITY POSTURE

In 1999, the Diet approved a new set of defence guidelines that clarify the cooperation and support that US forces can expect from the Self-Defense Forces (SDF) under a variety of different contingencies [**Doc. 16, pp. 141–3**]. The new guidelines commit the SDF to provide logistical support and to conduct search-and-rescue operations during emergencies in areas surrounding Japan. These provisions sound quite limited, but in the context of Article 9 and the long-standing taboo on deployment of Japanese forces for collective defence, they represent a controversial expansion and clarification of what Japan will do in an emergency.

The revised guidelines were a response to the ambiguities in what the SDF was permitted to do in the event of hostilities. They were also a response to the perception of the new threats to regional peace and stability that emerged in the post-Cold War era. The assumption of enhanced and wider security responsibilities marks a significant change from the marked reluctance to do so that characterized Japan's defence policies in much of the post-Second World War era. There have been growing concerns that if American forces became engaged in conflict in Asia and did not receive even limited Japanese support, the security alliance and bilateral relations would suffer severe damage.

Suggestions in Washington that Japan is getting a cheap ride on defence are invoked to ratchet up pressure on Tokyo to accommodate US security demands. Ironically, the United States imposed the constitutional constraints on the Japanese military but seems to have been regretting it ever since [**Doc. 17, p. 144**]. Since the outbreak of the Korean War in 1950, the United States has continually pressured Japan to beef up its military forces and assume more responsibility for regional defence. US demands that Japan establish military forces for its own defence were parried by Prime Minister **Yoshida** who emphasized the need to focus on economic recovery from wartime devastation. At this time Japan did create a small, armed force that evolved into the SDF, but did so in a minimalist way, reflecting strong national reservations about remilitarization. Japan steadfastly refused to participate in collective defence, maintaining that the Constitution only permitted the right of self-defence. President Nixon renewed US pressure in 1969 when he requested Japan to assume a greater role in ensuring the stability of East Asia.

In 1978 the United States and Japan agreed for the first time on guidelines on defence cooperation and it is at this time that Japan agreed to pay for hosting US troops. However, the security relationship remained a sensitive

Yoshida Doctrine: The policy of Prime Minister Shigeru Yoshida (1946–47, 1949–54), emphasizing the need of Japan to concentrate resources on economic recovery as a way to deflect US demands that it rearm in the early 1950s.

political issue in Japan. In 1983 Prime Minister **Yasuhiro Nakasone** provoked strong domestic criticism when he declared his intention to turn Japan into 'an unsinkable aircraft carrier', and agreed to extend the scope of Japanese navy patrols in surrounding sea lanes. It was also under his leadership that Japan openly breached the informal limit on defence spending of less than 1% of GDP. His willingness to tread on taboo topics and sensitivities offended many, but paved the way for a more vigorous security debate in Japan.

Moves to strengthen the bilateral security alliance with the United States since the 1990s have challenged sentiments in Japan that favour enhanced reliance on multilateral arrangements and organizations. The euphoria that greeted the end of the Cold War dissipated in the face of growing security problems in Asia. Moreover, it was soon apparent that multilateral approaches in the absence of a multilateral security architecture in Asia would not suffice. Asia has no shortage of frictions over islands, natural resources and history that impinge on Japan's security. In addition, the neighbourhood has grown riskier with North Korean missile tests and its nuclear weapons programme. In this atmosphere, during the Bush administration (2001–09) **defence cooperation** proceeded apace despite citizens' reservations. In the wake of 9/11, Prime Minister Koizumi quickly pledged support for the 'war on terror' and also sent a symbolic contingent of troops to Iraq. In addition, Japan supported US-led NATO coalition forces in Afghanistan with a refuelling mission based in the Indian Ocean.

The change in Japan's security posture has been driven by the experience of the Gulf War (1990–91), modernization of the Chinese armed forces and the development of missile technology and nuclear capabilities in North Korea. In addition, the United States has steadily kept pressure on the Japanese leadership to take on a greater share of the burden of Asian security.

A NORMAL NATION

The 1990–91 Gulf War proved to be a humiliating experience for the Japanese government. Never has a nation contributed so much, some $13 billion in financial support, for so little appreciation. Japan found itself subjected to criticism for its chequebook diplomacy and unwillingness to place its troops in harm's way. In a war that clearly involved Japan's vital strategic interests – unimpeded access to oil – this passive, risk-free approach to security and shifting of the heavy lifting to other nations made a mockery of Japan's ambitions to join the UN Security Council. In response, a leading conservative

Nakasone   Yasuhiro (1918–): Conservative LDP politician who served as prime minister (1982–87) under the aegis of Kakuei Tanaka, his most important supporter. His cabinets were referred to as the Tanakasone governments in recognition of his mentor's power behind the scenes. A personable statesman, he enjoyed close relations with President Ronald Reagan and Prime Minister Margaret Thatcher. A hawk on security issues, he played a significant part in expanding Japan's defence profile. He oversaw ambitious fiscal and administrative reforms and the privatization of government-operated monopolies in telecommunications and the railways.

Defence cooperation: During the Bush administration (2001–09), the LDP-led Japanese government developed closer security ties with Washington, provoking considerable unease among the Japanese people. The Japanese public did not support the dispatch of troops to Iraq nor logistical support for US-led NATO forces in Afghanistan. The government made these gestures in light of the dangers posed by North Korea and the continued reliance on US defence.

politician, Ichiro Ozawa, stirred debate by calling for Japan to become a 'normal' nation. In Ozawa's view, Japan had failed the test of leadership and had not assumed the responsibilities commensurate with its global standing. For Ozawa, normal meant that Japan had to reassess the constitutional constraints on its security posture in a manner that would enable it to respond effectively to military crises and threats. In the context of Japan's determination to secure a seat on the UN Security Council, Ozawa argued that Japan could not merely look on while other nations took on the burdens of security and peace-keeping [**Doc. 18, p. 145**].

Ozawa criticized what he viewed as the self-serving pacifism that has constrained Japan's postwar security policies. He played a key part in passing legislation in 1993 that enabled Japan to participate in overseas peace-keeping operations (PKOs) and to support United Nations Transitional Authority in Cambodia (UNTAC). The participation of Japanese troops in various PKOs, albeit under tight restrictions mandated in the Diet, showed the world a different Japan. The rehabilitation of Japan's international reputation gained momentum with its generous and crucial $3 billion financial support for UNTAC. This effort was headed by a Japanese national, Yasushi Akashi, and featured extensive Japanese involvement in preparing for and monitoring democratic elections in Cambodia, garnering rare but appreciated international kudos.

The passage of the new defence guidelines in 1999 with barely a murmur of public debate was a far cry from the street protests that rocked Tokyo in 1960 when the Security Treaty was revised and renewed. However, protests against deployment of troops to Iraq, opposition to the Indian Ocean refuelling mission and revision of Article 9 suggest that many Japanese in the twenty-first century remain dubious about the desirability of becoming 'normal'.

NORTH KOREA (DPRK)

North Korea's emergence as a serious military threat from the mid-1990s with missile capabilities and a nuclear weapons programme helps explain why Japan has reassessed its security policies. Given the legacy of hatred generated by Japanese colonialism in Korea, the possibility that North Korea (Democratic People's Republic of Korea, DPRK) could strike Japan with nuclear weapons drastically altered the strategic landscape in Northeast Asia.

Suddenly North Korea became a major factor in Japan's foreign policy deliberations and reassessment of its defence posture. In the wake of the 1998 missile tests, the Japanese government warmed to the idea of joining with the United States in developing a system for ballistic missile defence (BMD). In 2003 the Koizumi government endorsed BMD and made it a national security priority. In 2005 it adopted new defence programme guidelines that lifted the existing ban on joint weapons development key to deployment of BMD. North Korean missile launches and a nuclear test in 2006 accelerated deployment of a multi-layered sea-based (Aegis) and land-based (Patriot) system. By 2011 Japan plans deployment of four Aegis-equipped destroyers and 16 ground-based Patriot units around major cities. The government has also changed the Basic Space Law in 2008 to lift a ban on operating satellites, allowing support of defensive military operations such as BMD. Beijing is worried that BMD will affect its nuclear deterrent, apply to Taiwan and otherwise destabilize the region by triggering an arms race. The Obama administration and the Democratic Party of Japan (DPJ) are not as keen on BMD as their respective predecessors, suggesting some scope for revision in plans and priorities.

Prime Minister Koizumi also pursued normalization of relations with Pyongyang, travelling there in 2002 in a bid to resolve divisive issues (McCormack and Wada, 2005). His efforts failed largely because Kim Jong-Il admitted that his regime had abducted Japanese nationals and could not provide details on the fate of many of the abductees. Those that did return to Japan became the focus of a sustained and intense national campaign to pressure North Korea to return all the abductees and provide further information on those that were dead or missing (McCormack, 2004). Conservative groups opposed to normalization and committed to regime change have orchestrated a national campaign about the abduction problem that draws on the palpable suffering of the abductees' families (Johnston, 2004). In this context, Japan has had a limited role in the Six-Party Talks (North and South Korea, China, United States, Russia and Japan) that were launched in 2003 following Pyongyang's withdrawal from the Nuclear Non-Proliferation Treaty (NPT). The fitful process of the Six-Party Talks is aimed, *inter alia*, at ending North Korea's nuclear weapons programme. However, Japan has insisted that the abductee issue needs to be resolved to its satisfaction before it will support undertakings to achieve this goal. Differences over the Six-Party Talks and the US decision to lift sanctions against North Korea in 2008 have strained bilateral relations with Washington.

PEOPLE'S REPUBLIC OF CHINA

The modernization of the Chinese military forces gained momentum in the 1990s, raising concerns in Japan. China's double-digit annual growth in defence spending over the past two decades has drawn extensive media coverage in Japan and fuels speculation that Beijing harbours hegemonic ambitions in Asia. It is one powerful reason why Japan places great value on its security alliance with the United States.

The legacy of war remains a significant but fading factor in bilateral relations. When Premier Zhang visited Japan in 1998, he made it clear that all is not forgotten or forgiven, pressing his hosts at every turn to come clean about the past and atone for the various atrocities inflicted on the Chinese people between 1931 and 1945. However, after Prime Minister Koizumi left office in 2006, Beijing has toned down the rhetoric on historical grievances and emphasized a forward-looking relationship focusing on mutually beneficial economic ties. China became Japan's leading trading partner in 2005 and has overtaken Japan as the second largest economy in the world as of 2010. Nonetheless, Japan and China have been at odds over Taiwan, missile defence and United States–Japan security cooperation. China points to the presence of US troops and forward-basing facilities for the US Seventh Fleet as destabilizing factors in the region. The DPJ government is more in tune than the LDP with Washington's desires to cultivate Beijing as a strategic stakeholder in the international system. The two nations remain at odds, however, over the sovereignty of what Japan calls the Senkaku Islands (Daiyotai in Chinese), rocky outcrops that lie between Taiwan and the Okinawan islands. More importantly, conflicting claims over the gas fields in the East China Sea remain unresolved, even as China exploits them. The Japanese government is also apprehensive that China's growing economic and soft power in the twenty-first century is undermining its regional influence.

LINGERING TABOOS – ARTICLE 9 AND THE THREE NON-NUCLEAR PRINCIPLES

Article 9 of the Constitution bans the development of military forces and eliminates Japan's sovereign right to wage war. This article is unique in the world and is the reason the Japanese Constitution is often referred to as the Peace Constitution. As the only nation to have experienced the devastation of atomic bombs, Japan has assumed a unique role in global efforts to halt nuclear proliferation and eliminate nuclear weapons. It has embraced three principles that have served as the basis of its nuclear policy: (1) no development of nuclear weapons; (2) no possession of nuclear weapons; and (3) no introduction of nuclear weapons on Japanese soil.

Article 9 and the three non-nuclear principles have established the parameters of Japan's debate over defence, but these parameters have been challenged for some time (Samuels, 2008). Japan's defence budget is $50 billion, putting it in the top five worldwide, with a total of 240,000 military personnel and the world's fifth largest navy. It has an army larger than the United Kingdom or France and the most advanced naval and air force capabilities in Asia. In addition, the gap between official policies and reality is highlighted by revelations that the Japanese government permitted the United States to maintain nuclear weapons in Japan and had a **secret agreement** allowing US naval vessels to transit its waters carrying nuclear weapons [**Doc. 14, pp. 139–41**].

It also appears that Prime Minister Eisaku Sato (1964–72), who won the Nobel Peace Prize for embracing the non-nuclear principles, confided to US diplomats in 1969 that he thought they were 'nonsense'. Public opinion in Japan has been strongly against the development of nuclear weapons throughout the postwar era, but not everyone is convinced. In 1999, Shingo Nishimura, the parliamentary Vice Minister for Defence, publicly suggested that Japan reconsider its ban on developing nuclear weapons and was sacked for his remarks. He went on to suggest that Japan needed a nuclear deterrent to protect against neighbouring nations. A decade on, in 2009, former Prime Minister Nakasone made similar remarks while later that year Toshio Tamogami, the former head of the Air Self-Defense Forces (ASDF), gave a speech in Hiroshima on the anniversary of the atomic bombing saying, 'As the only country to have experienced nuclear bombs, we should go nuclear to make sure we don't suffer a third time.' These views may not be mainstream, indeed polls indicate that 80% of Japanese continue to support the three non-nuclear principles, but demonstrate that conservatives are less reluctant to trample on hallowed taboos.

Despite Article 9, the Japanese Supreme Court has ruled that the SDF is constitutional because the military forces are solely for defensive purposes and Japan cannot project its military power because it lacks aircraft carriers, bombers or long-range missiles [**Doc. 19, pp. 145–7**]. Nevertheless, calls for constitutional revision have grown more strident since the 1990s, in no small part because of the gap between the pacifist ideals of the Constitution and the prevailing realities in contemporary Japan. Ardent nationalists would like to rid Japan of what they view as an alien imposition and remake Japan into a 'normal' nation. Others want to strengthen security constraints in the Constitution while many oppose any revision at all, fearing it would open a Pandora's box (Dore, 1997). The prospects for revision improved somewhat in 2007 with passage of legislation laying out the guidelines for a national referendum, but the mushrooming of Article 9 Associations all over Japan

Secret agreement: Several former Japanese diplomats have confirmed the secret agreement with the United States in which the Japanese government agreed on a 'don't ask, don't tell' policy regarding whether or not US naval vessels transiting Japanese waters and making port calls were in violation of Japan's restrictions on the introduction of nuclear weapons. The LDP consistently denied the existence of this agreement.

in the twenty-first century opposed to revising the Constitution, more than 7,000 as of 2009, suggest that security taboos remain resilient among the Japanese people. Prime Minister Abe passed the referendum legislation in order to abolish Article 9, but voters were not impressed. The DPJ's electoral victories in 2007 and 2009 were not driven by security issues, but did draw on popular anxieties about LDP support for shedding security constraints and developing closer defence cooperation with the United States. The DPJ does not support constitutional revision and is seeking to emphasize human security initiatives that focus on alleviating the conditions that breed poverty, human rights abuses, extremism and violence.

7

Women in Japan

As of 2007, the United Nations Development Programme ranked Japan 54th on the gender empowerment index out of 93 countries, down from 38th in 2003. Despite this and other assessments that paint a bleak picture of a society failing to tap the potential of its women, some Japanese counter that women enjoy high status and a privileged position in Japan. They reject criticism by Western feminists and other international observers, arguing that Japan's social and cultural context is different. Proponents of this view focus on the powerful role of women in the family as proof that women are seeking and finding fulfilment within the context of traditional roles. Women often control family finances, while also having a central role in making educational decisions affecting their children (Iwai, 1993). While some women do find fulfilment within traditional roles, or find few options, it is evident that a growing number of women are choosing to break the mould and many are critical of patriarchal biases in society.

The popular stereotype of meek, submissive **Japanese women** has become little more than a condescending caricature at odds with contemporary reality. Opinion polls in contemporary Japan indicate that women are not terribly fulfilled, nor do they feel that they are treated as equals in society or within the family. More importantly, more and more women are carving out roles that are not consistent with traditional ideals as patterns of employment, marriage and family are changing.

The consequent tension between lingering (but fading) attitudes and norms, and the changing reality of women in Japan, animates discourse on gender roles. As elsewhere, women desire equal treatment, respect, freedom from harassment, assault and discrimination. They also desire a society free from gender constraints that provides more support for their multiple responsibilities as wives, mothers, workers and caretakers for the elderly. Women remain the fulcrum of the family and, despite the tremendous transformation experienced in Japan, they have helped maintain a degree of family stability that has long been the envy of other industrialized nations.

Japanese women: Whereas wives' weekly housework hours are almost identical in Japan and the United States (33.5 and 32.4 hours in 2000, respectively), there are substantial differences in the housework hours of husbands. Japanese husbands spent an average 2.5 hours per week on household tasks whereas American husbands spent about 8 hours per week on those tasks. The percentage of husbands who did no housework at all was 43% for Japan, 33% for Korea, and 10% for the United States. Japanese wives spent on average more than 13 times as much time as their husbands on household tasks. From 1995 to 2005, daily housekeeping reported by Japanese men increased from 32 minutes to 46 minutes.

DIVORCE

Shotgun marriages: Certainly the phenomenon of shotgun marriages is not new, estimated at nearly 13% of marriages in 1980, but in the Heisei era it has become very public and the media has played a key part in promoting positive attitudes towards these inadvertent marriages. There was a television drama series based on this theme and in 1997 a pregnant Namie Amuro, one of Japan's hottest pop stars, tied the knot at age 20. Ironically, her husband, 16 years older, was chosen by the government to lead a public campaign encouraging young men to be responsible fathers. However, their marriage did not beat the odds and they later divorced. Flouting convention, again, Amuro ceded custody of their child to her husband so she could focus on reviving her career. For many young women, unlike the stars, this is a daunting choice because they face a grim life of poverty whether or not they give up custody because they have interrupted their education and/or career and Japan is not a society open to late bloomers.

Heisei: Era of 'achieving of peace' (1990–present) under the reign of Emperor Akihito.

Retirement allowance and pension: The media speculated that the new law giving wives the rights to up to half of their

Divorce rates have risen dramatically, soaring 48% between 1993 and 2003 and more than 20% of marriages now end in divorce. The rate of divorce has become similar to the average in the EU (2.1 divorces per 1,000 people as of 2005; 3.6 in the United States), a reality that sits uneasily with prevailing images of stable families (Fuess, 2004). The divorce rate for couples aged 45–64 years rose an incredible 15-fold between 1960 and 2005. **Shotgun marriages** (*dekichatta kekkon*) have also surged in recent years and now account for 25% of all marriages, but over 60% of such unions end in divorce within 5 years.

As of 2008, the total number of single-parent families stood at 1.22 million, up 28% from 1998, and nearly half live in poverty [**Doc. 5, pp. 126–7**]. Poverty is common because child support is not; only about 18% of divorcees regularly receive alimony from former husbands. Although 80% of single mothers work, they tend to work in marginal jobs where pay and benefits are low because many lack advanced degrees and work experience, and also need flexible schedules to accommodate childcare responsibilities.

Divorce has increased because the greater economic independence of some women means that they no longer have to endure unhappy marriages and the social stigma attached to divorce has attenuated over the years. Divorce also tracks business cycles and the prolonged downturn since the early 1990s means that many men in marginal and insecure jobs are vulnerable and thus unable to provide economic security. In addition, there are wide gaps in gender expectations of marriage and younger women expect more from their husbands, especially in terms of helping out around the house and in child-rearing. Often, these expectations are not met as husbands starting out their careers have to work long hours and firms have not adopted family-friendly policies that would facilitate couples sharing family responsibilities more evenly. It is also true that social norms have changed considerably and wives are no longer expected to tolerate domestic violence and philandering. There has also been a spike in divorces among couples married more than 30 years, initiated mostly by women who have fulfilled their child-rearing duties and decide to restart their lives rather than share their remaining years with a husband they cannot abide. In 2007 the government amended the law to grant divorcees access to their husbands' **retirement allowance and pension**, making divorce a somewhat more viable option for veteran wives.

The surge in divorce constitutes a significant change in a nation where government social programmes such as elderly care are based on the assumption that stable families will have a key supportive role. Divorce is also the main reason why 14% of children are now raised in poverty. The

Plate 1 DPJ leader Yukio Hatoyama celebrates historic victory in 2009
Source: Aflo. Co. Ltd.

Plate 2 Kobe earthquake in 1995

Source: Aflo. Co. Ltd.

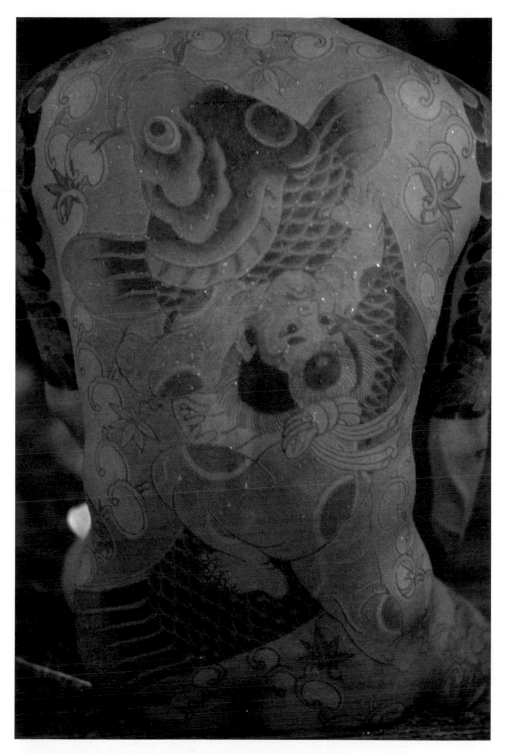

Plate 3 Yakuza often adorn their bodies with elaborate tatoos
Source: Alamy Images

Plate 4 Activists support contract workers who lost their jobs in wake of 2008 economic implosion

Source: Aflo. Co. Ltd.

Plate 5 Prime Minister Junichiro Koizumi made six visits to Yasukuni Shrine, a talismanic symbol for an unrepentant view of Japan's military aggression

Source: Press Association Images

Plate 6 The Yanba Dam project was cancelled in 2009, representing a downsizing of Japan's public works and shift in spending towards social programs under the DPJ

Source: Press Association Images

Plate 7 Shoko Asahara, leader of Aum Shinrikyo, a religious cult that carried out a sarin gas attack on Tokyo subways in 1995
Source: Gamma, Camera Press

Plate 8 Gesture of reconciliation: Emperor Akihito and Korean President Kim Dae Jung attend 2002 World Cup Soccer Final
Source: Reuters

Plate 9 Occupation leaders: General Douglas MacArthur and Prime Minister Shigeru Yoshida

Source: Press Association Images

Democratic Party of Japan (DPJ) is increasing family allowances, reinstating special subsidies for single-parent households and making public education free through high school in a bid to mitigate the consequences of higher divorce rates and try to ensure that these families do not become entrenched in poverty.

WOMEN AND WORK

As noted in Chapter 2, the Japanese Constitution is quite progressive regarding women's rights, but progress in realizing these rights in society has been dilatory. There has been a series of legislative initiatives since the mid-1980s aimed at improving women's position in the economy, but these have not yet produced the desired results. There is growing recognition that women have trouble balancing the competing demands for their time and energy at home and in the workplace. Government legislation aims to make it easier for women to balance the various roles they are expected to assume, but this goal remains elusive (Gelb, 2003). Despite the ratification of the UN Convention for the Eradication of All Forms of Discrimination Against Women in 1985, the enactment of the Equal Employment Opportunity Law in 1986 (revised 1999, 2006), the 1991 Childcare Leave Law and the 1998 Elderly Care Law, the 1999 Gender Equality Law and the 2001 Long-Term Care Insurance System for dispatching nurses and home helpers to ease the burdens of elderly care, women remain far behind men in the workplace in terms of job status and pay. On average, women earn only 60% as much as men and only 10% of managers are women. In addition, partly as a consequence of inadequate government policies, birth rates are dropping and families face unprecedented strains because of the need to provide care for the aged. These various laws reflect the fact that there is a growing number of women who are taking on multiple roles, but they face significant difficulties in assuming these varied responsibilities in the absence of necessary support mechanisms and helpful husbands. As Brinton points out, 'Thus, just at the point when legislation propounds equal opportunity for men and women, social conditions are promoting strongly unequal time obligations to the family' (Brinton, 1993: 236). She expresses pessimism, justified in retrospect, about the prospects for improvement in this regard because social attitudes about family roles change very slowly.

In most families in Japan, both the wife and husband work outside the home as paid workers. Since the 1980s, more married women have entered the paid labour force and currently about 45% of families depend only on the husband's earnings. However, the assumption that most women are full-time

husband's retirement allowance and pension would lead to a spike in divorces. The dip in divorces after the law was passed in 2003 and before it was enacted in 2007 suggested that many potential divorcees were waiting for the new law to take effect. In the event, there has not been a surge in retirement divorces, reflecting the fact that living on half of a pension involves considerable economic sacrifice. The courts do not have a good record in awarding equitable division of household assets and thus the economic penalties of divorce remain high. Nonetheless, the divorce rate among couples married more than 30 years has quadrupled since 1985.

housewives lingers despite this changing reality. Wives' earnings are critical to family finances and economic security and thus not working is not a viable option for most married women. This is an important phenomenon that confronts social attitudes and government policies that assume women will give priority to the family. In cities there are waiting lists for public **childcare** and government provided home-nursing for the elderly is only supplementary, assuming that a female relative will serve as the primary caregiver. The gap may be narrowing, but working women often find themselves confronting frustrations and difficulties in balancing their various roles because of the lag between their everyday reality and the social context within which they function.

Childcare: The competition to secure a slot in childcare is so intense that some couples actually time their child's birth to occur at the optimum time to join the waiting list. The catch-22 of childcare in Japan is that working mothers are given priority so that mothers who stop working to raise children find it difficult to resume careers because they have a low priority in securing childcare unless they are working which they cannot do unless they have childcare.

THE LABOUR FORCE PERIPHERY

As there is a strong assumption in society and within families that women should place a priority on household and family responsibilities, married women who work often require flexible work arrangements that enable them to juggle these various demands. Overall, only 40% of working age women are employed in the paid labour force, the lowest rate in the Organisation for Economic Co-operation and Development (OECD), and nearly two-thirds are non-regular workers (part-time, temporary, contract and dispatched workers). In general, full-time workers are expected to place a priority on their work duties and there are few concessions to working mothers. Women who need to work but also need flexible schedules that leave time for household duties are forced to seek non-regular jobs because flexitime, work sharing and similar innovations are rare in Japan. This means that women often take on less challenging jobs with fewer responsibilities, lower wages, less security, limited benefits and negligible prospects for promotion and wage increases.

Aside from the need for a flexible work schedule, the tax system is also credited with nudging women into part-time work. This is because if a man's wife earns over a certain amount (¥1.3 million, about $14,300), both of their incomes are taxed at a higher rate. In addition, in many firms the family would lose some important benefits, such as a housing subsidy or dependants' allowance, if the spouse works full-time. Thus, in considering why women seek non-regular work, it is important to bear in mind the tax penalty for working full-time, the potential loss of a husband's benefits, the difficulty in securing childcare, the need to reconcile long working hours with the shorter hours of childcare facilities and the inadequacy of elderly care that forces many women to adopt the main role in taking care of ageing relatives.

This tendency in women's labour supply behaviour is reinforced by labour demand conditions. As of 1997, 62% of working women were employed on a full-time basis compared with about 75% in the United States. By 2008, however, only 46% of working women in Japan held full-time jobs. This sharp drop illustrates the massive shift towards non-regular employment caused by deregulation of the labour market since 1998. Between 1990 and 2008 the percentage of non-regular workers nearly doubled to 34% of the total workforce. Women are disproportionately represented among non-regular workers, accounting for 62% as of 2008, while constituting only 42% of the total labour force.

Non-regular employment has surged because employers are eager to cut outlays on wages and social benefits. This trend has gained momentum due to deregulation of the labour market since 1998 which progressively removed government restrictions on which categories of work firms are allowed to employ non-regular workers.

Women workers are also shunted into dead-end jobs because corporate personnel officers expect that women will marry before they turn 30 years of age and leave the workforce to rear children. Thus, from the perspective of the firm, heavy investments in training women workers will not pay off. The logic of the lifetime employment system and continuous on-the-job training does not translate well in terms of the life-cycle needs of women workers. The failure to modify the employment system to accommodate the life-cycle needs and responsibilities of women workers often makes it an unviable option. Employment policies designed for men and based on the dated assumption that a wife will take care of family and household duties make it especially difficult for young women to pursue managerial careers.

During the prolonged recession since the 1990s, the 'flexible rigidities' of the Japanese employment system described by Dore have looked more rigid and costly while the flexibility has been largely at the expense of women workers (Dore, 1973). In this sense, mostly female, non-standard workers help subsidize the desirable but expensive 'rigidities' (lifetime employment, seniority wage increases, bonuses and various benefits) accorded to the mostly male core labour force.

EDUCATION

The structure of work opportunities means that the returns on education remain lower for women than men. Tachibanaki argues that discrimination explains why investment in women's education produces lower returns in terms of employment opportunities and career earnings (Tachibanaki, 1996).

Brinton suggests that because families know that the return on the education of daughters is lower than for sons, families are more inclined to spend more on their sons' education. In addition, Japan is the only industrialized nation, including Korea, in which there is a yawning gap between the expressed educational aspirations of mothers for sons and daughters (Brinton, 1993: 204–5). Brinton argues that the educational system and labour market have developed in ways that systematically disadvantage women. For example, the training system in firms that leads to promotion is tied to uninterrupted tenure, something that women with husbands and children can rarely manage. At university, women tend to be concentrated in humanities rather than departments with stronger **career orientations**. Women also represent less than one-quarter of undergraduate students at the elite universities that open doors and put graduates on fast-track careers. Women in the United States have benefited from professional degrees in law, medicine, business and accounting that give them more control over their careers, and allow them to resume careers after a hiatus for child-rearing. In this sense, education confers skills and status on women that enables them to get married, raise a family and maintain careers. In Japan, few women earn professional degrees and thus career and family is too often an either/or situation. Less than one-third of women continue to work while raising a child, and those who interrupt their careers for a few years to concentrate on their families can seldom resume their careers and are relegated to less responsible jobs at lower pay. This helps explain why many more highly educated women drop out of work altogether.

Although about half of women attend post-secondary educational institutions (slightly higher than the figure for men), more men attend 4-year university courses. This is a major change from 1960 when only 10% of women continued their education after high school. However, many women attend 2-year junior colleges or vocational schools rather than 4-year universities. This greater investment in the human capital of sons rather than daughters perpetuates differences in educational attainment that limits women's progress in the workplace. However, more families are having only one child, meaning that daughters' educational desires do not have to be sacrificed for their brothers. It is also possible that the impending labour shortage in Japan, due to shrinking family size, will eventually facilitate women's career advancement because there will not be enough male workers.

Career orientations: Women in Japan are increasingly starting up their own businesses and also making strides in the professions; women accounted for 2.8% of judges in 1980 and 10.8% in 2000, 3.8% of lawyers in 1980 and 8.9% in 2000. As of 2000, women account for two-thirds of all pharmacists and 15.6% of all doctors. Women also account for more than 15% of those who pass the National Civil Service Exam, up from 4.5% in 1980. The percentage of women undergraduates at the nation's two most prestigious universities, the University of Tokyo and Kyoto University, remains about 20% compared with over 50% in the Ivy League, but double the proportion in 1980.

LOW BIRTH RATE

The burdens of multiple roles carry important consequences for women and society. Most social scientists ascribe the low birth rate in Japan (1.37 children per woman in 2008 down from 4.3 in 1947) to the expense and difficulty of raising children. The consequences of this low birth rate are further discussed in Chapter 8. The support mechanisms common in other advanced industrialized societies that facilitate child-rearing and provide support to families are relatively limited in Japan. For example, the cost of giving birth is not covered by national health insurance. Women also complain that childcare services are in short supply and have rigid hours that do not mesh with work schedules. In addition, long working hours keep husbands at the office and limits their household contributions; just over 1% of eligible men take their childcare leave. Moreover, during maternity leave, only women working full-time receive 40% of their pay from social insurance, while those working as non-standard workers receive nothing, making it extremely difficult for many families to make ends meet. Because rearing children in Japan is costly in terms of educational and other child-specific expenses, derailed careers for women and frequently the loss of considerable income to have a child, the birth rate has declined well below the rate needed (2.07) to maintain current population levels.

THE BIRTH CONTROL PILL

In 1999 the Ministry of Health and Welfare approved use of the birth control pill for women, bringing an end to a more than three-decade campaign by women's rights organizations. The government had withheld approval of the pill since the 1960s out of concerns that its usage might promote promiscuity and lead to an erosion of traditional feminine roles. The medical community also opposed use of the pill, citing concerns about the effect on women's health and inconclusive data on its safety. In addition, critics argue that many doctors derived substantial income from performing abortions and thus opposed approval of the pill. Because condoms (80%) and withdrawal (17%) are the most widely used forms of birth control in Japan, there have been many unplanned pregnancies. As a result, Japan has had one of the highest abortion rates in the world, 9.3 per thousand women aged 15–49 in 2007 (United States 19.4 in 2005, England and Wales 18.2 in 2008) down from 40–50 in the 1950s (Jolivet, 1997; Norgren, 2001). At that time, there were over 1 million abortions per annum, before declining to an estimated 337,000 by 1997 and 256,000 in 2007.

The government had been planning to approve the pill earlier, but then the rising threat of AIDS and other sexually transmitted diseases led to the cancellation of approval out of a concern that it would lead to a rise in unsafe sex. Feminists and other critics argue that the ban on the pill reflected patriarchal biases. Some argue that concerns about Japan's declining birth rate also made bureaucrats reluctant to give women more control over their fertility. The government's decision to approve the pill is widely linked to the unprecedented, speedy approval for the anti-impotence drug Viagra in 1999. In this case, the government decided that foreign drug trial studies were sufficient and reliable. This undermined its position on the pill, which was based on the presumed need for further research and the unreliability of foreign research findings. The fast-track approval for Viagra made the government's stance on the pill increasingly untenable, opening it to a barrage of criticism for having a double standard on sexuality and reproductive health.

The pill has not become widely used, only 2.2% of women use it as of 2008, partly because it is not covered by national health insurance, but also because of negative publicity concerning the side-effects. The pro-pill lobby argues that the main point is to give families and women the right to make decisions free of government and patriarchal interference.

SEXPLOITATION

The sex industry is estimated to account for nearly 1% of GDP in Japan, a figure equivalent to the defence budget. Pornographic magazines, videos and *manga* (comic books) are widely available in shops and from vending machines. Tens of thousands of foreign women, mostly from Southeast Asia, were issued visas as entertainers, but most of these women work in the welter of '**soaplands**' and massage parlours (where many Japanese women also work) that are found in cities and towns all over Japan (Bornoff, 1991). After being criticized in a 2005 US State Department report for sex trafficking, the Japanese government has cracked down on this flesh trade, but it remains robust [**Doc. 20, pp. 147–8**].

Soapland: An establishment where men pay for sexual services.

Women's groups in Japan credit the enormous pornography industry with shaping and reinforcing demeaning attitudes and abusive actions among men towards women [**Doc. 21, p. 148**]. The Prime Minister's Office surveys report that one in three women in Japan is subject to physical assault and one in five has been subject to some form of sexual assault. There has been a rising awareness of **sekuhara** (sexual harassment) and many companies have instituted employee-sensitivity programmes. Costly settlements in sexual harassment lawsuits against Japanese companies in the United States including Mitsubishi in 1994 and Toyota in 2006 have focused the attention of corporate Japan on the need to take such workplace abuses seriously. In 2007 the government also upped the ante by passing legislation mandating proper handling of sexual harassment complaints by employees.

Sekuhara: Japan's sex industry has exploited this market niche, operating 'image clubs' where male customers pay to fondle women dressed up in various roles such as schoolgirls, train commuters or office ladies.

In cooperation with the police, subway and train operators have cracked down on the numerous *chikan* (molesters and exhibitionists) who frequent public transportation networks. In 2009 cameras have been installed on some train lines to curb such harassment and neighbourhood groups post anti-*chikan* signs to warn young women to be careful. It may not be that the situation has grown measurably worse, but rather that society has become more open in recognizing that these problems exist and more forceful in trying to stem such abuses. Cases of wife and child abuse are also reported with far greater frequency than previously, indicating that attitudes are becoming less tolerant of such behaviour towards women (Goodman, 2000; Kingston, 2004a). In the 1990s, Interpol named Japan as the largest source of Internet child pornography. After considerable lobbying by various citizens' groups, the distribution of such materials was made illegal in 1999, but possession remains legal, impeding effective enforcement. There are dubious cultural arguments suggesting that Japan is more tolerant about deviant sexuality, but Japanese women's groups argue that pornography, juvenile prostitution, sexual harassment and degradation of women is more about power than sexuality or culture.

It is a troubling sign of the times that in 2006 a video game maker in Japan released a game called RapeLay in which players act as sex perverts who score points and get revenge by molesting a mother and her two daughters with other chances to rape a selection of various female characters, including schoolgirls, in trains or other public places. Players can use the mouse to 'touch' selected body parts of their virtual victims. There is a gang rape feature and a movie mode for those who want to record their depraved feats. This game seems to draw on the same themes and market that made Rape Man a popular *manga* (1985–92), but is even more disturbing in terms of how points are scored and the choices players make to 'win'.

There is a robust market in Japan for games depicting sexual violence, but even within this genre RapeLay is notable for its molestation simulation. The games in this genre, offering virtual interaction, are often set in trains or schools, with young female targets dressed in their school uniforms, often sailor suits. Players typically score by groping, molesting or committing other indecent acts against these 'innocent' victims who inevitably, apparently fulfilling the players' fantasies, begin to enjoy what is being done to them by the virtual perverts. This *hentai* (pervert) genre has many variations in Japan drawing on the *lolicon* (Lolita complex) subculture and is ubiquitous in anime, *manga* and video games. The disturbing message for gamers is that casual sexual assault is normal, pleasurable and is what young women secretly long for even if they appear to initially resist and show signs of distress.

Given the popularity of video games, and the possibility that they do shape attitudes if not actions of gamers, activists in Japan and around the world are lobbying for a law banning such exploitative images. Illusion, the aptly named company that created RapeLay, claims its game was approved by an industry ethics watchdog body and that it complies with existing laws. This company and others like it seem to operate under the illusion that international norms do not matter. In their view, these products are for the domestic market and comply with domestic laws, end of the story. More importantly, they generate huge profits. Given the global fascination with Japan's anime, *manga* and video games, however, this industry and the *hentai* component is facing heightened scrutiny and pressures to stop depicting sexual exploitation and debasement as harmless fun.

Equality Now, a UK-based organization, led an international campaign against RapeLay, one that reverberates throughout Akihabara, the virtual centre of Japan's gaming industry where hundreds of similar *hentai* games are available. In 2009, Amazon withdrew the game from its online store, a sign that global values matter even in the world of virtual reality. Many fans around the world buy and play games that do not offend international sensibilities, but this niche market is too big to ignore. The international campaign is suggestive about the risks and limitations of globalizing aspects of Japanese culture that many Japanese also abhor.

8

Demographic Time-Bomb

Japan is one of the most rapidly ageing nations and 23% of the population is over 65 years of age. As of 2009, there were 29 million elderly (over 65) up from 21 million in 1999 out of a population of 126 million. Between 1988 and 2007 Japan's elderly population doubled. There are now 40,000 **centenarians** and 10% of the population is over 75 years old. It is predicted that by 2040, the elderly will outnumber the young by a ratio of four to one.

Japanese society is rapidly greying because of the drop in fertility, extended life expectancy and the ageing of the baby boomers (1947–49) born soon after the Second World War. The birth rate has fallen from 4.54 children per woman in 1947 to 2.1 children in the 1960s to 1.37 children in 2008. This decline is explained by the rising number of single women (the government estimates that one out of seven women born in 1980 will never marry), the preference for smaller families and the difficulties of securing convenient childcare. In addition, precarious job security and low incomes are discouraging many young workers from deciding to have a family. Smaller family size is related to the higher average length of education for women, rising levels of labour force participation by them and the difficulties of combining work and child-rearing. In addition, living space in cities is crowded and raising a child is expensive. There are often long waiting lists for public childcare and for couples in their thirties, career demands are especially onerous, leaving little time for family obligations. In 55% of married households, both spouses work.

Ageing in Japan has also accelerated because of the sharp rise in life expectancy. Average life expectancy for men increased from 50 years in 1947 to 79 years by 2009, while that for women rose from 54 to 86 years over the same period. Certainly there are many implications and one is that those with senile dementia will rise from an estimated 1 million in 1990 to nearly 3 million by 2015.

Centenarians: There are now so many Japanese who hit the century mark that municipalities are cutting costs by sharply reducing or eliminating cash awards for this achievement and have also reduced the silver content of commemorative sake cups.

Most experts agree that society is not yet ready to cope with the burdens and needs of a large elderly population. It is generally agreed that the ageing crisis is one of the most serious challenges facing Japan in the twenty-first century as it struggles to balance the needs and interests of the young and old. More Japanese commentators are raising the alarm that the future of Japan will be bleak and its influence will decline as a result of this ageing crisis [Doc. 22, p. 149]. It is expected that economic growth will slow as the labour force shrinks, savings drop and the level of business investments and residential construction fall because of a shrinking population. The government also faces a fiscal crisis, and citizens face higher taxes, because of the costs associated with pensions and medical care for the aged. Given the extent of these problems, how is society coping? In short, not too badly.

FAMILY-BASED ELDERLY CARE

In the postwar era there was an implicit assumption that families would take care of their ageing relatives. This assumption is based on the Confucian principle of filial piety and the deep respect accorded to the elderly. This respect is expressed at many levels, including an employment system in which status, power and wages are closely tied to seniority. Japan is a society where considerable deference is shown to elderly people and their experience is highly valued. Within the family, where patriarchal patterns remain strong, older males are accorded a position of dominance in their household. Given the practical and ideological importance of the family in Japanese society, it is not surprising that the government sees the family as the natural and desirable provider of care for the elderly. This inclination of the government to integrate the family into its social welfare policy is not only cultural; in general the government has refrained from the generous cradle-to-grave approach to social services and benefits that is common in Europe. Firms are expected to provide employment security and families are expected to take care of their own, meaning that until the 1990s the government mostly played a relatively limited part in providing the range of social welfare services and benefits common in other advanced industrialized societies.

It is important to bear in mind, however, that the ideals and values of society serve as an inspiration that may not always be realized in practice. Respect and deference to the aged is pervasive, but so is neglect, irreverence and frustration. Ever since the publication of Sawako Ariyoshi's 1972 novel, *The Twilight Years*, commentators have lamented the inadequacy of the elderly care system in Japan. The novel portrays a working woman at her wit's end trying to balance the competing demands on her time from office and home, including a senile but very active father-in-law, and how this difficult situation is complicated by her husband's failure to shoulder a share of the burden at home and the absence of adequate professional/community support. Since then, more and more women are working and facing a similarly impossible situation.

Government policies and societal norms, however, continue to place the burden of elderly care on the shoulders of women. Women, already busy as wives, mothers and workers, are also expected to become nurses for the aged. It is estimated that 85% of the elderly receiving care at home are cared for by female relatives (Harris and Long, 1999). This gender-based division of labour serves to make the care of the elderly an issue that strongly influences women's careers and their families.

To a degree, some women are willing to take on this task, internalizing the societal norm because of a feeling of *on*. Lebra defines *on* as 'a relational concept combining a benefit or benevolence given with a debt or obligation thus incurred' (Lebra, 1976· 91). In the context of the family, parents have bestowed much upon their offspring and thus reciprocating their accumulated kindness is considered natural and a way of assuming the responsibilities that *on* places on one. Some wives live up to social norms by caring for their husband's parents out of the same sense of *on* – the obligations assumed by the husband are internalized by the wife because they are jointly responsible for all that accrues to the family unit. Ultimately, they have little choice because there are very few options.

On: A personal sense of social debt or obligation created in a relationship by a benevolent act.

It has become increasingly apparent to the Japanese that this situation is not ideal and puts far too much pressure on families. Moreover, these traditional expectations are out of sync with transformations in the family, including residential patterns. Between 1980 and 2006, the proportion of older people living with a child declined from 70% to 44% while as of 2007, the percentage of three-generation households is only 18.3% of all households. The proportion of elderly living only with a spouse almost doubled from 20% in 1980 to 37% by 2007, while 16% of elderly now live alone. These figures suggest that family-based care is not viable for many elderly Japanese who live apart from their extended families, and if they are not living alone are often dependent on spouses who are also elderly. This significant change in the configuration of the Japanese family casts doubt on the efficacy of basing elderly care initiatives on the family.

The domestic media has also reported that many young women are reluctant to marry because they do not want to assume the onerous obligation of caring for their husband's parents, a trend that reportedly is making marriage more difficult for eldest or only sons whose wives are expected to take on this obligation. Those that do marry have their own families to raise and most want to also work. Women are reluctant to give up their jobs to nurse relatives as their income is often critical to household finances. Even if middle-aged women are willing to take on the task of caring for elderly relatives, there are not enough to cope with the surging numbers of elderly needing care.

NURSING CARE INSURANCE

What has been viewed as a family problem best dealt with at the family level has become a major public policy issue. The emphasis on home care versus institutional care means that there have not been enough nursing homes for the elderly who really do need institutional care. Instead, many have ended up as long-term patients in relatively expensive hospitals where they receive more care than they require. The government has reduced the available number of beds for such care significantly since 2005. In order to provide relief to families and to manage elderly care costs, in 2000 the government adopted the Long-Term-Care Insurance System (*Kaigo Hoken Seido*) which requires all Japanese workers over age 40 to pay premiums for nursing insurance. This system provides nursing and daycare services for everyone who needs care. There are various options for in-home services and services at local facilities which are determined in consultation with local care managers based on national criteria. The guiding principle emphasizes home and community-based systems that encourage older people to live with a minimum of dislocation and a maximum of independence for as long as possible. Not only is this approach economically more viable, but it is also in accordance with the wishes of more than 90% of elderly Japanese.

Caregivers: The government has negotiated Economic Partnership Agreements with Indonesia and the Philippines that allow for small numbers of nurses and caregivers to work in Japan, hundreds rather than the tens of thousands needed. However, the requirement that they all pass a difficult certification exam in Japanese within a few years of arrival means that almost none will be able to remain on a long-term basis unless the programme is modified. Given surging demand for nursing services and acute shortages of caregivers, the incentives for a pragmatic accommodation are high.

This long-term care (LTC) system has proven very popular, and demand for such services has surged, so much so that there are acute shortages of **caregivers**. There is high job turnover as conditions are difficult and pay relatively low. As of 2008, Japan already has some 9 million elderly enrolled in community-based adult daycare programmes and those receiving nursing care at home are projected to rise from 4.1 million in 2004 to 6.4 million by 2014. Premiums do not cover the costs of these programmes, weighing down already strained public finances. In addition, the LTC still relies on family members to serve as primary caregivers who only get limited help from the assigned professional caregivers. Because many family caregivers are elderly spouses, many lack the capacity to act as primary caregivers and some even need caregiving assistance themselves. In addition, as norms and labour force participation patterns change, it is unlikely that younger generations of women will take on these primary caregiving tasks to the same degree as their mothers and grandmothers. Certainly, there will be a growing demand for more nursing assistance for elderly still able to live at home but, for increasing numbers, assisted living facilities are a more appropriate option. However, there is a shortage of such facilities and long waiting lists. Progress towards meeting the ambitious targets of the central government's plans vary by region because local authorities are expected to assume responsibility for implementing the directives. Given the state of town and prefectural finances, in some areas national goals and standards will not be met unless there are generous subsidies.

PENSION AND MEDICAL CARE SOLVENCY

Coping with the challenges of the most rapidly ageing society, in which the number of elderly needing care will double between 1997 and 2020, is often described as 'mission impossible'. However, it is worth pointing out that Japan's elderly population doubled in the past two decades and the government has been able to manage medical costs. Japan spends less than half per capita than the United States on medical care and total health spending is about 8% of GDP compared with 17% in the United States. Even so, Japanese enjoy relatively good medical outcomes in terms of longevity and relatively healthy golden years. Certainly, Japan's demographic time-bomb poses enormous challenges to society and is straining both the medical care and pension systems, but by gradually and incrementally adjusting revenues and costs, the prospects may not be as cataclysmic as some commentators suggest. Clearly, taxes will have to rise and benefits will have to be trimmed or constrained in some fashion in order for society to accommodate the needs and interests of the elderly without sacrificing those of younger generations.

Is the pension system viable? As of 2000, there were 3.6 workers per retired person, but by 2025 it is estimated there will be only 1.9 workers per retiree and by 2030 only 1.5. In Japan's 'pay-as-you-go' system, this means that if benefits are not trimmed and eligibility for pensions remains unchanged, the pension contributions of workers will have to rise considerably. Currently, workers contribute 17.5% of their salaries towards the national pension scheme, but this would have to rise to an estimated 34% of basic earnings by 2025 to maintain the current benefit structure. Clearly, this is an undesirably high burden on the economically active population and would impinge on their quality of life.

To cope with this prospect, pension reforms enacted in 2004 are phasing in increased premiums and lowered benefits. The government seeks to ensure that pensions will equal 50.2% of after-tax working income, down from 62.3% in 2009, but there are good reasons to doubt the government will be able to reach even this target given high rates of pension delinquency among younger workers.

The government is trying to stabilize pension finances by raising the ratio of tax money used to cover the basic portion of the pensions from a little more than one-third to half, meaning this portion of pensions is less dependent on premium contributions. This is a response to the large number (40%) of those who are supposed to be making contributions to the pension scheme, but are not doing so. Managing pensions is critical not only in terms of the governments fiscal woes, but also in terms of the overall economy. Spending by retirees is becoming an ever more important mainstay of the economy.

The government's budget woes, most notably a public debt to GDP ratio of 200% as of 2010, are exacerbated by rising medical costs. After the age of 70, most elderly Japanese pay only 10% for health care (all other Japanese have a co-payment of 30%) and spending on them now constitutes more than one-third of the entire national health budget. As pension outlays rise more rapidly in Japan than anywhere else in the Organisation for Economic Co-operation and Development (OECD), by 2020 they could reach some 14% of Japan's GDP, nearly triple the average among the English-speaking countries of the OECD and even surpassing the level in some of the continental European nations. However, even if combined pension and medical outlays rise from 36% of GDP in 1997 to a projected 44% in 2025, this will put Japan comfortably close to the projected OECD average at that time [**Doc. 23, pp. 149–50**].

SOCIAL CONSEQUENCES

The ripple effects in society of a rapidly ageing population are diverse and complex. Since the mid-1980s, researchers have found a widening of income disparities in a society where equality is cherished and more than 90% of the population routinely identify themselves in annual surveys as part of the middle class. The Japan Institute of Labour has published research indicating that the ageing of society is the main factor behind widening income disparities in Japan (Ohtake, 1999). Ohtake finds that the degree of inequality within an age cohort increases with age due to the fuller realization of the rewards of human capital investments such as education and to what he calls the chance factors that affect individuals. He estimates that about half of the increase in inequality evident in Japan is due to an ageing population in which these factors are becoming increasingly influential. The cohort with the largest income disparities is growing fastest and thus the trend is towards greater inequality. As Japan rapidly ages, it will inevitably face the social strains and challenges of widening disparities. Society also has not coped well with the 20% of elderly living in poverty, one of the highest rates in the OECD. Their poverty and isolation have led to high rates of depression, suicide and also petty **crime** as they scramble to make ends meet.

As Coulmas *et al.* (2008) point out, the state has become a government for the elderly, redistributing income from the young to the elderly. One reason is that elderly voter participation rates are double those of younger Japanese so politicians seek to appeal to this growing bloc of voters with a vested interest in expanding social programmes for the aged. Even so, fiscal pressures will force the government to trim pension and medical care benefits. To the extent that pensions are cut, disparities are likely to widen, leaving those with fewer resources to fall back on more vulnerable.

The rapid ageing of society and depopulation carry the potential for igniting significant social change. For example, as the labour force shrinks, there will be a need to integrate women workers more fully into the workforce, creating incentives for work–life balance and gender equality employment practices. Society, employers and the state will also have to rethink retirement and cultivate a more active elderly population. This will depend on strengthening social networks that have atrophied in Japan's affluent society. The elderly are often looked on as a burden to society, but there is much they can contribute if given an opportunity to do so. Already community-based elderly volunteerism is filling some gaps in social programmes and retired professionals are increasingly making themselves available for development projects under the auspices of the Japan Overseas Volunteer Corps.

Elderly crime: Mostly shoplifting, has risen dramatically. In 2007, 31,573 senior citizens were convicted of theft, triple the total in 1998. Between 2002 and 2007, arrests of people over 65 more than doubled even as the overall crime rate declined. While the elderly population doubled between 1988 and 2007, the overall number of crimes committed by people aged 65 or over has risen fivefold. Between 2000 and 2006 the number of Japanese over age 70 charged with a crime more than tripled, to nearly 30,000 a year. Prisons are adjusting to the ageing of the prison population by constructing barrier-free facilities, introducing low-sodium diets and distributing hot water bottles during the winter months.

FURTHER REFORMS?

With the baby-boom generation retiring and the inexorable rise in the number of retirees per employed person, the financial circumstances of the elderly is generating considerable debate. Until the twenty-first century, taking care of the aged has been considered good and affordable. However, as the dependency ratio increases, political confrontation over the level of benefits and who qualifies for government programmes is intensifying.

Today's retirees are relatively well off and are receiving more in pension benefits than their contributions. In contrast, young people aged 24–34 today face an estimated ¥25 million deficit in their lifetime balance of tax and social security contributions to benefits. Given that people currently in their seventies are enjoying a ¥15 million benefit surplus, there is a ¥40 million generation gap. There is also resentment that civil servants and politicians have much better pensions than ordinary citizens. Premiums for low-income earners are relatively high, and it is difficult to enrol non-regular workers, one-third of the workforce, because employers are under no obligation to do so and few can afford to pay their premiums even if they enroll themselves. Marginalizing these workers in this way threatens social cohesion and raises questions about what will happen to them as they retire.

In the absence of means testing (determining who is eligible for benefits based on the economic situation of a given recipient), Japan's benefit structure is regressive because it does not favour relatively needy elderly, while those who are well-established financially usually receive higher benefits because of longer coverage and better pay. Because the well-off elderly tend to be asset-rich but cash-poor, mobilizing income from such assets is often suggested. However, because most assets are held in the form of a home, the sense of insecurity related to mortgaging it as a way of raising retirement income constitutes a considerable obstacle.

Instituting reform has been a difficult process and will not become easier as older voters will wield considerable power at the polls and can be expected to resist wholesale rollbacks. The government did move in 2008 to raise the means-tested medical insurance co-payment rate for elderly over age 75, reaching a maximum of 30% for those who have an income exceeding ¥5.2 million. Given the power of egalitarian ideals in Japan, there is public support for more means testing. Due to the pressing need of raising revenues and trimming costs, more decisive and unpopular actions are expected.

LABOUR SHORTAGE AND IMMIGRATION?

The dearth of babies and the rapid ageing of society threatens Japan with a labour shortage. By 2010, two workers are retiring for every new worker entering the workforce. It is hard to project what the shape of the future labour force will be, but there is growing concern that this labour shortage will make Japan the land of the setting sun. Technological advances could suddenly change this bleak outlook and there is also considerable room for more effectively tapping the vast pool of underemployed and unemployed women in Japan. Japan has in many respects squandered this significant reserve of human capital. However, in order to integrate women more fully into the labour force, attitudes must change, the employment paradigm must be modified to accommodate the life-cycle needs of women and public policies must be enhanced to lessen the obstacles to their labour force participation (see Chapter 7). This is a daunting agenda, but the alternative is a greater reliance on foreign workers.

There is a marked reluctance in Japan to accept greater numbers of foreigners in a society that thinks of itself as homogeneous and prizes an imagined ethnic purity. Compared with other large industrialized nations, Japan has relatively few non-Japanese residents, but the numbers doubled between 1990 and 2008 from 1.1 to 2.2 million, and they now constitute 1.74% of the population. Despite this surge, the percentage remains quite low compared with the United Kingdom (5.8%), Germany (8.2%) and Spain (10.3%). In the nation's non-Japanese community, there are about 590,000 Japan-born ethnic Koreans (*zainichi*), 655,000 Chinese and 312,000 *nikkeijin* (overseas-born Japanese from South America).

The *nikkeijin* were accorded a special working visa beginning back in 1990 by virtue of their shared ancestry. It was hoped that common ethnic origins would facilitate their integration in society, but these hopes have not been met. In 2009, as a result of the economic crisis, many lost their jobs and the government offered them airfare to return home. Chinese migrants tend to have better language skills than the *nikkeijin*, facilitating their adjustment. Many have been students who first came to Japan as scholarship recipients and decided to stay. As with the *zainichi*, they face considerable discrimination, but they have had a key role in Japan's booming economic relations with China.

Like everywhere else, Japan suffers from racism and discrimination against foreigners. There is little likelihood in the near future that there will be significant support for accepting a larger permanent foreign population. In April 2000, Governor Shintaro Ishihara of Tokyo stirred controversy in admonishing the Self-Defense Forces to be vigilant about *sangokujin* (third-country nationals – a seldom-used discriminatory and inflammatory reference to Koreans and Chinese resident in Japan) in the event of an earthquake. This remark was reminiscent of *senjin gari* ('Korean hunting' – massacres) conducted by vigilante groups in Tokyo and Yokohama in the wake of the 1923 Kanto earthquake.

The government seeks to prevent the emergence of a permanent community of **immigrants** (for a critical assessment of this situation see Shimada, 1994).

Japan does have immigrant workers and depends a great deal on their contributions, but the current situation allows the government considerable discretion in deciding to accept or deport foreign workers depending on business conditions. However, there will be a continuing demand for foreign workers because someone will have to work the *san-k* jobs (*kitanai*, *kiken* and *kitsui*, i.e. the dirty, dangerous and difficult jobs) not filled by Japanese.

Zainichi: Ethnic Koreans born in Japan who are descendants of Koreans brought to Japan during the colonial period (1910–45) as Japanese subjects, many as forced labourers. In many respects younger generations have been raised as Japanese, but face considerable discrimination and live in Japan as special permanent residents. In recent years there has been a rise in naturalization.

Nikkeijin: The controversial repatriation initiative involved the government paying each unemployed *nikkeijin* worker a one-time ¥300,000 payment to cover airfare, and ¥200,000 for each dependant, to return home. Initially, the government stipulated that anyone accepting the exit bonus would not be able to return to Japan and retain the special working visa status given to *nikkeijin*, rendering it a one-way ticket home. Denunciation of this plan within Japan and the international community forced the Japanese government to revise the plan to allow their return to Japan after 3 years.

Immigrants: In 2009 the Diet passed legislation that mandates residential cards (*zairyu*) for non-Japanese and substantial fines if they are found not carrying them. In addition, failure to report changes in personal information can lead to revocation of residential status. The Ministry of

Justice also took over control of issuing residential documents from local government offices that had been more compassionate in extending public services to visa overstayers. The new law also gives the government power to revoke a spouse visa for those who over a 6-month period fail to conduct without a legitimate reason 'activities spouses normally do'.

Human rights: Between 1982 and 2008 Japan accepted only 508 refugees, including a mere 49 through the entire 1990s; in 2007 alone the United States' target was 70,000. In 2008 the government granted refugee status to 57 asylum seekers, reflecting a sharp spike in applications from Burma. In 2010 Japan will begin a 3-year pilot program to accept third-country refugees (displaced Burmese living in Thai border camps) for resettlement, but only 30 per year, similar to the annual refugee intake of Iceland, population 300,000. Given that there are more than 100,000 Burmese in Thai refugee camps, advocates hope the pilot programme grows substantially.

Foreign workers are also needed to provide services to the elderly and to support the pensions of retirees through their social insurance contributions. Moreover, the shortage of skilled workers in the IT sector also increases the attraction of permitting expanded immigration of skilled workers and has led the government to make it easier for such workers to receive long-term visas.

It seems unlikely that the government will follow the suggestions of a recent UN report to accept 600,000 immigrants per annum, or a total of 17 million by 2050, to cope with its demographic time-bomb [**Doc. 24, pp. 150–1**]. How to accommodate migrant workers already here and respect their **human rights** remains a significant challenge.

9

Requiem for Japan, Inc.

THE LOST DECADE

Crisis and turmoil have a way of defining a people and their society. Japan has experienced prolonged and pervasive adversity in the recession-plagued 1990s, shaking beliefs, inclinations, relationships and patterns of behaviour. The ongoing transformation of Japan in the twenty-first century is driven in no small part by the wave of developments in the tumultuous 1990s that have acted as a curtain call for the postwar era. The verities of postwar Japan are fading rapidly or have disappeared altogether, signalling what some commentators refer to as the third great transformation in modern Japan. Perhaps one of the most profound changes has occurred in the way that citizens view their government as a series of scandals and exposés of negligence, incompetence and mismanagement have undermined the edifice of power and status of those who rule.

The discourse favouring deregulation and reform that emerged at the end of the 1990s owed its popular appeal to widespread scepticism about the wisdom and skills of those who make and enforce the regulations and wield power. The sweep of reforms and dynamics unleashed in the 1990s bear some resemblance to the changes instituted after the Meiji restoration (1868) and during the American Occupation (1945–52). It is too soon to comprehend the shape, breadth and pace of change in this emerging era of transformation, but limning the depths of the final decade of the twentieth century sheds light on why more and more people believe that the ways of the past are discredited and part of the problem, and thus why there is a growing consensus that reform is imperative [**Doc. 25, pp. 151–2**].

THE EMPEROR'S DEATH

In 1989 Emperor Hirohito died, bringing an end to the Showa Era (1926–89). His reign witnessed Japan's descent into military expansionism, the devastation of the Second World War and the incredible postwar recovery. The Japan he left behind was unimaginably different from the Japan he inherited from his father and yet despite extensive transformation there are also elements of continuity. Given the hardships inflicted and suffered under his name during the war, it is worth pointing out how well respected he remains among the Japanese who lived longest under his reign. The contradictions of society were perhaps best exposed during the funeral ceremonies, attended by foreign dignitaries from around the globe, whose presence indicated just how far Japan had been rehabilitated in the eyes of the world community. A god-king once likened to Hitler by the Allies, subjected to the disapprobation of the Allies during the Second World War was now, in death, accepted as the respected symbol of a renovated nation boasting a supercharged economy and a degree of peace and prosperity scarcely imaginable to those who surveyed the rubble that was urban Japan in 1945. The contradictions and ambivalence of the Japanese people were also on display. There was a public outpouring of grief throughout the archipelago, with mourners thronging the streets of Tokyo and visiting the Imperial Palace in their hundreds of thousands to offer condolences, while older Japanese tearfully shared reminiscences and the nation fell into a somber mood. This public evocation of loss was matched by record business in video rental shops as many Japanese switched off the extensive TV coverage of the traditional rites and retreated into their private spheres and interests. Soon after his death the economy also swooned, marking the beginning of the end of the miracle economy.

THE BURST BUBBLE

The bubble is a retrospective term that refers to the steep appreciation in asset prices that occurred in Japan during the late 1980s. Bubbles and subsequent crashes have occurred throughout history and are usually described as irrational, involving a collective mania spurred on by contagious optimism that what is bought today can be sold tomorrow for a higher price. At some point the crowd realizes that prices cannot be sustained at stratospheric levels, resulting in panic selling, an implosion in prices and economic crisis. Stock and urban land prices soared to unprecedented heights in Japan, with the stock average doubling between 1987 and 1989 and land prices in central Tokyo rising even more furiously. Just as suddenly as asset prices rose, however, they plummeted in 1990 and have remained depressed since then. This correction in asset prices is known as the bursting of the bubble. Twenty years later the Nikkei stock average was still less than one-third the level it reached at the peak and urban land prices remain down by a similar proportion.

Why did the asset bubble occur? There are a variety of theories and many factors are seen to have contributed to the dizzying spiral in asset prices. Like speculative spirals throughout history, price increases were fed by greed and a herd mentality, and were made possible by excessive liquidity and easy credit. In addition, a continuing escalation in prices for both stocks and land became a matter of faith and investors remained confident, even as prices plummeted, that there was still untapped upward momentum if they remained invested and patient. There was a powerful group psychology that encouraged people to suspend their judgement and worry more about being left out of the boom. As more punters poured more and more money into land and stocks, prices escalated out of control.

The bubble was not merely a result of this speculative frenzy. It is argued that Japan's current account surpluses and government restrictions on overseas investment by individuals and institutions during the late 1980s created a huge pool of excess money sloshing around Japan. The decision to allow a steep appreciation in the value of the yen in the Plaza Accords of 1985, aimed at reining in Japan's rising trade surpluses, is also thought to have contributed to the conditions that produced excess liquidity. In the absence of alternative investment vehicles, and with extremely low interest rates on bank deposits and government bonds, this surplus capital was funnelled into stocks and land, driving an appreciation in asset prices and wildly optimistic speculation. At one point, the **land in Tokyo** alone was supposedly more valuable than all of the land in the United States. The average price to earnings ratio on the Nikkei exceeded 65, more than quadruple the historic price to earnings ratio of the Dow Jones stock index in the United States.

Land in Tokyo: At the height of the bubble some analysts appraised the value of the 7.41 km^2 of the Imperial palace grounds in central Tokyo as being worth more than all of the real estate in California.

The government interest rate policy also contributed to the speculation by making it very cheap to borrow money, injecting huge sums of money into a system already awash in capital. The government was promoting expansion with cheap money and managed to spur growth averaging 5% between 1986 and 1989, at a time when other leading economies languished in recession. With interest rates at low levels, bankers had to lend more money to turn a profit and thus they aggressively expanded lending without careful credit assessment. Nor did they or government banking authorities monitor how the money was used. With what seemed like a green light from bankers and government officials, companies borrowed vast sums of money to expand production facilities and also engaged in *zaitech* – asset speculation designed to boost company balance sheets. With the government running a loose money policy and bankers eager to lend money, risks were thought to be minimal and mega-projects were launched without concern for returns or worst-case scenarios.

Zaitech: The speculative activities by corporations in land and stock unrelated to core business activities.

Lavish spending, speculation, over-investment and an absence of risk assessment made for a volatile combination. The government popped the bubble by raising interest rates five times in 1989 as a way of trying to prevent asset inflation from spilling over into the rest of the economy. The Central Bank's efforts to contain inflation burst the bubble, but the house of cards built by speculative fever was fragile anyway and it was only a matter of time before a shock sent it crashing down. The government may have hoped for a soft landing, but instead Japan was mired in recession throughout the 1990s. In the wake of the bubble, Finance Ministry bureaucrats have been blamed for mismanaging economic policy, causing the crash and failing to pursue policies that would effectively address the problems that had accumulated during the bubble era. Bankers have been accused of lax lending policies and incompetent credit risk assessment while the *yakuza* (gangsters) stand accused of manipulating bankers and bureaucrats to secure huge loans for speculative and illegal activities. Whiting argues that many of the **jusen** had *yakuza* ties known to both the bankers and government overseers (Whiting, 1999). A lot of the loan default problem can be traced back to these *jusen*, suggesting that the bubble was a giant con game that enriched the mob at public expense.

The collapse of land and stock prices sent shock-waves throughout the Japanese archipelago and brought the financial sector to its knees. Suddenly the land that served as collateral for almost all of the bank loans was worth less than the original loans. Those who had borrowed money for stock speculation were also unable to repay their loans. Until the end of the 1990s the government tried to keep the lid on how bad the problem of loan defaults was, mostly out of concern that revelations would spark a panic and further worsen already severe economic conditions. There was also hope that economic conditions would improve and that with an upturn in the business cycle, bankers and lenders would be able to work their way out of the mess. However, business conditions in the 1990s remain depressed and the **bad-loan problems** festered. The government could no longer stand by while the nation's entire financial system teetered on the edge of insolvency.

Taxpayer-funded bailouts of the banks and related financial institutions restored stability to a wobbly financial system, but at the expense of public confidence in the credibility of government leaders and bankers. Official estimates of the total bad debt run as high as $600 billion, about the same as the US Savings and Loan Bank crisis of the 1980s in an economy half the size. Unofficial estimates peg the bad debt at closer to $1 trillion. It would not be until Prime Minister Koizumi (2001–06) took charge that banks managed to write down their bad debts and restore their balance sheets.

Jusen: Real estate lending subsidiaries of banks that incurred massive unrecoverable loans in the wake of the bubble, threatening the collapse of the Japanese financial system in the mid-1990s and forcing a government bailout despite strong public criticism.

Bad-loan problems and the *yakuza*: The *yakuza* along with everyone else also lost a lot of money when the value of their assets imploded. But their penchant for violence discouraged banks eager to collect on loans outstanding to them or foreclose on *yakuza* properties put up as collateral. This proved a valuable niche for the *yakuza*, playing to their skills in debt collection, meaning that they helped banks recover from their mob brethren a fraction of what they were owed and in the process made considerable fees and often retained control of the collateralized assets. In the mid-1990s, following the murder of a banker pushing his luck by pressuring *yakuza* to repay, the government allowed banks to write off loans deemed difficult to recover.

THE BINGE

The shortlived bubble era, 1986–91, was a time of ostentatious and conspicuous consumption. Corporate entertainment money flowed in record levels and the **narikin** vied to outdo each other in exuberant, if not tasteless, excess. Restaurants sold noodles topped with gold flakes, imported designer goods sold at grossly inflated prices, flashy sedans became common sights in the entertainment areas and a society that placed great value on restraint and understatement went on a collective binge. Art was purchased at astronomical prices, with Van Gogh's *Sunflowers* fetching some $40 million. Marketers even advised foreign companies to sell their products at high prices in Japan because Japanese consumers associated high prices with quality and would thus shun **bargains**.

Narikin: The nouveau riche who emerged during the bubble at the end of the 1980s who engaged in conspicuous and often garish consumption fuelled by wealth generated by spiralling land and stock prices.

The real estate market overheated, pricing affordable housing out of the reach of the average salaryman. An apartment of 75 m^2 within 90 minutes from the office in central Tokyo cost 8.5 times the average annual salary of a salaryman, more than double the housing cost to salary ratio in other advanced industrialized nations. 'Reasonably' priced apartments in Tokyo's 23 wards cost 1 million yen per square metre. A million US dollars in Tokyo would buy a relatively small, shoddily built house with virtually no garden. But there was a pervasive faith that land prices only rose and indeed that had been the case in the postwar era. So even when prices seemed astronomical, families mortgaged their futures to the hilt, confident that 20 years down the road their investment would be considered a shrewd coup.

Bargains: From the mid-1990s, ¥100 stores proliferated and the price of all products, including imported goods, fell considerably while consumers revelled in *kakkaku hakai* (price destruction), demonstrating that Japanese also enjoy a good bargain.

The wealthy collected golf club memberships and they too became a field for speculation and incredible valuations. Second home and resort communities sprouted up around the country, bringing the influence of the bubble to some rural areas. It seemed as if the cult of mammon had suddenly spread a mass hysteria among a people not inclined to crass materialism.

The bubble gave rise to immense wealth for the lucky individuals who had bought land or stocks at the right time, suddenly creating significant socio-economic differences among people who all viewed themselves as 'middle class'. Japan had been enormously successful in evenly spreading the fruits of the economic miracle, but this achievement and the social cohesion it generated was tested by the sudden and sharp disparities fuelled by the asset bubble. Society suddenly faced the challenges generated by the emergence of 'haves' and 'have nots' and the tensions caused by evident differences in means and lifestyle in a nation that values conformity and uniformity.

HANGOVER

The bubble-induced hangover is still felt in the twenty-first century. The human toll has been enormous. Observers remark that the post-bubble experience in Japan has been relatively benign compared to the restructuring that swept through corporate America following the 1987 stock market crash. It is true that layoffs and unemployment have been relatively limited, but the misery index can be measured by other means. Many families had assumed massive, multi-generation mortgages to acquire housing, only to see the value of their property plummet below the level of their outstanding loan. This phenomenon of negative equity has helped depress consumption in Japan as families spend as little as possible to compensate for the folly of bubble-era purchases. Some landowners who had pledged their land as collateral for loans lost their land. Many families lost everything in the crash, not having hedged their heavily leveraged bets, and the media carried reports of debtors disappearing, presumably to escape creditors and assume new identities. Families suffered a rising divorce rate and children were yanked out of university because tuition had become an unaffordable expense. The media focused on the rising number of heads of households committing suicide so that their families could collect money from life insurance policies. Since 1998 Japan's number of suicides has surged, topping 30,000 every year, many linked to severe financial distress, including rising numbers of men in their 30s and 40s [**Doc. 26, pp. 152–3**]. The growing cardboard-box communities of homeless men gathered in train station areas bore testimony to the hardship not captured in the rosier official statistics on unemployment. So too did the shift of many young female university graduates into the sex industry and the rise in juvenile delinquency.

The crash also affected corporate Japan, but weighed more heavily on small and medium-sized businesses. Larger corporations still enjoyed favoured access to credit, especially if they were connected to a *keiretsu* group. Smaller firms suddenly found it difficult and expensive to borrow and the business downturn made it more difficult to service outstanding loans. Record numbers of corporate bankruptcies were reported throughout the 1990s, leaving ruin and dislocation in their wake.

Big Bang: Financial deregulation programme initiated by the government of Prime Minister Ryutaro Hashimoto in 1996 often characterized by the media as the 'little whimper' for failing to meet expectations for sweeping liberalization.

Even the larger corporations suffered as domestic consumption also crashed. Perhaps the most significant impact involved the financial sector. The government's '**Big Bang**' was implemented beginning in 1997 to rectify the moribund state of the financial sector. It was driven by the belated realization that the absence of deregulation and competition had accentuated the problems and left Japan lagging behind international competitors [**Doc. 27, pp. 153–4**]. Thus, the bursting of the bubble forced a reconsideration of prevailing practices and an embrace of reform discussed in Chapter 10.

The bubble has also unleashed unprecedented criticism of Japan's corporate culture and its values of slavish conformity, personal sacrifice and reverent loyalty. The 1999 hit film, *Jubaku: Archipelago of Rotten Money*, sends a powerfully subversive message in lashing out at the basic tenets of the business world. The redeeming features of Japanese-style capitalism are depicted as the cause of the decline and as an impediment to recovery. The emerging mood of frustration, scepticism and fear is changing the way Japanese view the world and act in it. Popular author Ryu Murakami struck a chord with the 1999 publication of his satirical, *The Bubble: What Could That Money Have Bought*. He lampoons the taxpayer bailout of bankrupt financial institutions by listing 123 alternatives for spending the same $600 billion. Rather than pay the 'gambling debts' of profligate bankers, Murakami points out that Japan could have done something useful with this huge sum of money that would have had a lasting benefit. Such films and books are popular precisely because they question the powers that be, increasingly common sentiments in Japan. It is telling that the once revered officials in the Ministry of Finance, the most powerful institution in Japan, were mocked in the media for their once frequent attendance at **nopan shabushabu** as honoured guests of bankers and others under their purview. Such behaviour is neither new, nor a revelation to reporters, but is no longer tolerated, less out of prudishness than out of concern about collusion and violation of the public trust.

AUM SHINRIKYO (SUPREME TRUTH SECT)

On 20 March 1995 members of the **Aum Shinrikyo** released sarin gas in Tokyo's metro, killing 12 people and making 5,500 other commuters ill. This act of terrorism was preceded by an attack against court officials in Matsumoto (Nagano Prefecture) not originally tied to Aum and was followed by a failed attempt to spread hydrogen cyanide at Tokyo's busiest commuter station, Shinjuku, on 5 May 1995. On 16 May, police arrested the guru of the cult, Shoko Asahara, and rounded up as many of his lieutenants and cult members as they could find. Train stations in Japan as of 2010 still have large wanted posters of cult leaders alleged to be involved in planning and carrying out these terrorist acts. Cult members have been charged with the subway deaths, 15 additional killings and an assortment of other crimes.

Aum was established in 1984 in Tokyo, one of the tens of thousands of new religions that have emerged in Japan in recent decades, and was initially involved in selling quack medicines. In 1989, the government extended it recognition as a religion and the half-blind Asahara, whose real name is Chizuo Matsumoto, began to attract attention with his syncretic new religion

Nopan shabushabu: Notorious restaurants featuring beef, mirrored floors and waitresses wearing short skirts and no panties. The wining and dining of Ministry of Finance bureaucrats at such establishments by businessmen under their jurisdiction provoked public outrage in the late 1990s and became symbolic of the collusion between corporate Japan and the government, and the special favours involved.

Aum Shinrikyo (Supreme Truth Sect): A new religion centred on the teachings of Shoko Asahara. It staged an attack on Tokyo subways in 1995 using sarin gas.

drawing on Buddhism, Hinduism, yoga and the apocalyptic sixteenth century predictions of Nostradamus. At its peak, Aum claimed some 40,000 members, with an estimated 20,000 in Japan and other members scattered in Russia, Sri Lanka, Germany, the United States and Australia.

Aum preached that the end of the world was near and that the United States would ignite the apocalypse in 1997. New recruits signed over their worldly assets and lived communally in the cult's compounds where, according to critics, they were subjected to training sessions involving headgear with attached electrodes to synchronize brain waves (or erase memory), solitary confinement, food and sleep deprivation, beatings and other techniques of brainwashing. Loyal members maintain that they merely followed the teachings of their beloved leader. Sometime in 1994 Asahara is believed to have changed tack and rather than merely preparing for Armageddon, Aum began planning to initiate it. At this point Aum used its considerable assets and highly educated followers for developing weapons of mass destruction (laser, nuclear, chemical and biological).

Following the police crackdown in 1995, the majority of members left Aum and tried to return to a normal life. Four of Asahara's lieutenants were found guilty and sentenced to death in 1999 and 2000 for their role in the subway gas attacks, the murder of those who campaigned against Aum or the murder of members who tried to leave the cult. Asahara was sentenced to death in 2004. In 1996 the cult was declared bankrupt in a court ruling and in 1997 the government decided not to invoke the Anti-Subversive Activities Law (1952) to ban the cult, asserting that it was, for all intents and purposes, defunct.

However, as of 2009 the cult still had an estimated 1,200 members and several compounds scattered around the country. The detention centre where Asahara is held has been declared a holy site and over 100 cult members have taken up residence in surrounding buildings. Communities have formed vigilante groups to prevent Aum from occupying purchased premises, maintaining 24-hour vigils, and local governments, with the muted acquiescence of the central government, have refused to register Aum members as residents, thus depriving them of voting rights, health insurance and other social welfare services. The central government passed legislation in 1999 empowering the police to monitor and curb the activities of any group whose members are guilty of carrying out or attempting indiscriminate murder and whose leader still holds sway over the membership, effectively making Aum the only organization affected by this legislation.

In 1995, Aum became a media phenomenon comparable to the O. J. Simpson case in the United States. Coverage was equally obsessive and dominated the airwaves and the printed media. Everyone wanted to know why Aum launched the worst terrorist attack ever experienced in Japan.

More intriguingly, why were many of the **cult's top members** young gradu-ates of Japan's best universities? Presumably, these young men and women had bright futures and had enjoyed the best educational experience that Japan could offer and yet they opted to join a marginal cult and participated in planning the destruction of Japan. These technologically savvy recruits had a key role in producing a variety of chemical weapons and conducting experiments with various biological agents. They also helped it establish a lucrative computer business.

It is hard to determine why Asahara decided to plan the destruction of Japan and the world. The apocalyptic predictions of Nostradamus played a key part, but much remains unknown about the guru's motivations. Various commentators have grappled with the issue of why elite students would turn their backs on good careers and plunge into an obscure new religion (Murakami, 2001). It is often argued that they reacted against a strait-jacket society, the suffocation of youth and a pressure-cooker educational system; joining Aum was an extreme backlash against the conformity that is often the cost of success in Japan. Others argue that they were cajoled and flattered into joining, given enormous powers and influence at an age when they would still have relatively low-level corporate or bureaucratic positions if they continued on their 'fast track' paths in a seniority-weighted system. Still others pointed to the crass materialism and spiritual void of modern Japan as a cause for their alienation and rejection of the status quo. Yet none of these explanations seem compelling or fully satisfying; the mystery continues to haunt the Japanese. The sense of security that the postwar Japanese came to view as a birthright and as an expression of the solidarity of the people was shattered by this cataclysmic event, forcing an uncomfortable reassessment of modern Japan and the social forces that percolate beneath the surface (Reader, 1996; Lifton, 1999).

Cult's top members: 'A' and 'A2', documentary movies by filmmaker Tatsuya Mori about Aum, are attempts to help explain what happened. The documentaries are surprisingly sympathetic, portraying rank-and-file cult members as ordin-ary people who found something in the cult that was lacking in their lives. Asked about the actions of their leaders in carrying out the attacks, they do not try to deny or shift blame, but rather seem baffled and unable to provide answers to the questions the nation was asking. More unsettling for many Japanese, they did not seem like villains or weirdos.

THE KOBE EARTHQUAKE

The Great Hanshin-Awaji earthquake struck Kobe on 17 January 1995, leaving a path of destruction and raising questions about construction safety standards and the government's disaster relief preparations and slow response. The deadly tremor registered 7.2 on the Richter scale. The details of the damage include 6,200 deaths, 180,000 badly damaged or destroyed houses and some $100 billion in estimated damages. At the peak of the relief effort, there were nearly 1,300 shelters for more than 320,000 evacuees. About one-third of Kobe was partially or completely destroyed and more than half of the central district was razed by the fires feeding on ruptured gas lines and flimsy wooden housing. Most of the modern high-rise buildings fared reasonably well, but 20% of structures over six stories suffered significant damage. The manmade islands in the port also suffered some liquefaction and container port facilities were devastated. Part of an urban expressway keeled over, some landmark commercial buildings were badly damaged and the urban infrastructure was clogged with debris.

The degree of the destruction and the inept response of the municipal and central governments took the nation by surprise. Some commentators at the time suggested it was an omen foreshadowing the end of Japan's heyday. High safety standards and well-planned earthquake preparedness drills offered no relief from this devastating natural disaster. Incredibly, there were no prearranged emergency relief centres and no contingency disaster plan. Offers of assistance by foreign relief agencies and NGOs were initially turned down and the Self-Defense Forces (SDF) remained in nearby barracks while Kobe burned. The *yakuza* embarrassed the government by opening the first soup kitchens for displaced survivors. It became apparent that some of the damage was due to **shoddy construction** and human error. The slow response of government authorities and the inadequate relief efforts left a lasting impression on a nation accustomed to believing that government officials knew best because they were the best and the brightest. Their incompetence and inflexibility were seen to have considerably worsened the human toll and damaged the already waning credibility of government institutions.

Shoddy construction: It was reported that construction companies had cut the amount of rebar in some structures and also had stinted on use of expensive chemicals that stabilize reclaimed land and stops liquefaction.

Beyond these profound political repercussions, the tremor hit hardest the low income, elderly population who had inhabited the central districts. They had the least resources to fall back on and were least prepared for the costs of rebuilding. The government has tried to help with loan relief and interest rate subsidies, but many citizens have had difficulty getting back on their feet and carry burdensome mortgages for both destroyed housing and the costs of rebuilding.

Recovery was slow and as late as 1999, 4 years after the earthquake, 5,000 out of the original 50,000 evacuated households remained in temporary housing. This was widely considered to be a manmade disaster reflecting poorly on the government authorities responsible for rebuilding the city and coping with the human tragedies that befell the community. Many earthquake survivors have returned to normal lives, shaken and impoverished, but others remained unemployed and forgotten.

By contrast, the response of young Japanese to the earthquake was widely praised as reflecting a charitable disposition not often evident among their elders. From all over the country over 1 million student volunteers poured into Kobe, offering their energy and willingness to help during the first few months following the tragedy. The enthusiasm and good intentions of these hordes of volunteers offered a stark contrast to the widely deplored sluggish and stiff bureaucratic response. As is usual in charitable endeavours in Japan, Christian groups took the lead in organizing volunteer work, but in the case of Kobe the overwhelming majority of volunteers were prodded by their own consciences and were not Christians. This has been interpreted as a welcome sign that a sense of community is alive and well in Japan. More often the media focus on signs of decay in community spirit and the rise of individualism imperiling the future of Japan.

NUCLEAR MISHAPS AND MISGIVINGS

Japan has experienced a string of nuclear accidents in the 1990s that raise serious concerns about public safety in an earthquake-prone nation with 55 reactors as of 2001. Japan is totally dependent on imported energy and has thus invested billions of dollars since the 1950s in developing its nuclear energy programme. In the early twenty-first century, Japan derives about one-third of its electricity from nuclear power facilities and in response to growing power demand the government has aggressively proceeded with ambitious expansion plans.

Public concerns about the safety of nuclear power contrast sharply with official insistence that the nation's facilities are both safe and necessary. Polls consistently reveal that 70–75% of Japanese harbour deep misgivings about nuclear power and express fear that serious accidents will happen.

The world's most serious nuclear accident since the Chernobyl meltdown in 1986 occurred in Tokaimura in September 1999. This small village, about 70 miles from Tokyo, is known as 'Nuclear Alley' because it is home to 15 nuclear processing facilities. In 1999, workers at a uranium reprocessing plant accidentally triggered a runaway chain reaction that lasted for 20 hours in a facility that had no containment barriers; they had been preparing fuel for an experimental fast-breeder plutonium reactor. A stunned nation learned that the accident occurred while the workers were transferring enriched uranium in stainless steel buckets; mixing the uranium by hand and then pouring it into a holding tank. The workers made a serious error in the quantities of the solution they mixed, and in order to save time and money they did not use the sophisticated processing equipment at hand that had automatic controls to prevent such an accident from occurring. Investigators found out that the workers were untrained and were actually following instructions from a company manual in illegally cutting corners and violating safety protocols. Because there would have been almost no risk of an accident if regulations were followed, there was no contingency plan for such an accident and no form of containment to protect area residents from the radiation.

Tokaimura's public authorities were slow to react and the Prime Minister's Office did not learn of the mishap for 5 hours. Lacking a formal request for assistance, nearby SDF troops remained at their base. The town authorities had no contingency plans and poorly informed firefighters arrived at the reprocessing plant during the chain reaction without protective clothing. Inexplicably, it took 2 days to arrange proper medical care for the three workers directly exposed to the nuclear fission. The one hospital designated for the treatment of radiation victims in every one of the emergency plans in the nation's 15 prefectures with nuclear facilities was not, in the end, prepared to handle such cases. This exposure of official bungling and the consequences of a business more concerned about profits than safety left the public deeply sceptical about a nuclear programme that has been plagued by safety flaws, radiation leaks, shutdowns, fires and cover-ups.

Tokaimura: JCO, the company operating the Tokaimura facility, was fined 1 million yen (about $10,000) in 2002 and its president an additional 500,000 yen ($5,000). The court granted suspended prison terms of 2–3 years for the six managers prosecuted. The cost of nuclear negligence, thus, proved rather modest.

Prior to the criticality incident at **Tokaimura**, the most serious accident occurred at the Monju fast-breeder reactor in 1995. This $6 billion facility features the fast-breeder plutonium-producing technology that has been abandoned elsewhere in the world because of safety problems. Of the 10 known accidents at fast-breeder plants, the Monju accident is considered the most serious. If an accident happens at a uranium-fuelled reactor, the nuclear core has a meltdown while plutonium fuelled reactors can explode. Since the sodium leak and fire at Monju, the plant was shut down until 2010. It has never performed up to expectations and has generated very little electricity. The public learned of an attempted cover-up and the destruction of evidence related to the extent of the 1995 accident when the chief investigator committed suicide and left a note implicating his superiors.

In addition to the concerns raised by the poor safety record of Japan's Power Reactor and Nuclear Fuel Development Corporation, the responsible government office, Japan's choice of plutonium-based, fast-breeder technology has given rise to suspicions that it is pursuing a civilian nuclear energy programme with military implications. Plutonium does not make economic sense as a fuel because it is much more expensive than uranium. Moreover, it turns out that fast-breeder reactors are not as efficient at producing plutonium suitable for fuel as they are in producing weapons-grade plutonium. Given the large amounts of plutonium in Japan, neighbouring countries are wary of its intentions despite official policy barring the development of nuclear weapons.

SYMBOLS THAT DIVIDE

In 1999, while the economy languished and various social issues demanded urgent attention, the government spent a great deal of effort on legalizing the national flag and national anthem. The flag-and-anthem bill was hurriedly passed despite the misgivings of a large segment of public opinion. The *Hinomaru* flag and the **Kimigayo** anthem have long been national symbols, but passing a bill conferring legal sanction to this status resonates powerfully in a nation still divided over its past. The sun flag is not much of an issue for most Japanese, but many consider that *Kimigayo* is a throwback to the era when the Emperor was an absolute monarch and, as such, is incompatible with the postwar Constitution which gives sovereignty to the citizens. Moreover, the song is a paean to the Emperor and a reminder of a painful time when Japan was waging war throughout Asia in the name of the Emperor.

To the extent that the anthem is reminiscent of Japan's militaristic past, it is rejected by progressive groups in society who feel that their nation has done too little to atone for the past. Passage of the bill in the Diet by an overwhelming majority is indicative of the dominance of conservative political forces although polls reveal greater hesitation and misgivings among the public. Some high school teachers have opposed raising the flag and sing the national anthem at school ceremonies and have suffered disciplinary actions for doing so. Under pressure from the Ministry of Education, more **schools** are forcing compliance, but there is a determined resistance to such directives because many liberal educators remain distrustful of nationalism and its symbols. In other nations this might seem like much ado about nothing, but these national symbols are also symbols of the political fault lines that persist in society between progressive and conservative forces.

SOCIAL MORES AND DELINQUENCY

As the twentieth century drew to a close, there was palpable concern about deteriorating ethics, morals and social order. Throughout the postwar era, the young generation has been the subject of censure by their elders and they were dubbed the **shinjinrui**. This inter-generational divide is common everywhere, but in Japan, where there is a strong ideology of filial piety, the repercussions are powerful for the national psyche.

A perusal of subway courtesy signs indicates just how much has changed in Japan, a nation rightly known for a generally high level of politeness. Until the mid-1990s there were only small signs suggesting that passengers surrender certain designated seats to the elderly or pregnant. Since then, however, train companies have gone to the trouble and expense of posting signs suggesting that passengers refrain from punching train company employees, groping women, smashing ticket machines and chatting on their

Hinomaru: The national flag with a red circle in the middle of a white background.

Kimigayo: Your Majesty's Reign. The national anthem is controversial because of its apparent reference to the days when the Emperor was an absolute monarch, making it a divisive political issue between conservatives and progressives.

Schools: There have been a series of lawsuits since then by teachers who have been reprimanded or penalized for refusing to comply with directives to sing the anthem at school assemblies. Some district courts have sided with the plaintiffs, and agreed that the directives infringe on their constitutional rights, but these decisions have been overturned on appeal. The Education Ministry has issued new guidelines in 2008 aimed at boosting patriotism by, *inter alia*, requiring anthem singing by elementary school children. Interestingly, Emperor Akihito made a rare political gesture by expressing opposition to mandatory anthem singing.

Shinjinrui: New species. A negative reference by older people used when criticizing the various presumed failings of the younger generation.

Ijime: Bullying is a pervasive practice in society that is aimed at imposing conformity within a specific group and ostracizing those who do not conform or meet expectations. High-profile suicides among students show this problem to be especially evident in schools.

Mura hachibu: Village ostracization imposed on those who do not meet social expectations in rural Japan.

mobile phones, indicating the sorts of problems that seem to be occurring with greater frequency.

Ijime is a problem that suffuses Japanese society, stretching from the classroom up to the office. Even young mothers fret about their 'park debut', the first time they visit the local park with their baby, because of the strict hierarchy of neighbourhood mothers and the need to conform to the group. Wrong choices in clothes or strollers, or parenting that does not measure up, can have a devastating impact on these mothers' social life and sense of self. Bullying encompasses a variety of common social sanctions in Japan, including the tradition of **mura hachibu** at the village or neighbourhood level. Those who do not conform to or meet local expectations are subject to a form of psychological harassment. At school, in university, on the baseball field and even in the office, bullying is intrinsic to the precise and rigid sense of hierarchy and order. It is an effective method of keeping people in their place and as such is tolerated, and indeed, to some extent, encouraged. This is not a new phenomenon, but society has become more open in discussing it. A number of student suicides and killings since the 1980s have been directly attributed to bullying at school, raising questions both about the high-pressure atmosphere of a school system that produces such behaviour and a society that sanctions it as a means of social control.

Rising rates of truancy are partially attributed to bullying as targets stay away from school to avoid mistreatment. Truancy is also seen to be a rejection of the stifling conformity and rigid curriculum in a school system widely criticized in Japan for not accommodating growing diversity or stimulating creativity. In addition, truancy and the breakdown of classroom order are seen to be symptoms of a wider social problem. Compared with other societies where violent crime is far higher, Japan's problems may seem almost quaint, but they are a cause for alarm in a nation that places great value on orderly behaviour. There is widespread concern that the deference to authority, willingness to accept strict discipline and **messhi hoko** that many Japanese believe have been crucial to social order in Japan seem to be ebbing [**Doc. 28, pp. 154–5**].

Messhi hoko: Self-sacrifice.

Enjo kosai: Compensated dating, usually between junior or high school girls and middle-aged men, often involving sex.

In the 1990s, **enjo kosai** became the focus of intense public scrutiny. There is no reliable information about the extent of *enjo kosai* and participation of young women in telephone date clubs, but most guesstimates suggest that less than 5% of female students are involved. Stricter laws governing sexual relations between minors and adults have been enacted and teachers, monks, government officials, company executives and others with high social status have been arrested for their involvement in *enjo kosai*. Based on media reporting, it does not seem a rare phenomenon. Commentators point out that unlike most women who engage in prostitution, the girls involved in *enjo kosai* and date clubs are usually from middle class backgrounds and not in dire economic circumstances. It is reported that the girls are desperate for spending money so that they can purchase expensive designer clothes and accessories and pay their *keitai* (mobile phone) bills. While this materialism and exploitation of sex is lamented, few doubt that this behaviour is an emulation of what is widely evident in society. For example, it was not until 1999 that Japan joined the international community in banning child pornography, and then it was mostly because of the bad publicity associated with being identified as the number one source of this seedy commodity.

The rising levels of truancy, bullying, materialism, moral laxity and delinquency among youth have spurred a national introspection, focusing on what has gone wrong. Conservatives argue that stressing ethics in school, encouraging respect for national symbols and seeking inspiration from Japan's rich traditions and culture can help alleviate the anomie and alienation that plague society. Progressives tend to focus on recasting society to permit more individuality and self-fulfillment as a means of encouraging people to identify with a community that currently seems unattractive, stifling and overly demanding of self-sacrifice for reasons that appear uncompelling to increasing numbers of Japanese.

DISCRIMINATION

Discrimination against non-Japanese and minority Japanese groups remains strong in Japan [**Doc. 29, pp. 156–7**]. At the end of the twentieth century, ethnic Koreans (*zainichi*) constituted the largest minority in Japan, numbering nearly 600,000. Of this total, as many as 150,000 are thought to be loyal to North Korea, and the political divisions on the peninsula are also evident in Japan. Most Koreans arrived in Japan during the 1930s and 1940s to work in the mines and factories to replace the Japanese males fighting in the Imperial Army. Many of the Koreans came to Japan under conditions of forced labour and endured harsh conditions. At that time, Koreans were considered subjects of the Emperor because Korea was a Japanese colony. However, after the Second World War, Koreans living in Japan were not granted rights as citizens and subsequent generations have remained in Japan under a special permanent resident visa status. Thus, ethnic Koreans have been raised and educated in Japan and their native language is Japanese, but they are treated as if they are foreigners. All Koreans are required to apply for residence visas and until 1998 were routinely fingerprinted, a requirement that became symbolic of Koreans' second-class status. In terms of education, jobs, housing and marriage, Koreans face pervasive discrimination, and negative stereotypes abound among Japanese. Increasingly, younger *zainichi* are naturalizing to avoid the consequences of discrimination.

The persistence of discrimination against successive generations of Korean residents raises questions about tolerance and diversity in Japan. Because of impending labour shortages, there is a compelling logic to relaxing immigration restrictions, but little enthusiasm among Japanese to do so.

Ainu: In 2007 the Diet unanimously approved a resolution that recognizes the Ainu as an indigenous people with their own language, religion and culture. The government also acknowledged they had suffered from discrimination.

The **Ainu**, an indigenous ethnic group now largely resident in Hokkaido, has been subjected to forced migration, prolonged assimilation and extensive discrimination [**Doc. 30, pp. 157–8**]. Like Okinawans to the south, they have not been explicitly recognized by mainland Japanese as a distinct ethnic group, but when they are recognized as such they are often the target of derogatory comments, negative stereotypes and marginalization. Okinawans, the indigenous people of the Ryukyu Islands, have endured similar treatment and see their relative poverty and hosting of a disproportionate share of US military bases as an indictment of Japanese rule.

Burakumin: 'Hamlet people' is term used to refer to some 1 million Japanese today. Visually indistinguishable from other Japanese, 'hamlet people' suffer discrimination in jobs, housing, marriage, etc. because they are identified as being members of this class. During the Tokugawa era (1603–1868) this class became hereditary and was linked to 'polluting' activities such as slaughtering animals.

The **burakumin** (also *eta* or *hinen*, literally 'hamlet people', – a derogatory term used to refer to the lowest caste of people) constitute a Japanese minority that has suffered discrimination since the seventeenth century. Prior to the Tokugawa era, people who engaged in activities that made them ritually impure in terms of Buddhist precepts temporarily entered into a polluted state from which they could exit once they had undergone ritual purification. However, since the Tokugawa era, this class of 'untouchables' has been hereditary and permanent. Those who worked with leather, for example, became *burakumin*, and to this day, tanning and curing of leather is dominated by them. They face discrimination in education, housing, marriage, jobs, etc., and are usually from lower economic strata. For employers and parents investigating potential marriage partners for their children, there are reportedly lists in circulation that purport to designate which districts are known to be inhabited by *burakumin*. Usually their status can be determined from the **koseki** maintained by government offices. Since the 1970s there have been activist citizen groups advocating affirmative-action policies, social welfare programmes and an end to pervasive discrimination. For the estimated 1 million Japanese who live with this stigma, greater sensitivity to their plight and supportive government programmes have brought some limited relief, but they remain an underclass and a target of discrimination.

Koseki: A family register, maintained over the generations with information about births, deaths, marriages, etc.

Gaijin: Foreigner(s).

Gaijin from around the world encounter both the kindness and hospitality of Japanese and petty discrimination. In general, whites are treated better than other foreigners but do suffer some of the indignities and discrimination that Asians, Middle Easterners and Africans are frequently subjected to. Some real estate agencies refuse to assist foreigners. Shops, bars and restaurants still have signs barring entry for non-Japanese and other forms of harassment are regularly experienced (Arudou, 2004). Many foreigners have good experiences in Japan – getting married, raising families and settling – but for too many *gaijin* significant negative experiences resulting from racism leave a lingering impression. The Ministry of Education has facilitated the arrival of large numbers of foreign students in Japan by offering scholarships in the hopes of building cultural bridges. However, government surveys indicate that for many of these foreign students the rich educational opportunities are offset by the negative images they bring home because of discriminatory treatment. In many cases this may not be a result of overt racism, but more a reflection of the closed nature of Japanese society that leaves many visitors with a feeling that they are not entirely welcome. Even *gaijin* who become fluent in Japanese and knowledgeable about Japan's history and culture often assert, and resent, that they are left on the outside.

Given the importance that the government places on **kokusaika** and the new demands that globalization is placing on Japanese society, the experiences of foreigners in Japan raise troubling questions about the future integration of Japan in the world community. Hall (1997) charges that Japanese insularity has fostered 'cartels of the mind' that perpetuate prejudice. Such narrow-mindedness among the elite of Japan leads to non-reciprocal and unsatisfying interactions with the rest of the world and the foreigners who come to Japan. He identifies the intellectual attitudes, institutional structures, ideological defences and cultural hubris that drive Japanese parochialism, arguing that this undermines the interests of nations that interact with Japan. In his view, Japan benefits greatly from the opportunities available to Japanese journalists, academics and lawyers overseas, but fails to make the same compromises and accommodations that would enable foreigners to enjoy similar benefits in Japan. Ultimately, the double standards he identifies in Japan constitute significant impediments to Japan's participation in the world community and run counter to its interests.

Kokusaika: Internationalization. A concept that is frequently invoked with mixed results to broaden horizons among Japanese and inculcate a positive value for interaction with foreigners and their cultures.

10

Paradigm Shift

Mired in recession since the early 1990s, Japan is facing the consequences of prolonged economic malaise, ones that are driving the paradigm shift we explore in the following pages. The post-Second World War Japan, Inc. model is no longer delivering and seems inadequate to the challenges the nation faces in the twenty-first century. Fitfully, incrementally and in zig-zagging fashion, the nation is questioning and shrugging off the norms, patterns and inclinations of the Japan, Inc. paradigm, one that centralized power in the Iron Triangle, nurtured a one-party democracy, emphasized the interests of producers over consumers and prioritized the pursuit of economic goals at the expense of alternative aspirations. This paradigm no longer has the capacity to inspire hope for a better future or deliver the benefits of rapid economic growth, job security and strong social cohesion. It is also at odds with the rising expectations and evolving sense of identity among growing numbers of Japanese in the twenty-first century.

The Japan, Inc. paradigm leaves behind a bankrupt legacy of profligate spending, a damning indictment for a system often lauded for responsible and effective economic management. As of 2010, Japan has a total public debt amounting to about 200% of GDP, highest by far in the OECD, a result of successive counter-cyclical government-spending packages aimed at stimulating recovery and rescuing the financial sector from insolvency. For a nation that enjoyed double-digit growth and minimal unemployment throughout the miracle years discussed in Chapter 4, growth has sputtered while unemployment and a sense of insecurity have sky-rocketed. This crisis, combined with the rash of corruption scandals discussed in Chapter 9, has discredited the government and aroused the ire of a people who are known for their stoic patience and fortitude in the face of adversity. They expressed their impatience with the powers that be at the polls in 2007 and 2009 when they voted the Liberal Democratic Party (LDP) out of power and handed government to the Democratic Party of Japan (DPJ), perhaps less in hope than with a certainty that it could do no worse. The DPJ mobilized their anxieties and rode their desperation into power.

The twin pressures of recession and economic deregulation since the early 1990s have generated a powerful riptide with considerable consequences for an employment system geared towards security. This system seems to be unravelling as companies discover that measures that saw them through past slumps are exhausted. Corporate Japan can no longer afford the rigidities and high costs of lifetime employment and seniority-based wage scales (*nenko*). The social contract between employers and employees based on security and loyalty has faded as firms pursue more aggressive restructuring. What went wrong [**Doc. 31, pp. 158–9**]?

A SYSTEM THAT SOURED

Katz (1998) argues that the system that propelled Japan to economic success in the 1950s and 1960s has soured. In his view, the policies, priorities, regulations, institutions, protectionism and practices that generated the economic miracle were appropriate for the recovery and catch-up phase of development, but were less relevant as the Japanese economy matured. He argues that the Japanese government shifted from industrial policies aimed at picking winners and encouraging success in certain promising sectors to protecting sunset industries and postponing the adjustments and restructuring needed as a consequence of Japan's economic transformation. In its attempts to facilitate a soft landing for troubled sectors in heavy industry, the government saved jobs but also saddled Japan with a high-cost economy. Systematic protectionism irked trading partners and also harmed some of the more successful sectors of the economy that depended on Japanese-made inputs. The restrictions on competition generated by recession cartels (industry associations that divided market share and colluded to set prices with the acquiescence of the government) and protectionist practices that prevented, limited or marginalized foreign participation had a negative effect on productivity and innovation.

Since the 1970s, the success of Japan's leading firms obscured the backwardness prevailing in other sectors. In the wake of the oil shocks in the 1970s, the more dynamic firms carried the economy, but this situation proved untenable over time. Funnelling investments, loans and workers into moribund sectors, even after they lost their international competitive advantage to emerging rivals such as Taiwan and South Korea, made it ever more politically difficult to institute overdue reforms and a transition towards policies and practices that make more sense in a mature economy.

As a result, the problems of the sunset industries festered and the transition needed to ensure Japan's continued competitiveness has been delayed. It was not until the late 1990s that industry and government pursued restructuring and deregulation aimed at resuscitating the economy and making Japan more broadly competitive. In doing so, they have been setting in motion a paradigm shift.

THE CHANGING EMPLOYMENT PARADIGM

The bubble economy of the late 1980s, a time when the juggernaut of Japan, Inc. appeared ready to dominate global markets, proved to be the last gasp of a system that had outlived its usefulness. The prolonged downturn since then has exposed the weaknesses that resulted from prolonging policies, institutions and practices suited to the era of rapid growth. Overall productivity in Japan lagged behind the United States by over 30% in the early 1990s, ranking only ninth among the eleven largest economies. Japan's relatively efficient export manufacturing sector was offset by other sectors with dismal productivity such as services, agriculture and food processing. By 1990, real GDP per worker in Japan had tripled since 1960, but ranked only 17 out of the top 23 global economies. Japan seemed to emerge from recession at the beginning of the twenty-first century, thanks to the booming Chinese market for Japanese exports, but the economic crisis that began in 2008 with the collapse of Lehman Brothers investment bank, caused a nearly 6% decline in Japan's GDP in 2009. The official unemployment rate nudged 5.7% in the summer of 2009, an unusually high level by Japanese standards, but in the absence of government job subsidies covering up to 80% of wages involving 2.4 million jobs at 88,000 companies, the real unemployment rate would have been 9.3%.

In the twenty-first century there has been rapid growth in the ranks of the working poor in Japan – those earning less than 2 million yen a year – some 10 million strong. They are among the 20 million precariat who work on limited duration contracts at low wages with little job security. Growing income disparities and the emergence of 'winners' and 'losers' in a society that values egalitarian ideals has generated considerable turmoil. This is not the Japan most Japanese want. The ouster of the LDP from control of the government in 2009 after more than half a century in power owed much to widespread discontent about this trend towards greater inequality in Japan and the absence of an adequate safety net for the most vulnerable.

From the end of the 1990s, the LDP-led government promoted a series of neo-liberal, market-oriented reforms aimed at reinvigorating the economy and boosting productivity while shredding job security. This trend has created precarious jobs while widening disparities. At the end of 2008 and into 2009 nearly 250,000 of these contract workers were abruptly fired, mostly in the manufacturing sector, victims of labour market deregulation championed by the LDP. Clearly, the rules of the game are rapidly changing, but at a cost to social cohesion and the sense of security that prevailed under Japan, Inc.

Liberalization of labour regulations heralded the advent of a more flexible, less secure employment system and a retreat from the rigid, secure and costly employment system that has characterized Japan since the Second World War. The three jewels of the Japanese employment system discussed in Chapter 4 – lifetime employment, seniority wages and enterprise unions – are all gradually fading in importance. Given the importance of work to personal identity, the spread of riskier employment and the rise of a **precariat** are having profound consequences.

Under the seniority wage system, as workers' tenure increased, so did their wages. By the 1990s, firms were top-heavy with these more expensive workers just as the nation plunged into prolonged recession. Workers were now collecting on their loyalty just as firms faced difficulties in keeping up their end of the bargain and cost-cutting became the new management mantra [**Doc. 32, pp. 159–60**]. This situation created incentives for firms to expand insecure jobs on fixed term contracts with low wages and benefits. As Genda (2005) argues, the interests of younger workers are sacrificed to protect the jobs and salaries of older workers. There is a sense of betrayal among these younger, expendable workers who had expectations rooted in the more paternalistic employment system that prevailed in the latter half of the twentieth century. This sundering of the social contract by corporations constitutes one of the bitter legacies of restructuring in Japan, eroding the trust that had been nurtured between employers and employees during much of the postwar era. Thus, it has been a time of losing faith in both government and business; the search for a new social contract is also shaping the emerging paradigm.

The shift towards more flexible and insecure employment arrangements is driven by the new logic of the Japanese economy, one that is marginalizing one-third of all workers. This new logic driven by cost-cutting and competitive pressures involves firms retaining a smaller core workforce and expanding non-standard employment. The downside has been growing risk, lower morale, growing disparities and a larger number of young workers who lack the sense of security and hope necessary to start their own families. In this sense, the employment adjustments undertaken by firms are exacerbating the demographic trends that are also shaping the new paradigm.

Precariat: The precarious proletariat of contingent workers who have no job security and low pay. The growing numbers of such workers in the first decade of the twenty-first century has generated apprehension about the implications for the future, especially as many workers in their twenties or thirties are being marginalized, undermining social cohesion.

The transition to a new paradigm is being driven by the demographic time bomb, the discrediting of Japan, Inc., the prolonged recession and globalization of norms and practices. Prolonged economic stagnation since the 1990s has undermined national self-confidence and forced a reassessment of existing practices. As the recession persisted, ideas that once seemed anathema, such as restructuring and deregulation, suddenly seemed compelling. The nose-dive of the financial sector put significant pressure on the bank-centred *keiretsu* (large industrial groups) and the cosy relationships that existed among member companies. Massive debts and losses began to unravel long-standing business relationships, and practices that had permitted low returns, low profitability and ill-considered investments could no longer be accommodated. As Japanese leaders sought to integrate Japan into the world economy more fully and reciprocally, the prospects of heightened international competition in the midst of this meltdown of Japan, Inc. generated considerable anxiety. Integration also meant reforming established practices to conform with international norms and expectations, ranging from accounting rules to transparency.

THE UNRAVELLING NEXUS

The nexus of power in Japan has been described as an Iron Triangle between big business, the bureaucracy and LDP politicians. The collusive and co-operative relations that prevailed among these groups defined and drove Japan, Inc. This Iron Triangle may better be described as a loose coalition of interest groups that worked together when common interests dictated. These groups can claim credit for overseeing the economic miracle, but they are now considered responsible for the malaise that hangs over the archipelago.

Kanson mimpi: Bureaucratic arrogance towards the public.

The days of **kanson mimpi** are numbered and the relations between the state and its citizens are changing perceptibly. The DPJ won a landslide victory in the 2009 Diet elections partly by promising to rein in the bureaucrats. This is a message that resonated powerfully with voters fed up with the negligence, incompetence and venality of bureaucrats exposed in a series of scandals since the 1990s. The misdeeds of the mandarins came to light due to growing transparency, one of the key elements of the paradigm shift we examine below. The more people knew about how officials were spending and squandering their tax money the more they wanted to know. There was a grassroots movement beginning in the early 1980s in support of information disclosure that spread from towns to prefectures and finally in 1999 to the national scene. From a modest beginning in 1982, by 1997 every large town and every prefecture has passed information disclosure legislation. Suddenly the people could look over the shoulders of their officials and what they found out about the shenanigans of the ruling class made them want to know more. Transparency came to be viewed as a litmus test of good governance and the media stepped in, along with citizens' groups, to use the new laws to ferret out malfeasance and hold those who govern accountable for their actions. Routine pilfering in the form of claims for fictional business trips (*kara shucho*) and standard procedures for obscuring this theft from the public purse angered Japanese. So too did reports of lavish wining and dining at the public expense by officials entertaining each other (*kankan settai*) at exclusive restaurants, also ensnaring some of the auditors ostensibly sent out to investigate such excesses. As the outraged public learned about the unscrupulous habits of the bureaucrats at the local and prefectural levels, pressure mounted on the central government to embrace greater transparency (*joho kokkai*). The opaque practices that had prevailed under Japan, Inc., and the privileged cocoon of immunity they conferred, became increasingly untenable and out of touch with popular sentiments. Finally, the government responded in 1999 by adopting information disclosure legislation that enables the public to find out more about what the government is doing. The media and non-profit organizations (NPOs) have become the most ardent users of this law and despite shortcomings and grudging compliance, have made headway in promoting transparency and forcing those in power to comply. This sea change in the relationship between citizens and the state in Japan – based on transparency and accountability – is a manifestation of the new emerging paradigm in Japan [**Doc. 33, pp. 160–1**]. Civil society is growing more robust and this is being made possible by the spread of NPOs and a supportive judiciary.

Following the Kobe earthquake and the government's bungled response, the media drew attention to the positive part played by volunteer groups, mostly of young Japanese, in helping residents in the aftermath. It was obvious that these young Japanese had a strong sense of community and desire to contribute to society. The media campaign drew support from corporate leaders and politicians who lobbied for legislation that would facilitate establishment of NPOs which was eventually adopted in 1998 (Schwartz and Pharr, 2003). Activists remain concerned about shortcomings in the legislation, but since then there has been a mushrooming of civil society organizations, which says a great deal about the interests and aspirations of Japanese in the twenty-first century. Most NPOs are small and underfunded, but they are having an influence well beyond what such constraints would suggest. They are giving a voice to citizens, lobbying government officials, promoting transparency and accountability, and providing services needed and valued by the diverse groups they serve (Kingston, 2004a). The

Kara shucho: Claiming expenses for fictional business trips became standard operating procedure for bureaucrats throughout the nation.

Kankan settai: Lavish wining and dining of central government bureaucrats by prefectural officials as part of lobbying efforts for budget allocations.

Joho kokkai: Information disclosure permitting citizens access to official documents, thus promoting transparency and accountability.

working relationship with government is in many cases infused with mutual distrust, but there are also many examples of fruitful cooperation. The key is that there are now over 80,000 civil society organizations working on a range of issues and programmes that are helping to shape the emerging paradigm with greater input from citizens. NPOs have gone from being a non-presence in Japan to often significant actors enjoying widespread support. It is not lost on the Japanese that in times of crisis when the government has not risen to the task at hand NPOs have done so, most notably at Kobe in 1995 and at the outset of 2009 in Tokyo. There a tiny NPO working on homeless issues mobilized other NPOs to set up a tent village in Hibiya Park for recently fired contract workers (Shinoda, 2009). This New Year's spectacle drew extensive media attention and deeply influenced public discourse about the fate of the workers and what kind of society Japan was becoming. Criticism focused on the LDP's deregulation measures and the growing disparities in Japan between 'winners' and 'losers'. This NPO-orchestrated media event forced the government to respond to a problem it preferred to ignore and was a key factor in the ouster of the LDP in the Diet elections in August 2009. As in Kobe, the NPOs held up a mirror to society and people did not like what they saw. In the aftermath, the government invited representatives of NPOs to work with it in crafting appropriate responses to the needs of these workers at risk. Thus, in trying to assess the power of NPOs it is not only a matter of staff and funding, although more of both seems likely as their valuable role gains attention and the government seeks to expand social services on limited budgets. Here, as in the United States during the Great Society programmes of President Lyndon Johnson in the 1960s, NPOs can have a critical role and in doing so gradually become a more crucial and influential actor in shaping the new paradigm.

Judicial reform is another powerful element shaping the new paradigm. This process, begun in the first decade of the twenty-first century, aims to make the judiciary more accessible and active. Law schools began operating in 2004 to train future generations of lawyers. Until then, lawyers crammed for the bar exam but only about 1% passed each year. Those that did were enrolled in a government-run training institute. One of the ideas behind law schools is to reduce state influence over training lawyers and thus change the relationship between those who practice law and those who enforce it. It also aims to double the number of lawyers, making the judicial system more accessible. In addition, aspiring lawyers will be exposed to a more varied curriculum and have a broader background in jurisprudence. It is interesting that a number of these law schools have incorporated an internship programme experience, ranging from helping citizens file freedom of information requests to advising asylum seekers. Certainly law schools are not a panacea, but they will help nurture a more diverse profession [Doc. 34, pp. 161–2]. Along with this shift in the nature of legal education, the government has also raised the pass rate for the bar exams. These reforms have not lived up to initially high expectations as the pass rate has risen but not as much as anticipated and a number of law schools will not survive if not enough of their students can pass the bar exam. However, it is worth bearing in mind that judicial reform is a long process and is part of a mutually reinforcing and wider set of economic, political and administrative reforms.

More immediate consequences have resulted from procedural reforms (2003) that have led to speedier trials, and the creation of an intellectual property rights court (2005) that helps firms protect and benefit from their intellectual property rights (IPR) while reassuring foreign firms that they can expect speedy dispute resolution for IPR infringement based on the rule of law. These reforms mark significant changes in how the law functions in Japan as does the establishment of a lay judge system in 2009. Under this system, six citizens serve with three professional judges on cases involving serious crimes that could involve life imprisonment or the death sentence. Public interest in serving as a lay judge remains low despite concerted efforts by the judiciary to encourage participation, but public interest in the proceedings has been high as people line up for seats in the court galleries. The media has provided extensive coverage and has aroused considerable interest in how the courts function. In this sense, the lay judge system can be judged a qualified success because it has served a public relations purpose of making people feel more involved, thereby narrowing the gap between the public and judiciary that motivated this reform. Finally, the courts have supported greater transparency and have ruled against the government more often than not in cases in which information requestors have sued because of incomplete or non-compliance with information disclosure legislation. Given that the courts are usually viewed as compliant to the state and normally rule against it in only about 10% of cases, it is significant that judges are strictly holding government officials to their statutory obligations. Certainly, officials remain reluctant to divulge and the habits of transparency are still a work in progress, but the judiciary is contributing to the changing relationship between the people and the state.

The ouster of the LDP from control of the Diet is one of the most dramatic manifestations of the wider trend towards greater transparency, accountability and a more robust civil society. The LDP and the bureaucracy, as central actors in the Iron Triangle, did not measure up to rising expectations among voters, a shortcoming amplified by the economic crisis. The DPJ tapped into popular desires for improved governance and resentment concerning the special treatment accorded bureaucrats embodied in the practice of *amakudari* (descent from heaven), long tolerated by the LDP, wherein elite officials retire into lucrative sinecures in companies they supervised or in quasi-public entities that are subsidized by their ministries. Such practices fuel mistrust of government and undermine its legitimacy.

The cascade of scandals and setbacks in the 1990s discredited Japan, Inc., as people came to understand the seamy ways and means that prevailed. Revelations about relations between bankers, bureaucrats, *yakuza* and politicians undermined the credibility of the paradigm, reinforcing discontent with a system that was no longer delivering. The insider deals involving cash-for-favours, bid-rigging, *amakudari*, shady real estate deals, favouritism, petty and large-scale embezzling, cover-ups, etc., exhausted the patience of a citizenry that had good reason to expect more from those in charge.

UNDER CONSTRUCTION

Japan is in the midst of a quiet revolution, one that is not on media radar screens because the reforms that are driving this transformation will not solve today's problems tomorrow, will not revive the stock market, will not alleviate unemployment and will not boost growth. The new paradigm emerging from this quiet revolution is driven by NPOs, information disclosure legislation and judicial reforms which are strengthening Japan's civil society and changing popular expectations about good governance. These institutional and legal developments are empowering citizens and have aroused greater awareness among them about the need for greater transparency, accountability and open government. The media may be more beholden to the powers that be than in other advanced industrialized nations, but in Japan it has become somewhat feistier about exposing the malfeasance, profligacy and dysfunctionality of Japan, Inc. In doing so it is promoting transparency and accountability and supporting civil society.

To reiterate, the new paradigm is being shaped by this discrediting of Japan, Inc., by the prolonged economic crisis, the demographic time-bomb and globalization of norms and practices. This is a time of policy experimentation as Japan tries to come to grips with its enormous challenges. Cobbling together a new paradigm involves improvisation by policy-makers as they assess and reassess what makes sense, relying far more than in the past on input from citizens and civil society organizations. Moreover, they are more mindful of public expectations in addressing Japan's problems.

The downsizing of the construction state (*doken kokka*) is emblematic of how Japan's problems are driving its transformation and how public sentiments are shaping this paradigm shift (Kingston, 2004b). The tawdry deals and systemic corruption that prevail in public works projects drew public criticism as symbols of the worst excesses of Japan, Inc. The media and citizens pilloried bureaucrats and politicians for bankrupting the nation with wasteful and often unnecessary pork-barrel projects, ones that were also having an adverse impact on the environment and natural beauty. People wondered with good reason why a country the size of California was laying as much cement in a year as the United States. Suddenly in the late 1990s the public mood shifted decisively against ready-mix politics and the logic of the *doken kokka* and politicians began running against it. Roads and bridges to nowhere infuriated exasperated taxpayers who saw the ruling elite lining their pockets while mortgaging the nation's future. Prime Minister Koizumi (2001–06) sought to restore fiscal discipline by cutting public works spending by 30% during his tenure in office and also moved to privatize the post office. The post office had served as a ready source of funding for special deficit bonds issued by the government to cover public works projects. Privatizing it was seen as a way to subject such bond issues to greater scrutiny and the logic of market sentiments. Thus, in the first decade of the twenty-first century there was a significant downsizing of the massive construction state, one that had generated 20% of GDP, double that of the United States, and employed some 12% of the workforce at the end of the 1990s, compared with 1% in the United States. The DPJ is continuing with this downsizing agenda (although reconsidering the privatization of the post office) as it seeks to shift spending towards expanding social services. The **doken kokka** was unsustainable and was starving other programmes of sufficient resources. Certainly public works spending remains large in Japan, but relatively large cuts rapidly implemented in response to public pressure, fiscal realities and the need to do more to prepare for the rapid ageing of Japan are revealing about the state of the nation and efforts to create a new paradigm.

Doken kokka: The Yamba Dam project in Gunma Prefecture has become a symbol of the wasteful spending associated with the *doken kokka*. This massive flood control and drinking water project exceeded any plausible need, but did generate lots of local jobs. It also divided residents of Kawarayu Onsen, a hot springs resort that was set to be engulfed by the dam's reservoir over whether to support or oppose the project and the disruptive relocation scheme. As the project entered the last phase of construction, the DPJ took over in 2009 and promptly cancelled it, provoking the ire of residents who feel the government has treated them cavalierly. Most Japanese support downsizing the construction state, knowing that it involves excessive waste and that the money could be better spent elsewhere.

Part 3

ASSESSMENT

11

In Retrospect

The transformation of Japan over the second half of the twentieth century and into the twenty-first century has been momentous, recasting the social, political, economic and cultural landscape. The pace and breadth of change has been staggering and yet some aspects of Japan seem unchanged or only slightly modified. Pockets of rural Japan remain repositories of a vanishing era while the small shops, factories and *nomiya* (bars) of **shitamachi** (downtown) remain redolent of the sounds, smells, flavours and relationships conjured up by nostalgic memories about how Japan used to be, almost frozen in time. Time-honoured traditions persist and some aspects of society still function on established patterns, but the scope of continuity has been overwhelmed by the metamorphosis of modern Japan.

Postwar Japan has experienced success in reconstructing a war-ravaged nation, raising living standards, renovating democracy, taming militarism and rejoining the community of nations. This far-reaching rehabilitation of Japan marks an extraordinary achievement and has led to significant advances in the lives of Japan's citizens. It is stunning that despite this whirlwind of tumultuous and deracinating transformation, Japan has preserved and augmented its social capital and avoided the worst of the scourges that plague other advanced, industrialized nations. The relative absence of deep cleavages in society, the highly developed sense of community and success in containing the dislocation and social ills of modernization are a source of considerable strength in Japan. People are better housed, better educated, healthier, live longer and are, by virtually any yardstick, better off than their predecessors and most other people in the world. They have enjoyed political stability, economic security, low crime, good health care, decent schools, adequate housing and an extraordinary level of public politesse. Even during the prolonged adversity the early 1990s, the social fall-out has been limited. Japan has not avoided the usual problems of industrialized societies, but seems to have done a better job in containing, and coping with, these problems.

Shitamachi (downtown): Refers to a simpler time and way of life adopted by blue-collar workers, tradesmen and artisans gathering in less fashionable districts where they frequent public baths, bars and restaurants as regulars and where traditional housing, pursuits and sense of community linger. This is the increasingly rare, urban enclave where the spirit of the common people and strong sense of collective values remain vibrant.

The postwar model, however, has run out of steam and has lost much of its credibility [**Doc. 35, pp. 162–3**]. In the 2000s, the limits and constraints of this model have become ever more apparent. People are apprehensive about the wide range of reforms that are currently being implemented to address the problems of a system no longer thought capable of meeting the challenges of contemporary Japan. Whether these reforms will succeed in turning the tide is unclear, but they promise more volatility and uncertainty.

There is considerable ambivalence about the rapidity of change and the erosion of tenets and verities many Japanese feel have been important to their identity as a people, their cohesion as a community and their success as a nation. This turmoil is reflected in the mix of progressive yearnings and conservative inertias that animate contemporary Japan. The knowledge that transformation is happening and that more is needed does not mean that the reshaping of Japan is entirely welcome. People are caught between what they see as the loss of defining values and a pragmatic assessment that it is time for modifying and discarding many of these ideals and patterns of the past which are no longer tenable in vastly altered circumstances. There is a pervasive recognition that the various quandaries facing Japan, which have been discussed in preceding chapters, are forcing change, some of which is considered overdue and necessary for improving the prospects of individuals and the nation as a whole. The vested interests of the status quo have vigilantly and successfully defended their prerogatives and interests over the decades, slowing the pace of change and diverting the impetus of reform. They continue to do so but with less success because more and more people chafe under the current system and see it as a threat to their interests.

The logic of the economic and political arrangements that prevailed in postwar Japan is changing. The concatenation of common interests and agendas that bound the Iron Triangle (big business, the bureaucracy and the LDP) was never seamless and is growing less so. The ouster of the LDP is emblematic of this changing of the guard as is the emergence of a more robust civil society. There have been profound changes in relations between people and the state and their employers involving an erosion of trust and credibility. The singular devotion to economic recovery and growth that helped forge a common identity and a sense of shared destinies in postwar Japan has faded away. A society that emerged from the devastation of war naturally accorded priority to economic security, but this too has been sacrificed as corporate Japan tries to reinvent itself and become more productive and competitive.

The Japan emerging in the early twenty-first century is one profoundly affected by prolonged economic stagnation and efforts to mitigate its consequences. It is a society confronting uncomfortable realities that strike at the heart of national identity, collective values and shared norms. The *kakusa shakai* is at the heart of public discourse in the early twenty-first century as growing disparities challenge cherished egalitarian ideals and myths of a ubiquitous middle class. The changing employment model means that more jobs are risky and poorly paid with few prospects that workers can move to more secure, better paid work. About one-third of workers are now engaged on such adverse terms, creating a precariat of working poor with little hope for a better life. Such circumstances threaten social solidarity and community values. Economic misery is not the only reason for Japan's prolonged spike in suicides – more than 30,000 per year since 1998 – but is certainly a significant factor, especially for men in their thirties. People are eager for a new paradigm that can mitigate the consequences of growing disparities among 'winners' and 'losers' and restore hope for those who have lost it.

Kakusa shakai: Unequal society, a term symbolizing growing discontent with neo-liberal economic reforms that have widened disparities in society and created 'winners' and 'losers'.

In assessing the prospects for reform, profound changes in the attitudes of individual Japanese are encouraging. People act less subserviently and reverently towards their elected officials, civil servants, teachers, corporate titans and others who hold positions that once conferred status, power and respect. There is a sense that the edifice of power is slowly eroding, as are the foundations of that system. As a result, society is in flux and entering uncharted waters, looking for new solutions to growing social and economic problems. Uncertainty, angst and despair have inspired an incremental and hesitant social movement with no nerve centre or impetus other than the rising aspirations of people and their frustrations with a sclerotic status quo. Over the decades, holding the government and corporations accountable for their actions or negligence has slowly become normal, while demands for transparency are no longer viewed as the dangerous demands of radical idealists. When faced with problems, many Japanese shrug their shoulders and seek refuge in expressions such as *shigatakanai* ('nothing can be done') and *akirameru* ('reluctant resignation'), but these inclinations are slowly fading, giving way to greater assertiveness and higher expectations among a growing number of people. This is not so much a rise of political consciousness or activism as it is a reflection of people's growing sense of entitlement and awareness of the way things are in other advanced societies around the world. The power over disseminating information that was a key component of the status quo is ebbing quickly in the face of a more questioning polity and a society in which the flow of information is relatively unhindered. People know more, trust less and are thus less tolerant of the opaque ways of the past. Politicians, bureaucrats and corporate leaders often may not measure up to these rising expectations and standards, but episodically and gradually they are responding. The conduct of government, business and individuals is subject to more intensified scrutiny and being assessed by a better informed and less tolerant public, creating an atmosphere conducive to improved performance, lapses notwithstanding.

Are the Japanese enjoying a more robust democracy and greater freedom and justice? There is no consensus on this question. On balance, in this writer's view, there is a great deal more freedom in society, and a greater accommodation and tolerance of diversity and alternative lifestyles. Although voter participation rates have grown anaemic, the disaffection of voters may not necessarily signal a decline in democracy. The media and public have become more aggressive in holding the government accountable and exposing malfeasance, negligence and incompetence. In addition, citizens' groups and non-governmental organizations have proliferated while the status quo parties seem to have begun a wrenching and slow process of political reform in response to pressure and criticism. It is too early to assess what the impact of current reformist tendencies will be, but the information revolution is making it ever more difficult to bamboozle and muzzle the public and it is difficult to see this trend abating. In that sense, the prospects for a more robust democracy seem reasonably good.

In terms of justice, the record is mixed. Critics charge that the judiciary regularly appears reluctant to exercise its independence in cases that involve government interests, but as we have seen in information disclosure cases, the courts have been supportive of citizen's rights. Outrage over the favourable treatment sometimes accorded to high-ranking politicians and bureaucrats is muted. For minorities, foreigners and women, justice has proved more elusive, but recent court rulings suggest that the trend is towards somewhat more justice for those who have been burdened by more extensive experience with injustice. Some of the more onerous and egregious discriminatory requirements, regulations and abuses have abated and there is no reason to doubt the prospects for further, if only gradual, improvements. The significant judicial reforms enacted in the first decade of the twenty-first century are part of a wider set of reforms aimed at transforming Japan from the *rule by law* to the *rule of law*, thereby reducing the scope for favouritism.

Rule by law encompasses arbitrary, biased actions by officials exercising their discretionary powers to enact laws and regulations to achieve specific desired goals or benefit/penalize specific actors, whereas the **rule of law** refers to a situation where laws and regulations are enacted and enforced in ways that are fair, transparent, equal and support general rules of the game that ensure a level playing field.

TRANSFORMATION?

Paradoxically, as Japan plunges further into the twenty-first century there is both nostalgia for the security of the Japan, Inc. paradigm and recognition that jettisoning this model is crucial to improving prospects. In ousting the LDP in 2009, voters gave their verdict, but they remain anxious about the direction of reform. This is a time of confusion and uncertainty as the success of transforming postwar Japan into a global economic powerhouse has given way to introspection about what went wrong. Why have the fruits of success been both so fleeting and so unsatisfying? The Lost Decade of the 1990s was a time when unprecedented amounts of wealth evaporated, legions of companies went bankrupt, employment security began to fade and the public's confidence in its leaders reached a nadir in response to a cascade of corruption scandals involving government bureaucrats, politicians and corporate managers. It has been a time when trust in the elite and faith in their competence has given way to widespread scepticism. The mantra of reform, deregulation and restructuring echoing throughout the archipelago during the Koizumi era (2001–06), signified that the norms and ways of the past have been irretrievably discredited and are no longer sacrosanct. By 2009, however, voters came to realize that the benefits of such neo-liberal reforms were oversold while the risks grossly underestimated. The DPJ has been tasked with expanding the safety net for those at most risk, addressing disparities and revitalizing the economy, tasks that are not always compatible. There is an acknowledgement that Japan needs far ranging reforms, even though various groups and vested interests are working to ensure that this proceeds slowly or bypasses their turf. The key is whether Japan can repeat the success it had in overcoming the odds to transform its institutions radically as it did in the mid-nineteenth century following the Meiji restoration and during the mid-twentieth century during the American Occupation. At these crucial junctures, Japan did meet the challenges of a changing world, but this does not mean that it can do so again.

The jury is still out on whether contemporary Japan is doing what it needs to do with sufficient dispatch. Will the government's zeal for managing change end up stifling and limiting the positive consequences of reform? There is evidence on both sides of this question and it will take time before anyone can answer with certainty whether or not Japan has managed yet again to turn calamity to its advantage. For those who focus on the demographic time-bomb, there is scant basis for optimism because there do not seem to be any policies that can alleviate the dire economic consequences of a rapidly ageing society. And, even if policy changes might help mitigate some of these problems, the voting public will become increasingly aged and thus more conservative, disinclined to support radical reform measures and protective of their perquisites. How can change occur in a society that will have so many elderly people who favour risk-averse policies consistent with minimal disruption to the status quo?

Yet Japan has demonstrated a great capacity for change. It still has some of the most dynamic global companies, boasts leading technologies and has an enormous store of social capital. Many people are favourably disposed to reform and most see the need for retreating from key features of the current paradigm that are no longer seen to serve the interests of society. The ongoing proliferation and dissemination of technology is creating new frontiers and breathing dynamism into what had become a relatively moribund nation, forcing the reconsideration of what is possible and undermining confident predictions about what society will be like a few decades down the road. Japan is also well poised to tap the growth in China and India and the opportunities in environmental technologies and products. As it is still early on in the process of forging a new paradigm, what appear to be intractable troubles today may become manageable in ways that cannot be foreseen now. In this sense, the rapid ageing of society may prove far less cataclysmic than some are predicting. Also working in Japan's favour is the prospect of more fully tapping the potential of its women, a highly educated pool of human capital that has, in many respects, been squandered due to antediluvian attitudes and practices. The impending labour shortage is expected to open up opportunities for women and they will be given a greater chance to develop and use their skills. In this way perhaps Japan can address the overdue transition from an economy based on 'perspiration' (growth based on increasing inputs of labour and/or capital) to one that relies on 'inspiration' (growth based on innovation and rising productivity) (Krugman, 1994). It is also promising that the rising generation of workers are far more adept with IT than their predecessors, allowing Japan to tap this potential more fully. Finally, there is also reason for cautious optimism about the future because of the accumulated frustration with being a country that enjoys wealth without prosperity (McCormack, 1996). Japan can look forward to this new frontier where the economic development and wealth that has been generated in the postwar era becomes the basis for spreading the amenities of prosperity.

Part 4

DOCUMENTS

Document 1   THE 1947 CONSTITUTION

The Constitution was written in February 1946 at the orders of General MacArthur who was the Supreme Commander of the Allied Powers (SCAP) which ruled Japan during the Occupation (1945–52). The initial Japanese attempt to revise the Meiji Constitution was judged inadequate by MacArthur and his aides in correcting the problems of overly concentrated power and did not go far enough in terms of promoting civil liberties and making the government accountable to the people. The new Constitution was drafted in 2 weeks by a small group of Americans who lacked formal training in constitutional law. General MacArthur has been credited with inserting Article 9 renouncing war. This Constitution was translated into Japanese and presented to the Japanese political leadership for their approval at SCAP insistence. It was promulgated with minor revisions in 1947.

Preamble,

We, the Japanese people, acting through our duly elected representatives in the National Diet, determined that we shall secure for ourselves and our posterity the fruits of peaceful cooperation with all nations and the blessings of liberty throughout this land, and resolved that never again shall we be visited with the horrors of war through the action of government, do proclaim that sovereign power resides with the people and do firmly establish this Constitution. Government is a sacred trust of the people, the authority for which is derived from the people, the powers of which are exercised by the representatives of the people, and the benefits of which are enjoyed by the people. This is a universal principle of mankind upon which this Constitution is founded. We reject and revoke all constitutions, laws, ordinances and rescripts in conflict herewith.

We, the people, desire peace for all time and are deeply conscious of the high ideals controlling human relationships, and we have determined to preserve our security and existence, trusting in the justice and faith of the peace-loving peoples of the world. We desire to occupy an honored place in an international society striving for the preservation of peace and the banishment of tyranny and slavery, oppression and intolerance for all time from the earth. We recognize that all peoples of the world have the right to live in peace, free from fear and want.

We believe that no nation is responsible to itself alone, but that laws of political morality are universal; and that obedience to such laws is incumbent upon all nations who would sustain their own sovereignty and justify their sovereign relationship with other nations.

We, the Japanese people, pledge our national honor to accomplish these high ideals and purposes with all our resources.

Chapter 1. The Emperor

Article 1. The Emperor shall be the symbol of the State and the unity of the people, deriving his position from the will of the people with whom resides sovereign power.

Article 2. The Imperial Throne shall be dynastic and succeeded to in accordance with the Imperial House Law passed by the Diet.

Article 3. The advice and approval of the Cabinet shall be required for all acts of the Emperor in matters of state, and the Cabinet shall be responsible therefore.

Article 4. The Emperor shall perform only such acts in matters of state as are provided for in this Constitution, and he shall not have power related to government.

Chapter 2. Renunciation of War

Article 9. Aspiring sincerely to an international peace based on justice and order, the Japanese people forever renounce war as a sovereign right of the nation and the threat or use of force as means of settling international disputes.

In order to accomplish the aim of the preceding paragraph, land, sea and air forces, as well as other war potential, will never be maintained. The right of belligerency of the state will not be recognized.

Chapter 3. Rights and Duties of the People

Article 11. The people shall not be prevented from enjoying any of the fundamental human rights.

These fundamental human rights guaranteed to the people by this constitution shall be conferred on the people of this and future generations as eternal and inviolate rights.

Article 13. All of the people shall be respected as individuals. Their rights to life, liberty, and the pursuit of happiness, to the extent that it does not interfere with the public welfare, will be the supreme consideration in legislation and other governmental affairs.

Article 14. All of the people are equal under the law, and there shall be no discrimination in political, economic, or social relations because of race, creed, sex, social status, or family origin.

Peers and peerage shall not be recognized.

No privilege shall accompany any award of honor, decoration, or any distinction, nor shall any such award be valid beyond the lifetime of the individual who now holds or hereafter may receive it.

Article 15. The people have the inalienable right to choose their public officials and to dismiss them.

All public officials are servants of the whole community and not of any group thereof.

Universal adult suffrage is guaranteed with regard to the election of public officials.

In all elections, secrecy of the ballot shall not be violated. A voter shall not be answerable, publicly or privately, for the choice he has made. . . .

Article 20. Freedom of religion is guaranteed to all. No religious organization shall receive any privileges from the State nor exercise any political authority.

No person shall be compelled to take part in any religious act, celebration, rite, or practice.

The State and its organs shall refrain from religious education or any religious activity.

Article 21. Freedom of assembly and association as well as speech, press, and all other forms of expression are guaranteed.

No censorship shall be maintained, nor shall the secrecy of any communication be violated. . . .

Article 24. Marriage shall be based only on the mutual consent of both sexes, and it shall be maintained through mutual cooperation with the equal rights of husband and wife as a basis.

With regard to choice of spouse, property rights, inheritance, choice of domicile, divorce and other matters pertaining to marriage and the family, laws shall be enacted from the standpoint of individual dignity and the essential equality of the sexes. . . .

Article 28. The right of workers to organize and bargain and act collectively is guaranteed. . . .

Article 37. In all criminal cases, the accused shall enjoy the right to a speedy and public trial by an impartial tribunal.

He shall be permitted full opportunity to examine all witnesses, and he shall have the right of compulsory process for obtaining witnesses on his behalf at public expense.

At all times the accused shall have the assistance of competent counsel who shall, if the accused is unable to secure the same by his own efforts, be assigned to his use by the State. . . .

Chapter 4. The Diet

Article 41. The Diet shall be the highest organ of state power and shall be the sole lawmaking organ of the State.

Article 42. The Diet shall consist of two Houses, namely, the House of Representatives and the House of Councilors.

Article 43. Both Houses shall consist of elected members, representatives of all the people.

Article 60. The budget must first be submitted to the House of Representatives.

Upon consideration of the budget, when the House of Councilors makes a decision different from that of the House of Representatives, and when no agreement can be reached even through a joint committee of both Houses, provided for by law, or in the case of failure by the House of Councilors to take final action in thirty days, the period of recess excluded, after the receipt of the budget passed by the House of Representatives, the decision of the House of Representatives shall be the decision of the Diet.

Chapter 5. The Cabinet

Article 65. Executive power shall be vested in the Cabinet.

Article 66. The Cabinet shall consist of the Prime Minister, who shall be its head, and other Ministers of State, as provided for by law.

The Prime Minister and other Ministers of State must be civilians.

The Cabinet, in the exercise of executive power, shall be collectively responsible to the Diet. . . .

Chapter 6. The Judiciary

Article 76. The whole judicial power is vested in a Supreme Court and in such inferior courts as are established by law.

Source: From *The Columbia Guide to Modern Japanese History*, 1 ed., Columbia University Press (Allinson, G. 1999) pp. 223–6. Copyright © 1999 Columbia University Press. Reprinted with permission of the publisher.

JOHN DOWER ON THE US OCCUPATION OF JAPAN **Document 2**

Dower is the pre-eminent historian of the Occupation and won the National Book Award for his book, Embracing Defeat: Japan in the *Wake of World War II. He focuses on the paradoxes and ironies of Americans imposing democracy, leading a revolution from above with minimal consultation with the people. His work is especially useful in providing details about how the Japanese people perceived and participated in the Occupation and how the Americans fell short of their ideals and principles in remaking Japan.*

[T]he contradictions of the democratic revolution from above were clear for all to see: while the victors preached democracy, they ruled by fiat; while they espoused equality, they themselves constituted an inviolate privileged caste. Their reformist agenda rested on the assumption that, virtually without exception, Western culture and its values were superior to those of 'the Orient.' At the same time, almost every interaction between victor and vanquished was infused with intimations of white supremacism. For all its uniqueness of time, place, and circumstance – all its peculiarly 'American' iconoclasm – the occupation was in this sense but a new manifestation of the old racial paternalism that historically accompanied the global expansion of the Western powers. Like their colonialist predecessors, the victors were imbued with a sense of manifest destiny. They spoke of being engaged in the mission of civilizing their subjects. They bore the burden (in their own eyes) of their race, creed, and culture. They swaggered, and were enviously free of self-doubt.

It was inevitable that relations between the victors and the vanquished be unequal, but this inequality was compounded by authoritarian practices that were part and parcel of the American modus operandi independent of the situation in Japan. To begin with, the administrative structure that the Japanese encountered was itself organized in the most rigid hierarchical manner imaginable. MacArthur's command, after all, was a military bureaucracy, the very organizational antithesis of democratic checks and balances.

This working model of authoritarian governance was compounded by the manner in which the occupation regime implemented its directives. Contrary to the practice of direct military government adopted in defeated Germany, this occupation was conducted 'indirectly' – that is, through existing organs of government. This entailed buttressing the influence of two of the most undemocratic institutions of the presurrender regime: the bureaucracy and the throne.

Source: From *Embracing Defeat: Japan in the Wake of Defeat*, W. W. Norton & Co Ltd (Dower, J. 1999) pp. 211–12. Copyright 1999 by John W. Dower. Used by permission of W. W. Norton & Company Inc. Reproduced by permission of Penguin Books Ltd.

Document 3   THE TREATY OF MUTUAL COOPERATION AND SECURITY BETWEEN JAPAN AND THE UNITED STATES, 19 JANUARY 1960

This revision of the 1951 Security Treaty sparked riots, demonstrations and polarized politics in Japan. While it did remove the right of US forces to intervene in the event of domestic disorder, it extended the right of the United States to maintain and use military bases in Japan. Critics looked upon this extensive US military presence as a continuation of the Occupation and an encroachment on Japanese sovereignty. The resulting controversy forced the resignation of Prime Minister Kishi and made the US alliance the focal point of opposition politics in the 1960s.

Japan and the United States of America,

Desiring to strengthen the bonds of peace and friendship traditionally existing between them, and to uphold the principles of democracy, individual liberty, and the rule of law,

Desiring further to encourage closer economic cooperation between them and to promote conditions of economic stability and well being in their countries,

Reaffirming their faith in the purpose and principles of the Charter of the United Nations, and their desire to live in peace with all peoples and all governments,

Recognizing that they have the inherent right of individual or collective self-defense as affirmed in the Charter of the United Nations,

Considering that they have a common concern in the maintenance of international peace and security in the Far East,

Having resolved to conclude a treaty of mutual cooperation and security,

Therefore agree as follows:

Article I

The Parties undertake, as set forth in the Charter of the United Nations, to settle any international disputes in which they may be involved by peaceful means in such a manner that international peace and security and justice are not endangered and to refrain in their international relations from the threat or use of force against the territorial integrity or political independence of any state, or in any other manner inconsistent with the purposes of the United Nations.

The Parties will endeavor in concert with other peace-loving countries to strengthen the United Nations so that its mission of maintaining international peace and security may be discharged more effectively.

Article II

The Parties will contribute toward the further development of peaceful and friendly international relations by strengthening their free institutions, by bringing about a better understanding of the principles upon which these institutions are founded, and by promoting conditions of stability and well-being. They will seek to eliminate conflict in their international economic policies and will encourage economic collaboration between them.

Article III

The Parties, individually and in cooperation with each other, by means of continuous and effective self-help and mutual aid will maintain and develop, subject to their constitutional provisions, their capacities to resist armed attack.

Article IV

The Parties will consult together from time to time regarding the implementation of this Treaty, and, at the request of either Party, whenever the security of Japan or international peace and security in the Far East is threatened.

Article V

Each Party recognizes that an armed attack against their Party in the territories under the administration of Japan would be dangerous to its own peace and safety and declares that it would act to meet the common danger in accordance with its constitutional provisions and processes.

Any such armed attack and all measures taken as a result thereof shall be immediately reported to the Security Council of the United Nations in accordance with the provisions of Article 51 of the Charter. Such measures shall be terminated when the Security Council has taken the measures necessary to restore and maintain international peace and security.

Article VI

For the purpose of contributing to the security of Japan and the maintenance of international peace and security in the Far East, the United States of America is granted the use by its land, air and naval forces of facilities and areas in Japan.

The use of these facilities and areas as well as the status of United States armed forces in Japan shall be governed by a separate agreement, replacing the Administrative Agreement under Article III of the Security Treaty between Japan and the United States of America, signed at Tokyo on February 28, 1952, as amended, and by such other arrangements as may be agreed upon.

Article VII

This Treaty does not affect and shall not be interpreted as affecting in any way the rights and obligations of the Parties under the Charter of the United Nations or the responsibility of the United Nations for the maintenance of international peace and security.

Article VIII

This treaty shall be ratified by Japan and the United States of America in accordance with their respective constitutional processes and will enter into force on the date on which the instruments of ratification thereof have been exchanged by them in Tokyo.

Article IX

The Security Treaty between Japan and the United States of America signed at the city of San Francisco on September 8, 1951, shall expire upon the entering into force of this Treaty.

Article X

This Treaty shall remain in force until in the opinion of the governments of Japan and the United States of America there shall have come into force such United Nations arrangements as will satisfactorily provide for the maintenance of international peace and security in the Japan area.

However, after the Treaty has been in force for ten years, either Party may give notice to the other Party of its intention to terminate the Treaty, in which case the Treaty shall terminate one year after such notice has been given.

Source: US Department of State (1961) *United States Treaties and Other Agreements*, Vol. 2, part 2 (Government Printing Office, Washington, DC), pp. 1633–5.

CHALMERS JOHNSON ON THE JAPANESE MIRACLE   Document 4

Johnson represents what is loosely termed the revisionist camp among scholars and commentators specializing on Japan. He and others since have challenged the more benign and less critical interpretations of Japan by orthodox Japan-hands, such as Edwin Reischauer, who are sometimes termed the Chrysanthemum Club, a reference to the flower used in the Imperial crest. This seminal work came out at a time of rising Japanese trade surpluses with the United States and gained considerable attention for its elucidation of the Japanese government's role in guiding and nurturing the economy. His views continue to influence public perceptions in the United States and stoke concerns that the Japanese government has orchestrated predatory and unfair trading practices harmful to US interests.

One clear lesson from the Japanese case is that the state needs the market and private enterprise needs the state; once both sides recognized this, cooperation was possible and high speed growth occurred.

Japan offers a panoply of market-conforming methods of state intervention, including the creation of government financial institutions, whose influence is as much indicative as it is monetary; the extensive use, narrow targeting, and timely revision of tax incentives; the use of indicative plans to set goals and guidelines for the entire economy; the creation of numerous, formal, and continuously operating forums for exchanging views, reviewing policies, obtaining feedback, and resolving differences; the assignment of some governmental functions to various private and semiprivate associations (JETRO, Keidanren); an extensive reliance on public corporations, particularly of the mixed public–private variety, to implement policy in high risk or otherwise refractory areas; the creation and use by the government of an unconsolidated 'investment budget' separate from and not funded by the general account budget; the orientation of anti-trust policy to developmental and international competitive goals rather than strictly to the maintenance of domestic competition; government-conducted or government-sponsored research and development (the computer industry); and the use of the government's licensing and approval authority to achieve developmental goals.

Perhaps the most important market-conforming method of intervention is administrative guidance. This power, which amounts to an allocation of discretionary and unsupervised authority to the bureaucracy, is obviously open to abuse, and may, if used improperly, result in damage to the market. But it is an essential power of the capitalist developmental state for one critical reason: it is necessary to avoid overly detailed laws that, by their very nature, are never detailed enough to cover all contingencies and yet, because of their detail, put a strait jacket on creative administration. . . . The Japanese political economy is strikingly free of lawyers; many of the functions performed by lawyers in other societies are performed in Japan by bureaucrats using administrative guidance.

Source: Chalmers Johnson (1982) *MITI and the Japanese Miracle: The Growth of Industrial Policy, 1925–1975* (Stanford University Press, Stanford, CA), pp. 318–19.

———————◀◉▶———————

Document 5   END OF THE MIRACLE: GROWING DISPARITIES AND POVERTY

The rate of relative poverty in Japan is now one of the highest in the OECD area. Population ageing is partly responsible for boosting inequality as it raises the proportion of the labour force in the 50 to 65 age group, which is characterised by greater wage variation. However, the key factor appears to be increasing dualism in the labour market. The proportion of non-regular workers has risen from 19% of employees a decade ago to over 30%. Part-time workers earn on average only 40% as much per hour as full-time workers, a gap which appears too large to be explained by productivity differences. Although the increase in non-regular workers has been partly caused by cyclical factors, there is a risk that labour market dualism will become entrenched, given that thus far only a small proportion of non-regular workers have become regular workers. One important key to reversing the rise in inequality and poverty is to reduce labour market dualism. This requires a comprehensive approach including reducing employment protection for regular workers and thereby weakening the incentives of firms to hire non-regular workers. In addition, it is important to increase the coverage of temporary workers by social insurance and to enhance the employment prospects of non-regular workers.

The serious fiscal problem limits the scope for boosting social spending to reduce relative poverty. It is necessary, therefore, to reallocate social spending to increase the share received by low-income households, while taking care to limit the creation of poverty traps and work disincentives. About three-quarters of social spending is allocated to the elderly. More than half of single working parents were in relative poverty in 2000, compared with an OECD average of around 20%. Moreover, Japan had a higher poverty rate for single parents who work than for those who are not employed. In 2002, the government reformed the single parent allowance to provide work incentives. Significant poverty among single parents is a factor boosting the child poverty rate to 14% in 2000, well above the OECD average. Given the relatively high proportion of education costs borne by the private sector, it is essential to ensure that children in low-income households have adequate access to high-quality education to prevent poverty from being passed to future generations.

Source: OECD Policy Brief, Economic Survey of Japan, 2006.

THE WAR APOLOGY RESOLUTION: THE PRIME MINISTER'S ADDRESS TO THE NATIONAL DIET, 9 JUNE 1995

Document 6

The war apology resolution passed by the National Diet in June 1995 was a compromise hammered out among political parties. Progressives in Japan sought to use the 50th anniversary of the end of the Second World War to make an unequivocal apology to victims of Japanese aggression and thereby overcome lingering resentments and suspicions in Asia. Conservatives opposed such a gesture because in their view, Japan's actions were justified. The final wording of the apology resolution clouded the issue of responsibility and thus, in the eyes of many Japanese and other Asians, undermined the sincerity of the apology. The reference to 'colonial rule and acts of aggression in the modern world' has been interpreted as an attempt to mitigate Japan's actions and spread blame in a way that deflects attention away from the widespread atrocities committed by the Imperial armed forces.

RESOLUTION TO RENEW THE DETERMINATION FOR PEACE
ON THE BASIS OF LESSONS LEARNED FROM HISTORY

House of Representatives, National Diet of Japan

The House of Representatives resolves as follows:

On the occasion of the 50th anniversary of the end of World War II, this House offers its sincere condolences to those who fell in action and victims of wars and similar actions all over the world.

Solemnly reflecting upon many instances of colonial rule and acts of aggression in the modern history of the world, and recognizing that Japan carried out those acts in the past, inflicting pain and suffering upon the peoples of other countries, especially in Asia, the Members of this House express a sense of deep remorse.

We must transcend the differences over historical views of the past war and learn humbly the lessons of history so as to build a peaceful international society.

This House expresses its resolve, under the banner of eternal peace enshrined in the Constitution of Japan, to join hands with other nations of the world and to pave the way to a future that allows all human beings to live together.

Source: Ministry of Foreign Affairs website: *www.mofa.go.jp*

Document 7　PRIME MINISTER MURAYAMA'S APOLOGY, 15 AUGUST 1995

Prime Minister Murayama, leader of the Japan Socialist Party (JSP) coalition government with the Liberal Democratic Party (LDP), used the 50th anniversary of Japan's surrender to articulate the progressive view of the war, to take unequivocal responsibility for the suffering inflicted on fellow Asians and to make a sincere apology for the atrocities caused by Japanese aggression. His remarks were well received in Asia and went a long way in dispelling the ill will and negative impressions generated by the Diet's war resolution of June 1995.

The world has seen 50 years elapse since the war came to an end. Now, when I remember the many people both at home and abroad who fell victim to war, my heart is overwhelmed by a flood of emotions.

The peace and prosperity of today were built as Japan overcame great difficulty to arise from a devastated land after defeat in the war. That achievement is something of which we are proud, and let me herein express my heartfelt admiration for the wisdom and untiring effort of each and every one of our citizens. Let me also express once again my profound gratitude for the indispensable support and assistance extended to Japan by the countries of the world, beginning with the United States of America. I am also delighted that we have been able to build the friendly relations which we enjoy today with the neighboring countries of the Asia-Pacific region, the United States and the countries of Europe.

Now that Japan has come to enjoy peace and abundance, we tend to overlook the pricelessness and blessings of peace. Our task is to convey to younger generations the horrors of war, so that we never repeat the errors in our history. I believe that, as we join hands, especially with the peoples of neighboring countries, to ensure true peace in the Asia-Pacific region – indeed, in the entire world – it is necessary, more than anything else, that we foster relations with all countries based on deep understanding and trust. Guided by this conviction, the Government has launched the Peace, Friendship and Exchange Initiative, which consists of two parts, promoting: support for historical research into relations in the modern era between Japan and the neighboring countries of Asia and elsewhere; and rapid expansion of exchanges with those countries. Furthermore, I will continue in all sincerity to do my utmost in efforts being made on the issues arisen from the war, in order to further strengthen the relations of trust between Japan and those countries.

Now, upon this historic occasion of the 50th anniversary of the war's end, we should bear in mind that we must look into the past to learn from the lessons of history, and ensure that we do not stray from the path to the peace and prosperity of human society in the future.

During a certain period in the not too distant past, Japan, following a mistaken national policy, advanced along the road to war, only to ensnare the Japanese people in a fateful crisis, and, through its colonial rule and aggression, caused tremendous damage and suffering to the people of many countries, particularly to those of Asian nations. In the hope that no such mistake be made in the future, I regard, in a spirit of humility, these irrefutable facts of history, and express here once again my feelings of deep remorse and state my heartfelt apology. Allow me also to express my feelings of profound mourning for all victims, both at home and abroad, of that history.

Building from our deep remorse on this occasion of the 50th anniversary of the end of the war, Japan must eliminate self-righteous nationalism, promote international coordination as a responsible member of the international community and, thereby, advance the principles of peace and democracy. At the same time, as the only country to have experienced the devastation of atomic bombing, Japan, with a view to the ultimate elimination of nuclear weapons, must actively strive to further global disarmament in areas such as the strengthening of the nuclear non-proliferation regime. It is my conviction that in this way alone can Japan atone for its past and lay to rest the spirits of those who perished.

It is said that one can rely on good faith. And so, at this time of remembrance, I declare to the people of Japan and abroad my intention to make good faith the foundation of our Government policy, and this is my vow.

Source: Ministry of Foreign Affairs website: *www.mofa.go.jp*

Document 8   REPARATIONS AND RECONCILIATION

Japan has provided little in the way of reparations to victims of Japan's wartime aggression and forced labour. Critics argue that the absence of redress is an impediment to improving regional relations. The following op-ed makes the case for compensation.

During visits to South Korea and China in October (2009), Prime Minister Yukio Hatoyama revealed his vision for an East Asian community built on a spirit of 'fraternity.'

A peaceful and stable regional bloc would certainly ensure greater prosperity for all, but Japan cannot hope to attain that goal until it addresses some long-outstanding grievances – in particular the settlement of compensation for wartime misdeeds.

These include, for example, forcibly bringing Koreans and Chinese to Japan as laborers, and subjecting prisoners of war from allied powers to forced labor.

The sad truth is that 64 years after the end of World War II, so many people continue to suffer from the mental and physical scars left by atrocities.

Since 1990 alone, there have been more than 70 damage lawsuits brought to courts in Japan. Some of the rulings acknowledged the illegality of the acts, showed sympathy to the victims and urged new legislation to provide for settlements. But with the exception of a small number of cases that sought court-mediated settlements with companies involved in forced labor, the courts dismissed all of the claims by plaintiffs.

For nearly six decades, Liberal Democratic Party administrations continued to sidestep issues such as this one. But their failure to own up to Japan's wartime atrocities and offer compensation has only exacerbated the suffering of victims and undermined trust in Japan throughout the international community, especially in Asia.

The government should clarify its responsibility and secure necessary funds in a step toward building trust and peace in the region.

Source: Ken Arimitsu, coordinator of the Lawyers and Citizens' Association for Post-War Judicial Implementation. Redress for war is 1st step to regional fraternity. *Asahi*, 9 December 2009.

Document 9   KONO STATEMENT ON COMFORT WOMEN

After conducting an investigation into the involvement of the Imperial Japanese government and military in the recruiting of young women to provide sexual services to Japanese troops as comfort women, and establishing and running comfort stations, the Japanese government concluded that there was sufficient evidence proving extensive involvement. The Kono statement served as an official acknowledgement of responsibility and promised to inform Japanese about the comfort women issue and to make gestures of atonement. The Asia Women's Fund (1995–2007) was established to achieve these ends with limited success.

The Government of Japan has been conducting a study on the issue of wartime 'comfort women' since December 1991. I wish to announce the findings as a result of that study.

As a result of the study which indicates that comfort stations were operated in extensive areas for long periods, it is apparent that there existed a great number of comfort women. Comfort stations were operated in response to the request of the military authorities of the day. The then Japanese military was, directly or indirectly, involved in the establishment and management of the comfort stations and the transfer of comfort women. The recruitment of the comfort women was conducted mainly by private recruiters who acted in response to the request of the military. The Government study has revealed that in many cases they were recruited against their own will, through coaxing, coercion, etc., and that, at times, administrative/military personnel directly took part in the recruitments. They lived in misery at comfort stations under a coercive atmosphere.

As to the origin of those comfort women who were transferred to the war areas, excluding those from Japan, those from the Korean Peninsula accounted for a large part. The Korean Peninsula was under Japanese rule in those days, and their recruitment, transfer, control, etc., were conducted generally against their will, through coaxing, coercion, etc.

Undeniably, this was an act, with the involvement of the military authorities of the day, that severely injured the honor and dignity of many women. The Government of Japan would like to take this opportunity once again to extend its sincere apologies and remorse to all those, irrespective of place of origin, who suffered immeasurable pain and incurable physical and psychological wounds as comfort women.

It is incumbent upon us, the Government of Japan, to continue to consider seriously, while listening to the views of learned circles, how best we can express this sentiment.

We shall face squarely the historical facts as described above instead of evading them, and take them to heart as lessons of history. We hereby reiterated our firm determination never to repeat the same mistake by forever engraving such issues in our memories through the study and teaching of history.

As actions have been brought to court in Japan and interests have been shown in this issue outside Japan, the Government of Japan shall continue to pay full attention to this matter, including private research related thereto.

Source: Yohei Kono, Chief Cabinet Secretary, Government of Japan, 4 August 1993.

Document 10   THE NANKING MASSACRE

Conservatives still challenge established historical accounts of Japan's rampage through Asia between 1931 and 1945, arguing that this record has been falsified and distorted to discredit Japan and to extract concessions and reparations. They maintain that negative accounts of the Imperial armed forces reflect a 'victor's' history that demeans the sacrifices endured by Japanese on behalf of other Asians in trying to overturn the Western colonial order. This selective amnesia about wartime atrocities is not representative of public opinion in Japan, but angers many Chinese. Iris Chang's The Rape of Nanking *(1997) introduced this topic to a wide audience, while Honda (1999) presents a detailed account about the nature and extent of atrocities committed by Japanese troops. Wakabayashi (2007), Yoshida (2006), Fogel (2000) and Brook (1999) provide additional evidence that belies assertions by Japanese conservatives that the Nanking Massacre is a myth. For a thoughtful comparison of how Germany and Japan have coped with the legacy of the Second World War, see Buruma (1994).*

A conference intended to play down Japan's record of atrocities during its occupation of China has unleashed a storm of criticism from Beijing and drawn strong condemnation from some historians and others in Japan.

The topic of the one-day conference, scheduled for Sunday in Japan's second largest city, Osaka, is the 1937 Nanjing Massacre, which organizers have provocatively called 'the biggest myth of the 20th century.'

The site selected for the meeting further stoked the ire of many in Japan. The conference will be in the city's International Peace Center, which houses permanent exhibits on war, including the American atomic bombing of Japan in World War II and Japan's brutal military campaign in China in the 1930s.

For several days running, the Chinese government and news media have bitterly attacked the conference as the work of people eager to falsify history and raise tensions between the two countries.

'By planning the rally, Japanese rightists want to distort history, paper over the aggression and undermine Sino-Japanese friendship,' said a Chinese foreign ministry spokesman, Zhu Bangzao, in a statement published in the official *China Daily*.

Ryutaro Nakakita, an Osaka lawyer opposed to the event, said that the organizers' intention was 'to bring chaos to a hall that was meant to promote peace, and to muddle history.' City officials say, however, that the Peace Center is a public place and that to refuse to allow the conference to be held there would be an infringement on free speech.

Mainstream Japanese historians of the 1930s and 1940s, the period of Japan's aggressive militarism, say that to accept such an invitation is akin to legitimating the views of German extremists or others who would deny the existence of the Holocaust.

Although casualty estimates vary, it is widely accepted among scholars that after the sudden collapse of the Chinese defense of Nanjing in December 1937, rampaging Japanese soldiers executed thousands of prisoners of war, men suspected of being soldiers and civilians, and burned the homes of Chinese to keep warm. Thousands of Chinese women are also believed to have been raped.

In discussing this history, parallels with Germany are inevitably strained. Germany has broadly owned up to the horrors of its wartime past and has paid compensation to many of its victims. But Japan as a society has generally avoided any deep reflection and contrition over a period in which its army ran roughshod over much of Asia. It has generally refused to compensate its war victims and has even avoided paying veterans' benefits to Korean citizens forced to fight in Japan's defense.

Japan's aggression and the atrocities it entailed are treated only cursorily in most schools here. Even recent concessions to textbook reform in this area, like mention of the rape and sexual slavery of thousands of Korean and Chinese women, is under attack by conservatives, who cast doubt on the accounts and say these subjects should not be taught to young Japanese.

'The people claiming there was no Nanjing Massacre, including the organizers of this conference, are the people who would maintain that Japan's war in China was legitimate, that it was not an invasion,' said Tokushi Kasahara, a professor of Chinese modern history at Tsuru University in Tokyo. 'Many Japanese do not know much about these events, and the people of this camp are trying to influence them.'

But while fringe figures who deny the Holocaust exist in Germany and elsewhere, voices here dismissing or greatly playing down Japan's wartime crimes are regularly heard from the political, academic and media establishment. The governor of Tokyo, Shintaro Ishihara, for one, has frequently called the Nanjing Massacre a lie.

'People think by analogy that because Germans committed a Holocaust, that Japanese must have done something like that too,' said Dr. Shudo Higashinakano, a historian of social thought at Asia University in Tokyo. 'But you must look at the facts.'

Dr. Higashinakano, who is scheduled to speak at the Osaka conference, said the Nanjing Massacre, also commonly known as the Rape of Nanjing, was 'groundless war propaganda.'

Source: Howard W. French. Japanese call '37 massacre a war myth, stirring storm. *New York Times*, 23 January 2000, p. 4.

Document 11   THE ODA CHARTER

Japan was the world's leading donor of Official Development Assistance (ODA) throughout the 1990s. The government developed a set of criteria for determining the provision of aid in order to clarify under what conditions ODA might be withheld from a recipient nation. Critics have argued that Japan has not rigorously applied its own principles as articulated in the ODA Charter. This document from the Ministry of Foreign Affairs explains the government of Japan's position on aid, discussing various cases that illustrate its commitment to the ODA Charter. It is worth noting that sanctions against India have been lifted and it is one of the leading recipients of Japanese ODA.

Adopted as a cabinet decision in June 1992, Japan's ODA Charter demands the observance of several important principles with a bearing on the provision of aid. Though decisions on aid should be based on a comprehensive assessment of aid requests, economic and social conditions, bilateral relations, and other factors, the Charter also urges consideration of four key factors: namely, (i) pursuit in tandem of environmental conservation and development, (ii) avoidance of any use of ODA for military purposes or for aggravation of international conflicts, (iii) full attention to trends in recipient countries' military expenditures, their development and production of weapons of mass destruction and missiles and their export and import of arms, etc. and (iv) full attention to efforts for promoting democratization and introduction of a market-oriented economy, and the situation regarding securing basic human rights and freedoms in the recipient country.

In keeping with the principles of its ODA Charter, Japan has actively provided assistance to Mongolia, Vietnam, and several countries in Central Asia because they have all demonstrated acceptable progress in terms of democratization and the transition to free-market economic systems.

By contrast, the nuclear tests that India and Pakistan conducted in May 1998 forced Japan, in consideration of its ODA Charter, to adopt strict countermeasures. To be sure, the nuclear policies of both those countries had been in question for some time. Working through bilateral forums on aid, nuclear non-proliferation, and other policy dialogues, Japan and other countries concerned had urged that India and Pakistan rein in their nuclear weapons and missile development programs and sign the Non-Proliferation Treaty (NPT) as well as the Comprehensive Test Ban Treaty (CTBT). However, the Vajpayee Administration that assumed power in March 1998 raised further doubts about India's nuclear policies by declaring a policy guideline of the coalition government, in which India would exercise the option to become a nuclear-armed state. Though the Japanese government urged through high-level channels that it assume a policy of restraint, India decided instead to conduct underground nuclear tests in May 1998, going thus against the global trend toward a comprehensive ban on nuclear testing. Japan immediately and strongly protested, and, in consideration of the principles of its ODA Charter, decided to halt the provision of new grant aid (other than grant assistance for grassroots projects or of an emergency, humanitarian nature) and new yen loans, and to carefully consider any loans for India through multilateral development banks.

Following the Indian nuclear tests, Japan sent a Prime Minister's envoy to Pakistan and enlisted additional governmental channels to encourage Pakistan to exercise self-restraint. In late May, however, Pakistan also went ahead with underground nuclear tests, and Japan responded accordingly by imposing essentially the same measures it had taken against India.

Given that India and Pakistan are countries with which Japan has traditionally maintained friendly ties, it is disappointing that both have decided to act counter to the interests of the non-proliferation regime. It is expected that both countries will adopt revised nuclear policies that include abandoning the development of nuclear weapons.

China has actively pursued steps in openness and reform policy, and has also continued to show welcome progress toward a market-oriented economy. However, in 1995 it engaged in nuclear tests despite repeated requests from Japan. As a consequence, in August that year, Japan imposed a freeze on all grant aid to China other than aid of an emergency, humanitarian nature or for grassroots assistance. In July 1996, China enacted a moratorium on further nuclear testing and later signed the CTBT, thus prompting Japan to resume grant aid to the country in March 1997. Japan has also taken various opportunities to explain the position outlined in its ODA Charter on military spending and related issues, and has urged that China adopt a more transparent set of military policies, while China has taken some steps toward improved transparency, such as the publication of a document on Chinese arms control and disarmament in 1995 and another on national defense policy in July 1998.

Source: Ministry of Foreign Affairs website: *www.mofa.go.jp*

Document 12   BEYOND THE ASIAN CRISIS: SPEECH BY MR KIICHI MIYAZAWA ON
THE OCCASION OF THE APEC FINANCE MINISTERS' MEETING,
LANGKAWI, MALAYSIA, 15 MAY 1999

Finance Minister Miyazawa discusses how the Japanese government has responded to the severe Asian financial crisis in 1997 that triggered extraordinary currency devaluations, bankruptcies and a devastating regional recession. This is an important speech because Japan differed with the United States and the International Monetary Fund on how to deal with the crisis, arguing for a regional stabilization fund and capital controls at odds with the market-oriented solutions favoured in Washington. Japan's approach was initially rejected out of hand, but after the austerity measures advocated by the IMF were criticized for worsening the crisis, Japan's initiatives have gained more support, especially within the region.

The global economic crisis, which began in Thailand in July 1997 and spread rapidly throughout Asia, and then to Russia and Latin America, seems to have subsided, and it may be safe to say the immediate crisis is over. Now that we have entered a period of relative calm, it probably behooves [sic] us to look back and analyze what really happened and to come up with a perspective for the global economy, the Asia-Pacific economy in particular, for the next century.

The crisis caught most of us, particularly in this region, off-guard. Despite some earlier signs of vulnerability, market participants and analysts failed to predict the crisis from Thailand to South Korea. Risk premia for loans remained low, and rating agencies such as Standard & Poor's and Moody's maintained their relatively high ratings of sovereign bonds until the onset of the crisis. Many analysts and financiers argued, particularly at the outset of the crisis, that a lack of proper disclosure or an insufficient degree of transparency hampered a proper assessment of the risk. Objective evidence and data would seem to indicate, however, that the pertinent information, including real effective exchange rates, private sector short-term foreign debt, current account balances, and banking sector balance sheets, was largely available. The problem was, this information was not appropriately incorporated into the market risk assessment. An analysis of factors involving the behavior of hedge funds, pension funds and other non-bank financial institutions suggests that a herd mentality prevailed over the otherwise rational, detailed calculation of emerging market risk.

Thus, a more objective study of the circumstances surrounding these crises reveals that, in the globalized financial system we now have, sudden reversals of market confidence can cause periodic panics of varying magnitude and duration. Indeed, the substantial liberalization in 1993 and thereafter of the capital accounts of five Asian economies – South Korea,

Indonesia, Malaysia, Thailand, and the Philippines – led to the inflow of approximately $220 billion in private capital into the region during the three-year period from 1994 to 1996. The reversal of flows that occurred in 1997 as a result of a sudden shift in confidence amounted to roughly $100 billion. No economy or region can withstand this kind of sudden shift in market sentiment, from euphoria to panic, and the resulting huge reversal of private flows.

These shifts in capital flows interacted with the affected economies' domestic financial systems, which in hindsight, were grossly inadequate to deal with such an enormous amount of financial intermediation in such a short period of time. Looking at the crisis from the perspective of recipient economies, the problem was essentially one of a fund mismatch in currencies and maturities compounded by ineffective intermediation. Asia, which has quite strong economic fundamentals, including a high saving ratio and a diligent labor force, has traditionally invested most of its savings outside the region, mainly in the United States and in Europe. Funds flowed back to Asia in the form of foreign direct investment and, increasingly in recent years, in portfolio investment and bank loans with short maturities. In other words, Asia remained on the periphery of the global financial system, providing the bulk of the funds to the system while suffering from a mismatch in obtaining refunding from the center.

In this context, I would like to report that Japan has created a $3 billion guarantee fund in the Asian Development Bank, as well as providing ¥27.5 billion or $230 million, to subsidize interest payments. In addition, we passed legislation last month that will allow the Export-Import Bank of Japan to guarantee sovereign bonds to be issued by emerging economies, or to purchase them directly. With these new instruments, it is expected that a total of ¥2 trillion, or approximately $17 billion, of long-term sovereign debt could be raised from the markets. Although there have been some significant withdrawals of Japanese bank loans from the region in recent years because of the restructuring of Japanese banks, I expect a large amount of Japanese money primarily from institutional investors to flow back to Asia through these long-term debt instruments.

Given the diversity of cultures, races, histories and developmental stages of the Asian economies, it would clearly be extremely difficult to achieve unification of the European type in Asia. Nor would it be possible for Japan to play the type of role the US plays in the American continents.

In early October of last year, I came up with an initiative to provide $30 billion in financial assistance, short-term and medium- to long-term, to five crisis-hit economies in Asia, Thailand, Malaysia, the Philippines, Indonesia, and Korea. As of now, approximately two thirds of this assistance has been committed. Japan intends to continue to implement and even enhance this initiative both in substance and in scope in the coming years. In this context, we plan to extend financial support to Vietnam as well, apart from the $30 billion previously announced.

As the world enters the 21st century, the trend of 'globalization' would be accelerated. The 'globalization,' however, should be pursued with the due respect to the cultural and religious diversity on the globe. Achieving globalization amid diversity is a challenging task facing all of us.

Source: Speech delivered by Finance Minister Kiichi Miyazawa available at the Ministry of Finance website: *www.mof.go.jp/english/*

————————◄●►————————

Document 13   ON THE REVISION OF THE UNITED STATES–JAPAN SECURITY TREATY, 1960

Nishi articulates the concerns of many Japanese about Japan being dragged into war against its wishes because of its alliance with the United States. His remarks capture the ambiance of the Cold War and the threat perceptions that prevailed at that time. His opposition to revision of the Security Treaty was based on his belief that this would be interpreted as a provocation by the Soviet Union and the People's Republic of China with potentially dire consequences for Japan. His view that the Security Treaty actually increased Japan's security threats and vulnerability was widely shared by domestic critics of government policy, some of whom advocated neutrality rather than choosing sides in the Cold War.

I consider the proposed Security Treaty revision to contain enormous danger for our country when viewed from the perspective of our relations with the Soviet Union and China. The Soviet Union has steadfastly maintained that the Security Treaty was imposed on powerless Japan by the US at the time of the conclusion of the peace treaty. She has not condemned Japan on this account. However, the proposed revision of the pact will be carried out by the free will of Japan. . . . We must be prepared to face a protest coming from the Soviet Union and Communist China. . . . It goes without saying that the Soviet Union and Communist China will hold Japan responsible for all the provisions of the treaty, not just those articles that are being revised . . . the problem that concerns me most is the fact that US soldiers can embark from bases located within Japan. As it has been reported, after the treaty revision, consultation with or consent of the Japanese government will be required in this matter, and thus the American military's freedom of action will be somewhat more restricted than before. However within the limitation thus set on the action of the American military, Japan will become equally responsible in that she is party to the American action. In this sense there is potentially a great danger. For example, if the crisis over Qemoy and Matsu (Taiwanese islands) of last year is revisited, or the situation governing North and South Korea becomes worsened, it is conceivable that the American military will adopt a far stronger military measure to cope with the situation. And in this connection if American soldiers must take off from bases in Japan, we must be prepared to face a charge of joint responsibility in the military action that can be levied against us from the Soviet Union and Communist China. . . . We must always bear in mind that once the US accepts defense of Japan as an obligation under a treaty, the Soviet Union and Communist China will regard the treaty revision as merely a means to strengthen military cooperation between the US and Japan, and they may begin putting pressure on Japan. . . . In an emergency, would it not be more likely that the Security Treaty will give an excuse for the Soviet Union and Communist China to invade Japan by terming us a common enemy along with the US? . . . The national power of Japan, compared to the prewar era, has been reduced to such a level that if we commit one false move, we can even be completely annihilated. The country that will be exposed to that kind of danger as a result of the Security Treaty revision is Japan and not the US.

Source: Haruhiko Nishi Kaiso no Nihongaiko [Reminiscences on Japanese Diplomacy]. (1965) (Iwanami Shoten, Tokyo), pp. 183–9. As cited in David J. Lu (1997) *Japan: A Documentary History*, Vol. II (M. E. Sharpe, Armonk, NY), pp. 520–4.

—◄●►—

SECRET NUKE PACT HUSHED UP FOR DECADES   **Document 14**

For years, secrets and deceptions were the order of the day when government officials stood before the Diet and told lawmakers that US Navy ships never carried nuclear weapons into Japanese ports or when passing through its territorial waters.

That's the thrust of a report released Tuesday that was ordered by Foreign Minister Katsuya Okada soon after the Democratic Party of Japan took power last September to verify the existence of secret pacts between Japan and the United States.

Prime Minister Yukio Hatoyama said Tuesday that 'Japan will maintain as before' the three non-nuclear principles of not possessing, manufacturing or bringing nuclear weapons into its territory.

In an earlier exclusive interview with *The Asahi Shimbun*, Okada reiterated that US warships passing through Japanese waters or making port calls while carrying nuclear weapons would constitute the introduction of nuclear weapons.

Okada added that he did not believe any problems would arise with the United States since no US Navy ships currently carry nuclear weapons.

Experts studied about 300 documents to reach their conclusions.

The investigation found that since 1968 government officials gave approval to passage and port calls of all US Navy warships without asking whether they were carrying nuclear weapons. All prime ministers since were aware of the sub rosa pact.

Government officials were keenly aware the ships could be carrying nuclear weapons. But for decades, they insisted that no port calls were made by ships with nuclear weapons because there had been no prior consultation between the two nations to allow such port calls.

A number of important documents were not found, and the experts group recommended further investigation to determine if and why they were destroyed. The document used to demonstrate the existence of a secret nuclear pact was a confidential memo compiled by Fumihiko Togo, then director-general of the Foreign Ministry's North American Affairs Bureau, and dated January 27, 1968.

It describes the exchange Togo had with US Ambassador U. Alexis Johnson the previous day. Johnson explained the US interpretation of US Navy ships with nuclear weapons. The two sides agreed to stick to their own interpretation.

Thereafter, even though Japan now recognized that the American interpretation meant no prior consultation was needed for US ships carrying nuclear arms when making port calls or passing through Japanese waters, government officials still insisted in public that it was required.

The document was used in explaining the government policy to succeeding prime ministers and foreign ministers. In the margin of the document is a notation indicating that then Prime Minister Eisaku Sato had read it.

There are also notations indicating that Kakuei Tanaka, Yasuhiro Nakasone and Noboru Takeshita, among others, were all briefed when they took over as prime minister.

An attached memo compiled by Takakazu Kuriyama when he was foreign vice minister in 1989 shows that Toshiki Kaifu was briefed about the policy, indicating that the tacit approval was handed down for at least two decades.

A secret pact was also recognized by the experts group for an agreement made in conjunction with the 1960 revision of the Japan–US Security Treaty that would allow US troops based in Japan to deploy to the Korean Peninsula without prior consultation should a military conflict erupt.

Concerning a secret pact on whether nuclear weapons could be brought back into Okinawa after it reverted to Japanese sovereignty, the group said there was no evidence one existed.

The group agreed that a secret pact in the broad sense existed for the agreement to have Japan shoulder the cost of restoring land to its former condition in line with the Okinawa reversion even though no document was found.

Source: Nanae Kurashige. *The Asahi Shimbun*, 10 March 2010: *http://backup.asahi. com/english/TKY201003090385.html*

SHINTARO ISHIHARA ON JAPAN'S RELATIONSHIP WITH THE UNITED STATES

Document 15

The United States has not sufficiently appreciated Japan and even taken us all that seriously because, since 1945, we have been under Uncle Sam's thumb. . . . For our sake and that of the whole Pacific region, the special Tokyo–Washington relationship must be preserved.

The conflicts among nations will be increasingly economic in nature. With the Cold War over, friction on trade and investment will inevitably intensify. . . . Although I see the bilateral relationship as the dominant force in the next century, before we reach that level of cooperation, US policy towards Japan will approximate the stance against the Soviet Union at the height of the Cold War.

If we try to bend with the wind, making concessions and patchwork compromises as usual, the tempest will abate for a while, only to recur with even greater force. We must not flinch in the face of pressure. . . . When justified, we must keep saying no and be undaunted by the reaction.

A deal with the Soviet Union over semiconductors cannot be completely ruled out . . . microchips determine the accuracy of weapons systems and are the key to military power.

Source: Shintaro Ishihara (1991) *The Japan That Can Say No: Why Japan Will Become First Among Equals* (Simon & Schuster, New York), pp. 103–19.

THE 1997 GUIDELINES FOR UNITED STATES–JAPAN DEFENSE COOPERATION

Document 16

The new defence guidelines were passed in the Diet in 1999 with minimal public debate or opposition, indicating just how much Japan has changed since the 1960 anti-Security Treaty demonstrations. There were growing concerns in

Washington that in the event of a crisis the Japanese government would be paralysed and unable to act swiftly enough to authorize Japanese participation in any military operations, thus compromising combat effectiveness. The new guidelines also aim to avert a scenario in which US forces based in Japan would come under fire, but not receive any assistance from its ally. The potential threats of China and North Korea in the region created an impetus to clarify Japan's willingness to participate in collective defence by providing rear area support that does not violate the prevailing interpretation of Article 9 in the Constitution.

II. BASIC PREMISES AND PRINCIPLES

The Guidelines and programs under the Guidelines are consistent with the following basic premises and principles.

The rights and obligations under the Treaty of Mutual Cooperation and Security between the United States of America and Japan (the US–Japan Security Treaty) and its related arrangements, as well as the fundamental framework of the US–Japan alliance, will remain unchanged.

Japan will conduct all its actions within the limitations of its Constitution and in accordance with such basic positions as the maintenance of its exclusively defense-oriented policy and its three non-nuclear principles.

All actions taken by the United States and Japan will be consistent with basic principles of international law, including the peaceful settlement of disputes and sovereign equality, and relevant international agreements such as the Charter of the United Nations.

The Guidelines and programs under the Guidelines will not obligate either Government to take legislative, budgetary or administrative measures. However, since the objective of the Guidelines and programs under the Guidelines is to establish an effective framework for bilateral cooperation, the two Governments are expected to reflect in an appropriate way the results of these efforts, based on their own judgements, in their specific policies and measures. All actions taken by Japan will be consistent with its laws and regulations then in effect.

V. COOPERATION IN SITUATIONS IN AREAS SURROUNDING JAPAN THAT WILL HAVE AN IMPORTANT INFLUENCE ON JAPAN'S PEACE AND SECURITY

Situations in areas surrounding Japan will have an important influence on Japan's peace and security. The concept, situations in areas surrounding Japan, is not geographical but situational. The two Governments will make every effort, including diplomatic measures, to prevent such situations from occurring. When the two Governments reach a common assessment of the state of each situation, they will effectively coordinate their activities.

In responding to such situations, measures taken may differ depending on circumstances.

1.   When a Situation in Areas Surrounding Japan is Anticipated

When a situation in areas surrounding Japan is anticipated,

> the two Governments will intensify information and intelligence sharing and policy consultations, including efforts to reach a common assessment of the situation.

At the same time, they will make every effort, including

> diplomatic efforts, to prevent further deterioration of the situation, while initiating at an early stage the operation of a bilateral coordination mechanism, including use of a bilateral coordination center. Cooperating as appropriate, they will make preparations necessary for ensuring coordinated responses according to the readiness stage selected by mutual agreement. As circumstances change, they will also increase intelligence gathering and surveillance, and enhance their readiness to respond to the circumstances.

2.   Responses to Situations in Areas Surrounding Japan
     (b) Rear Area Support

Japan will provide rear area support to those US Forces that are conducting operations for the purpose of achieving the objectives of the US–Japan Security Treaty. The primary aim of this rear area support is to enable US Forces to use facilities and conduct operations in an effective manner. By its very nature, Japan's rear area support will be provided primarily in Japanese territory. It may also be provided on the high seas and international airspace around Japan which are distinguished from areas where combat operations are being conducted.

In providing rear area support, Japan will make appropriate use of authorities and assets of the central and local government agencies, as well as private sector assets. The Self-Defense Forces, as appropriate, will provide such support consistent with their mission for the defense of Japan and the maintenance of public order.

Source: Defense Agency (1997) Completion of the Review of the Guidelines for US–Japan Defense Cooperation, US–Japan Security Consultative Committee, New York, 23 September 1997. From the Defense Agency website: *www.jda.go.jp*

Document 17   NIXON ON US RELATIONS WITH JAPAN DURING THE COLD WAR

Nixon articulated the Cold War logic of the United States changing its position on Japanese disarmament, arguing that it was an honest mistake based on a miscalculation of communist intentions. At the time that the United States wrote the constitutional prohibition on maintaining Japanese armed forces in Article 9, disarming Japan was a reaction to its wartime aggression and a desire to prevent a recurrence.

If Japan falls under communist domination, all of Asia falls. There is no question about it and from Japan's standpoint, if the rest of Asia falls under communist domination, Japan will also fall under communist domination; and therefore if Japan desires to be free, desires to be independent, it is essential that they work with the free nations in maintaining adequate defenses and adequate strength – strength which will ensure that the communist aggression goes no further than it has already gone in this section of the world.

It must be admitted that the primary responsibility for Japan's defense must rest upon Japan and the Japanese people. It is true that there are grave problems. The nation's economic capabilities have been sapped by the war through which it has gone, but it is essential, if Japan is to survive as a free and independent nation, that we recognize frankly that its defense forces must be increased eventually to an adequate level . . .

There are those who say the US is taking a very inconsistent position about the rearmament of Japan. They might say: In 1946 who was it that insisted that Japan disarm? It wasn't the Japanese, although they were willing to embark on that program, but it was at the insistence of the US that Japan disarmed.

Now if disarmament was right in 1946, why is it wrong in 1953? . . . I am going to admit right here that the US did make a mistake in 1946.

We made a mistake because we misjudged the intentions of Soviet leaders. It was an honest mistake. We believe now as we believed then in the principle of disarmament.

In other words, in 1946, both in the US, in Japan and in most of the free world, we looked ahead to the future hoping against hope that it would be possible at long last to reduce the armaments of nations to a minimum level. But since that time, the communist threat has gained in power, wars have been begun – witness the one in Korea – and the threat has become so great that as we analyze it today we must change our opinion.

Source: Richard M. Nixon (1953) To the Japanese People. *Contemporary Japan*, XXII, 7–9, pp. 369–71. As excerpted in J. Livingston, J. Moore and F. Oldfather, eds. (1973) *Postwar Japan: 1945 to the Present* (Pantheon, New York), pp. 263–4.

BECOMING A NORMAL NATION   **Document 18**

Ozawa called on his nation to rethink how it participates in the international community, criticizing what he termed a selfish, inward-looking pacifism that shifted the difficult burdens and responsibilities onto other nations. He was responding to the reluctance of Japan to contribute anything but money to the Gulf War conflict and the opposition to legislation authorizing the government to commit troops to peace-keeping operations (PKOs) overseas because it flouted Article 9 of the Constitution.

What is a 'normal nation'? First it is a nation that willingly shoulders those responsibilities regarded as natural in the international community. It does not refuse such burdens on account of domestic political difficulties. Nor does it take action unwillingly as a result of 'international pressure'. This is especially relevant where national security is concerned. We don't need to return to the Gulf War or PKO bill debates to see how suddenly eloquent we become in self-righteous arguments about the constitution and other laws whenever security issues arise. We look for ways, however fallacious, to avoid a responsible role. The contradiction is clear: how can Japan, which so depends on world peace and stability, seek to exclude a security role from its international contributions? For many people, the thought of Japan playing any sort of role in the security arena conjures up images of a rearmed, militarist Japan. But this is, quite simply, not an issue of militarization or aspirations to military superpower status. It is a question of Japan's responsible behavior in the international community.

A second requirement of a 'normal nation' is that it cooperate fully with other nations in their efforts to build prosperous and stable lives for their people. It must do so on issues that affect all nations, such as environmental preservation. While Japan has made significant progress in this area, we still have a great deal to offer and can lead a worldwide effort toward making our planet more sustainable.

Source: Ichiro Ozawa (1994) *Blueprint for a New Japan: The Rethinking of a Nation* (Kodansha International, Tokyo), pp. 94–5.

THE GOVERNMENT'S POSITION ON ARTICLE 9 OF THE   **Document 19**
CONSTITUTION

Article 9 has been the source of considerable controversy, not least because it appears to render the Self-Defense Forces (SDF) unconstitutional. The Japanese government and higher courts have held that the wording does indeed permit Japan to maintain forces sufficient for self-defence. This interpretation is questioned both in Japan and by international jurists. This document conveys the government's position on this issue.

A. Self-Defense Capability Permitted to Be Possessed.
The self-defense capability that Japan is permitted to possess is limited to the minimum necessary by the constitutional limitations.

The specific limit of the minimum necessary level of armed strength for self-defense varies depending on the prevailing international situation, the standards of military technology and various other conditions. However, whether or not the said armed strength corresponds to 'war potential' stipulated in paragraph 2 of Article 9 of the Constitution is an issue regarding the total strength that Japan possesses. Accordingly, whether the SDF are allowed to possess some specific armaments depends on the judgment whether its total strength will or will not exceed constitutional limitations by possessing such armaments.

But in any case in Japan, it is unconstitutional to possess what is referred to as offensive weapons that, from their performance, are to be used exclusively for total destruction of other countries, since it immediately exceeds the limit of the minimum necessary level of self-defense. Therefore, for instance, the SDF is not allowed to possess ICBMs [inter-continental ballistic missiles], long-range strategic bombers or offensive aircraft carriers.

B. Conditions for Exercise of Right of Self-Defense.
The exercise of the right of self-defense is restricted to the following so-called three requisite conditions:

(i)   there is an imminent and illegitimate act of aggression against Japan;
(ii) there is no appropriate means to deal with this aggression other than resort to the right of self-defense; and
(iii) the use of armed strength is confined to the minimum necessary level.

C. Geographical Scope of Exercise of Right of Self-Defense.
The use of minimum necessary force to defend Japan as employed in the execution of its self-defense is not necessarily confined to the geographic scope of Japanese territorial land, sea and airspace. Generally speaking, however, it is difficult to make a wholesale definition of exactly how far this geographic area stretches because it would vary with separate individual situations.

Nevertheless, the government believes that the Constitution does not permit it to dispatch armed forces to foreign territorial land, sea and airspace for the purpose of using force, because such an overseas deployment of troops generally exceeds the limit of minimum necessary level of self-defense.

D. Right of Collective Self-Defense.

Under international law, it is understood that a state has the right of collective self-defense, that is, the right to use force to stop armed attack on a foreign country with which it has close relations, even when the state itself is not under direct attack. It is beyond doubt that as a sovereign state, Japan has the right of collective self-defense under existing international law. The government, however, is of the view that the exercise of the right of self-defense as permissible under Article 9 of the Constitution is authorized only when the act of self-defense is within the limit of the minimum necessary level for the defense of the nation. The government, therefore, believes that the exercise of the right of collective self-defense exceeds that limit and is constitutionally not permissible.

E. Right of Belligerency.

Paragraph 2 of Article 9 of the Constitution provides that 'the right of belligerency of the state will not be recognized.' As already mentioned, however, it is recognized as a matter of course that Japan can make use of the minimum force necessary for self-defense and that the use of such force is quite different from exercising the right of belligerency.

Source: Defense Agency website: *www.jda.go.jp*

HUMAN TRAFFICKING IN JAPAN   **Document 20**

The United States has criticized the Japanese government for not curbing human trafficking more aggressively, regularly citing lapses in its annual Trafficking in Persons reports.

JAPAN (Tier 2)

Japan is a destination and transit country for men, women, and children trafficked for the purposes of commercial sexual exploitation and forced labor. The majority of identified trafficking victims are foreign women who migrate to Japan seeking work, but are subjected upon arrival to debt bondage and forced prostitution. Male and female migrant workers are subjected to conditions of forced labor. Traffickers use debt bondage to exploit women in Japan's large sex trade, imposing debts of up to $50,000. In addition, trafficked women are subjected to coercive or violent physical and psychological methods to prevent them from seeking assistance or escaping. Traffickers also target Japanese women and girls for exploitation in pornography or prostitution. Many female victims, both foreign and

Japanese, are reluctant to seek help from authorities for fear of reprisals by their traffickers, who are often members or associates of Japanese organized crime syndicates (the Yakuza).

To date there have been no cases where the government actually provided legal assistance to a trafficking victim.

During the reporting period, the government did not take any steps to specifically reduce the demand for child sex tourism by Japanese nationals. Japanese law does not criminalize the possession of child pornography, and this continues to contribute to the demand for commercial sexual exploitation of children and child sex tourism.

Source: Trafficking in Persons Report, US State Department, 2008.

Document 21   THE SEXUAL EXPLOITATION OF WOMEN IN JAPAN

Since 1985 a new genre of sexually oriented literature has emerged called 'Lolita eros'. This style of comic magazine emphasizes sex with young girls . . . There is hardly any element of storytelling but, instead, portrayals of individual and gang rape . . . of young girls. Furthermore, girls who have been raped are described as . . . grateful for the ecstasy accorded them by their rapist.

While it is important to look at the great extent to which pornographic culture pervades contemporary Japan, it is also important to stress that women in Japan have been actively protesting the production of such images. . . .

In 1991 the Japanese Foundation for AIDS Prevention produced a set of posters . . . for World AIDS Awareness Day. These posters are interesting in terms of what they reveal about the prevailing attitudes concerning sexuality. One of these posters shows a businessman hiding his face with a Japanese passport, and the ad copy reads (both in Japanese and English): 'Have a nice trip! But be careful of AIDS.' Another poster features a naked woman enveloped in an enormous condom, with the caption, 'Thin, but strong enough for AIDS.' . . . Through our efforts these posters were withdrawn.

Source: Kuniko Funabashi (1995) Pornographic culture and sexual violence. In: K. Fujimura-Fanselow and A. Kameda, eds. *Japanese Women: New Feminist Perspectives on the Past, Present, and Future* (The Feminist Press, New York), pp. 255–63.

ECONOMIC CONSEQUENCES OF AN AGEING POPULATION   **Document 22**

Japan's demographic time bomb is generating concern that the nation is ill-prepared to cope with the financial consequences of this transformation. This report by a leading business consultancy suggests some dire implications

Demographic trends are expected to slow the rate of growth in Japanese household savings and financial wealth accumulation in the coming years, with potentially significant implications for economic growth in Japan and globally. MGI analysis suggests that – absent changes in population trends, savings behavior, or returns on financial assets – the net financial wealth of Japanese households will decline 0.2 percent annually between 2003 and 2024, after increasing 5.5 percent per year between 1975 and 2003. By 2024, this retreat will cause total household net financial wealth to fall nearly ¥1,000 trillion (or 47 percent) below what it would have been had historical growth rates continued.

The rapid aging of the Japanese population and the dramatic slowdown in population growth are often discussed as important forces that will slow household savings growth. As important, but less widely discussed, are the slowdown in the rate of household formation (implied by the slowing population growth), and the significant differences in saving behavior between younger and older generations.

New household formation is coming to a standstill, and in twenty years there will be nearly the same number of households available to save as there are today. Of these, there are an increasing number of older households that are moving into the lower saving or non-saving part of their life cycle. The remaining younger households tend to save less and borrow more than older generations at all ages. All of this results in a meager flow of aggregate new savings, and produces an actual decline in aggregate net financial wealth by 2024.

Source: Japan: The world's savers retire. In: *The Coming Demographic Deficit: How Aging Populations will Reduce Global Savings*. McKinsey Global Institute, January 2005.

HEALTH CARE COSTS: OECD   **Document 23**

According to the OECD, rising health care costs cast a cloud over Japan's future although it has a very good track record in containing medical outlays.

Looking ahead, population ageing is likely to put further upward pressure on health spending. Between 2000 and 2006, health spending increased at a 2.2% annual rate for the elderly, while it declined at a 0.6% rate for the rest of the population, reflecting the growing number of persons over 65 and the falling number under that age. Ageing will accelerate in the years to come, with the share of the population over age 65 projected to reach 26.9% by 2015 and 30.5% by 2025. The increase will be concentrated among the very old and will thus have a major budgetary impact. Indeed, the over 75 age group, which already accounts for almost one-third of health spending, will double from 9% to 18% of total population, while the share of the population in the 65-to-74 age group will rise only slightly from 11% to 12%. The National Commission on Social Security's report in 2008 projected that spending on health and long-term care combined will rise by about 3% of GDP to around 11% by 2025 under the current framework and utilisation patterns and by about 4% if reforms to improve quality and expand capacity were implemented. According to an OECD study (Oliveira Martins and De la Maisonneuve, 2006), public health and long-term care spending combined in Japan will rise from 6.9% of GDP in 2005 to 9.4% by 2050 due to demographic changes alone. Other factors, including technological advances and rising income and wealth, which make individuals seek more frequent and higher-quality treatment, are projected to boost spending by another 1.5 to 4 percentage points of GDP, depending on the degree of cost containment. As a result, public expenditures on health and long-term care are projected to rise to between 10.9% and 13.4% of GDP by mid-century, a larger increase than the OECD average.

Source: OECD Economic Surveys: Japan, September 2009, p. 100.

Document 24   IMMIGRATION AND THE DEMOGRAPHIC TIME BOMB

According to the UN, immigration needs to dramatically increase if Japan seeks to offset the negative consequences of population decline.

If Japan wishes to keep the size of its population at the level attained in the year 2005, the country would need 17 million net immigrants up to the year 2050, or an average of 381,000 immigrants per year between 2005 and 2050. By 2050, the immigrants and their descendants would total 22.5 million and comprise 17.7 per cent of the total population of the country. In order to keep the size of the working-age population constant at the 1995 level of 87.2 million, Japan would need 33.5 million immigrants from 1995 through 2050. This means an average of 609,000 immigrants are needed per year during this period. Under this scenario, the population of the country is projected to be 150.7 million by 2050. The number of post-1995 immigrants and their descendants would be 46 million, accounting for 30 per cent of the total population in 2050.

Source: Replacement Migration: Is it a Solution to Declining and Aging Populations? UN Population Division, 21 March 2000.

JAPAN'S THIRD TRANSFORMATION: PRIME MINISTER KEIZO OBUCHI   **Document 25**

In this speech, Prime Minister Keizo Obuchi (1998–2000) clearly enunciates what many Japanese people also think – Japan is commencing a third great transformation and the patterns and policies of the past are no longer appropriate for the challenges of the new century. Unusual in a policy speech, he calls for the 'fulfillment of our souls'.

It seems to me that Japan is now experiencing a Third Reform, which follows the great reforms effected during the Meiji Restoration and the Post-War era. In the years following the Meiji Restoration our nation, both government and private sector, made great efforts which gave birth to the foundations upon which a modern state was built. The amazing economic growth achieved by Japan, and the prosperity which we now enjoy, are the fruits of those efforts. As our very values diversify and the world undergoes great transformation, the systems and decision-making processes which once allowed us to effectively manage our country are now pulling us down as shackles.

We must remember that in addition to removing that which holds us back, we must build new systems to replace them, and at the same time we should make an effort to keep that which is good and wonderful in our society. It must certainly be clear to all that this Third Reform can not be realized only through the will of politicians. Indeed, nothing can succeed unless there is a reform in the consciousness of the people and unless the people participate in the process.

For more than a half century after the War we engaged in a single-minded pursuit of abundance. Although we have certainly met to some degree our target of becoming an abundant nation, no one would deny that we have conversely tended to forget that which is of ultimate importance to us as human beings – fulfillment of our souls.

Sound capitalism can not be maintained based purely on pursuit of profit. This precept rings clear in the words of the German sociologist Max Weber, as well as philosophers the world over. Unless our nation is a moral one enriched with great aspirations, there is no way that we can continue as an abundant nation and we most certainly will not gain the trust of the world.

As we review the overall structures of our society, it is imperative that we forcefully promote structural reform of those systems which make up the social safety net, including the pension, health, and nursing systems, so that stable administration can be guaranteed into the future. In order to ensure the necessary provision of those services while considering the burden to be born by future generations, and at the same time maintain the dynamism in our society and our economy, we must achieve a balance between provision and burden ratios while at the same time expanding the choices of users, including introducing private sector service providers as we increase the efficiency and rationality of our systems.

A society of mass production and mass consumption generates massive waste and places a great burden on the global environment. One of our most weighty responsibilities is to pass on to our children, and to their children, a beautiful and stable environment by creating a renewable economic society. In order to carry out this responsibility I intend to address global environment issues, to promote increased energy efficiency and further develop nuclear energy utilization and new sources of energy and promote their use and to strive for the creation of recycling systems which can process specific needs. Japan will lead the way in creating a society which respects nature and preserves natural resources in order to defend our irreplaceable earth.

The morals which have been formed over many years in our homes, in our communities and at our places of work, and the spirit of warm and friendly relations among people, as well as our excellent culture and traditions, are precious assets which must be handed down and continued on into the future by the next generation. Moreover, we must realize a society where the human rights of each individual are respected and build a judicial system which the people feel a part of.

Source: Excerpts from policy speech by Prime Minister Keizo Obuchi to the 145th session of the Diet, 19 January 1999 (abridged). From the Ministry of Foreign Affairs website: *www.mofa.go.jp*

Document 26   SUICIDE TOLL REMAINS HIGH

Japan's suicide rate is high by international standards and there are few signs of it abating given limited government intervention.

The figure, surpassing the 30,000 mark for the 12th year in a row, is roughly equal to the crowd of runners who pack Ginza-dori avenue in the annual Tokyo Marathon. Everything possible must be done to bring down the annual toll.

At the same time, we must not forget that the rising number of suicides leaves behind a larger number of families in sorrow. According to estimates by the suicide prevention nonprofit organization Lifelink and others, about 3 million people have experienced the suicide of a spouse, a sibling, a parent or a child in the past 40 years.

Whatever the circumstances, the sudden death of a blood relative is a horrendous event. This is doubly true of suicide, which deeply scars the hearts of families in ways that are quite different from death due to an accident or illness. Bereaved families tend to put the blame on themselves, even when they bear no responsibility, or encounter criticism for having failed to prevent the death of a loved one.

In cases where illness and debts were the cause of a suicide, many people might have been saved if sufficient social support had been available. With most suicides, however, the cause of the tragedy is written off as individual weakness. This is a stigma that the surviving family members must carry with them thereafter. Over the past decade or so, an increase in suicides by middle-aged and older men has kept the overall figure at a high level.

One result of this trend is the growing number of mothers forced to raise junior and senior high school student children without fathers. Many bereaved families relate tragic stories of how suicides occurring in apartments forced them to continue paying the rent, being saddled with debts due to ignorance about how to waive inheritance of debt liabilities and other problems. Such matters could have been avoided if they had the opportunity to consult with lawyers or other professionals.

Source: Asahi editorial, 30 December 2009.

————————◆——————————

JAPAN'S 'BIG BANG' Document 27

The costs of protectionism and exclusionary, non-reciprocal international economic interactions have been evident in Japan's beleaguered financial services industry. As a result, in 1996 the Ministry of Finance announced a Japanese 'Big Bang'. The gradual implementation of these reform measures over an extended period of time means that the 'bang' has been muted.

An efficient and competitive financial sector is absolutely essential for the vitality of the Japanese economy in the 21st century. The Financial System Reform, 'Japanese Big Bang', was commenced in November 1996 under the three principles of 'free, fair and global', aiming to rebuild the Japanese financial market into an international market comparable to the New York and London markets.

As the first step, the revised Foreign Exchange Law was changed to totally liberalize cross-border transactions in April 1998. Then, the Financial System Reform Law, a package of revisions of laws including the Banking Law, the Securities and Exchange Law, and the Insurance Business Law, that were required to implement the Financial System Reform, was enforced in December 1998.

. . . [E]fforts were made to provide attractive services through vital inter-mediary activities, such as promoting entry of banks, securities companies and insurance companies into each other's business, switching from the licensing system to a registration system for securities companies, liberal-izing cross-border capital transactions and foreign exchange business, fully liberalizing brokerage commissions, and eliminating the obligation to use premium rates set by the non-life insurance rating organization.

. . . [D]iversified markets and channels for fund raising were created by abolishing the requirements to trade stocks only through stock exchanges, and introducing proprietary trading systems (electronic trading systems). The Tokyo Stock Exchange established a new market for promising start-ups, so called Mothers (Market of High Growth and Emerging Stocks), in November 1999, and there is a plan to establish NASDAQ Japan stock market at the Osaka Stock Exchange in June 2000.

. . . [A] framework for reliable trading was established by improving the disclosure system, setting up fair trading rules, such as stricter insider trading control, and protecting customers in times of failure of financial institutions. Since the accounting period ending March 1999, financial insti-tutions are required by law to disclose information on their non-performing assets on a consolidated base according to standards equivalent to the ones set by the Securities and Exchange Commission of the United States, with possible penalties for non-compliance.

As a result of the financial system reform as well as ongoing restructuring, the . . . efficiency and profitability of financial institutions will improve.

Source: Ministry of Finance, *Japanese Big Bang*. From the Ministry of Finance website: *www.mof.go.jp*

Document 28   SOCIAL ORDER IN JAPAN

Masao Miyamoto, a psychiatrist who worked in the Ministry of Health and Welfare, was an outspoken critic of the bureaucracy and its role in promoting groupism and conformity through the educational system and deflecting pres-sures for change. His columns in the mass media proved enormously popular, tapping into growing public distrust and scepticism towards the government.

The interests of producers are consistently given priority over those of consumers because the bureaucrats see the enlargement of Japan Inc., as their overriding goal.

To expand Japan Inc., the bureaucracy introduced the philosophy of *messhi hoko*, or self-sacrifice for the sake of the group. This philosophy requires the subordination of individual lives to the good of the whole. Since all Japanese invariably belong to some sort of group, through this philosophy they end up sacrificing their personal lives, voluntarily or otherwise.

It is difficult to say no to *messhi hoko* and look for another job, since most Japanese companies are based on this philosophy. A person who rejects the concept of self-sacrifice can expect total isolation from the group. The fear of ostracism evokes strong anxiety in most Japanese, therefore the threat of removal from the group exerts a strong controlling influence on individual behavior.

In psychological terms, the stimulation of masochistic tendencies equals pleasure. The more you lose your personal life, the more pleasure you get, and as it is very difficult to resist the centripetal force of *messhi hoko*, this philosophy has become a very efficient way to control people. It has infiltrated the daily lives of the Japanese, particularly through the education system, which the bureaucrats control.

The Japanese are educated so that even if they are frustrated or unhappy, they will resign themselves to the situation. This education is very important since, if people do not complain, it is easier to propagate the philosophy of *messhi hoko*.

To accomplish the goal that every Japanese embrace the philosophy of *messhi hoko*, the bureaucrats introduced an educational program based on the idea that all Japanese should look, think, and act alike. This type of education does not allow for individual differences, and as a result, creativity is severely curtailed. From a psychiatrist's point of view, the bureaucrats are asking the people to embrace an illusion.

Ultimately the bureaucracy does not want people to be independent. Being independent means that a person expresses his thoughts openly, develops a capacity to say no, and questions the status quo. *Messhi hoko* prevents people from becoming independent. What this means in terms of personality structure is that a person's pride is fragile, and can be easily injured.

Once you belong to a group, freedom of expression disappears. Open expression of critical thoughts is not tolerated without approval by the entire group.

Source: Masao Miyamoto (1994) *The Staitjacket Society: An Insider's Irreverent View of Bureaucratic Japan* (Kodansha International, Tokyo), pp. 20–4.

Document 29   MULTI-ETHNICITY IN JAPAN

The myth of ethnic homogeneity is widespread and implicit in Japan. The government and media contribute to this misconception as do the social values of conformity and uniformity. In addition, ethnic diversity is not as visually apparent in Japan as in some other societies because most of its minorities are also Asian. This essay introduces some key features of Japan's multi-ethnicity.

Japan is a society with many ethnic and social minority groups and a large majority population of heterogeneous origins. Anthropological evidence describes a migration from Southeast Asia and later from East Asia, probably over land bridges that once existed.

Invasion and migration from China and Korea continued until the ninth century, by which time nearly one-third of the aristocratic clans in the Chinese-style Heian capital (present-day Kyoto) were of Korean or Chinese ethnicity. Immigrants were well received as they were recognized as bearers of a superior cultural tradition, not only as nobility but as craftsmen, priests, and educated professionals. Their traditions in literature, art, and religion were absorbed and became a foundation on which much of Japanese culture was based.

In more recent times, large numbers of people from Korea and Taiwan, who were at that time colonial subjects and Japanese nationals, settled in Japan or were pressed into prewar or wartime labor there. Despite efforts to repatriate them after the war, many stayed in Japan but lost their Japanese nationality when the postwar San Francisco Peace Treaty of 1952 designated them as foreigners. The Allied Occupation brought hundreds of thousands of people to Japan, mostly American men, and the maintenance of military facilities has led to the continued presence of a significant number of American military personnel.

In today's Japan, in addition to at least twenty-four thousand Ainu and a million Okinawans, ethnic minorities holding citizenship include recently naturalized persons from various ethnic backgrounds, particularly Korean. In addition, there are persons of mixed ethnic ancestry, such as the offspring of Korean–Japanese or American–Japanese parentage. There are also nearly a million resident foreigners, the majority of whom are Koreans, with smaller numbers of Chinese, Filipinos, Americans, and others.

In recent years, the ethnic composition of foreigners in Japan has changed dramatically with a flood of workers and students from around the world seeking opportunity in Japan. Students, mainly from China and other parts of Asia, are also rushing to Japan in rapidly increasing numbers to fill the government's stated goal of 100,000 by the year 2000, although many use their student status simply to enter the country to work.

The largest minority in Japan, the *burakumin*, are physically and linguistically indistinguishable from majority Japanese but exhibit the political and cultural traits of an ethnic group. They are the as many as three million descendants of the *eta*, a subclass legally distinguished during the Tokugawa period (1600–1868) and until their emancipation in 1871. The atomic bomb survivors of Hiroshima and Nagasaki, the *hibakusha*, and their descendants are a new minority group who, like the *burakumin*, may be plagued by fears that they are genetically defective or contaminated.

In all, about five percent of the Japanese population, or some six-million persons, are minorities who suffer much the same fate that ethnic and other minorities do in America and Europe. Most of Japan's minority groups have higher rates of unemployment, welfare, and crime, and lower levels of income and educational attainment, than the majority population.

Source: Stephen Murphy-Shigematsu (1993) Multiethnic Japan and the monoethnic myth. *MELUS*, 18:4 (Winter), pp. 63–80.

AINU RECOGNIZED BY GOVERNMENT   Document 30

The state has worked to erase Ainu identity since the nineteenth century, but finally in 2008 recognized them as an indigenous people after decades of struggle.

The Ainu celebrated a historic moment Friday as the Diet unanimously passed a resolution that recognizes them as indigenous people of Japan.

The unprecedented resolution was adopted by both chambers, acknowledging the Ainu's hardships from discrimination and poverty.

The resolution states 'the government shall recognize that the Ainu are indigenous people who have their own language, religion and culture.'

It also calls on the government to refer to the UN Declaration on the Rights of Indigenous Peoples and take comprehensive steps to advance Ainu policies while heeding the opinions of specialists.

After the resolution was passed, Chief Cabinet Secretary Nobutaka Machimura said the government now recognizes the Ainu as indigenous and promised policy measures on behalf of an ethnic minority that has been forced to lead underprivileged lives.

'The government would like to solemnly accept the historical fact that many Ainu were discriminated against and forced into poverty with the advancement of modernization, despite being legally equal to (Japanese) people,' Machimura said.

In 1869, one year after the Meiji Restoration, the government gave Hokkaido its current name and established Kaitakushi (the Development Commission) to rule and develop the prefecture. This marked the start of the forced assimilation of the Ainu, Uemura said.

The Family Registry Law, enacted in 1871, incorporated the Ainu as 'commoners'. At that time, the government also prohibited them from practicing certain traditions, including men wearing earrings and women getting tattooed, and 'encouraged' them to learn the Japanese language.

Many Ainu still live in poverty, with 38.3 percent of those in Hokkaido on welfare, compared with 24.6 percent of other Hokkaido residents, according to a 2006 prefectural survey. Also, only 17.4 percent of the Ainu receive a college education.

Source: Masami Ito. Diet officially declares Ainu indigenous. *The Japan Times*, 7 June 2008.

Document 31   RICHARD KATZ ON THE RISE AND FALL OF JAPAN'S ECONOMIC MIRACLE

In the following extract, from a contribution to the Japan Times, *Katz (author of* Japan: The System that Soured) *explores the reasons for Japan's economic success and the current malaise. He argues that overdue reforms have not been implemented because they would harm the vested interests that benefit from the existing arrangements and practices.*

In all likelihood, the era that began with the collapse of the bubble economy in 1990 will turn out to be the third great transition in Japan's modern history. By 1990, the political-economic system previously responsible for Japan's economic miracle had turned into the country's biggest ball and chain. The Catch-22 is that the very features that now obstruct economic growth also serve as pillars of Japan's political system. Consider the informal cartels pervading private industry. They not only sap efficiency; they also create high prices that siphon off consumer demand. . . . The political difficulty is that cartels, structural protectionism and high prices serve as disguised employment and income redistribution for moribund sectors like farming, construction, paper, glass and a host of others. Eliminating inefficiency in these sectors would also eliminate 10 million jobs. Sure, reform would eventually create even more new jobs. That, however, would take time and Japan has a thin social safety net. Hence the very things that make reform necessary also make it difficult.

Once Japan reached maturity in the early 1970s, there were no more infant industries. 'Developmentalist' techniques should have been ended. Instead, they were reinforced, with one big difference: In the high growth era, Japan primarily promoted future winners; after 1973, it protected losers.

The trigger for this shift was the oil shock of 1973. For a full decade, zero growth plagued industries accounting for half of Japan's manufacturing output and a third of its factory workers. Rather than accepting downsizing, companies and workers cried out for relief. The government gave it to them.

Gradually, Japan turned into a deformed dual economy – a dysfunctional hybrid of super-strong exporting industries and super-weak domestic sectors. . . . By the late 1980s, the exporters could no longer support the burden. They were caught in a squeeze between high costs at home and a rising yen, which made it more difficult to pass on those costs overseas. In response, the exporters fled. Today, Japan produces more cars outside of Japan than inside Japan; more consumer electronics outside Japan than inside Japan. As this flight progressed, the productivity of the entire economy was steadily dragged down to the level of the stagnant sectors.

Source: Richard Katz. Japan in the midst of a third great transition. *Japan Times*, 27 June 1999, p. 1.

CHANGING EMPLOYMENT SYSTEM   Document 32

Taichi Sakaiya was one of the first commentators to point out the need for transforming Japan's employment paradigm. In the mid-1980s when Western observers were penning best-selling books about the secrets of Japan's economic success, he warned about the high costs and inefficiency of white-collar workers and the burdens of a bureaucratic and stifling managerial culture. His ideas about merit- and performance-based pay and promotion were anathema at the time, but have proven remarkably prescient.

During the era of rapid economic growth, Japan was a country where salaried workers had things pretty much their way. Protected by lifetime employment and with a pay scale that gave them steady increases in income every year as they advanced in seniority, most secured a status befitting their age throughout their careers. As soon as they reached a certain level in the hierarchy, elite salaried workers were also granted one of the perquisites of the corporate scene: The authority to use 'entertainment funds'. This type of expense account was unknown in prewar Japan and much more lavish than expense accounts in other countries, and with it these workers would wine and dine the company's clientele.

The past few decades of Japanese history have been, in other words, a paradise for salaried workers. Not surprisingly, large numbers of youths left their home towns and family businesses to work for leading companies. But the good old days are over, or will be soon.

It was the hallmark of good management to have the stage set for implementation as soon as a company consensus had been reached. The patience with which consensus was awaited was not, however, the monopoly of top management; it was shared by management at every level from headquarters to individual sections. What evolved was a sort of waiting game style of management. The foremost requirement of any manager was bureaucratic-style administrative ability. . . .

In line with the reigning trend toward formalism and bureaucratic control of society, the worth of a salaried worker was judged chiefly on the basis of personal self-sacrifice. The number of hours and the amount of effort devoted to a job were more important than how a job turned out. It was the process, not the outcome, that counted.

Without doubt, the privileges of salaried workers in big business will disappear with the arrival of the new age. Specifically, the systems of seniority-based wages and lifetime employment will be gradually dismantled.

It will no longer be possible merely to wait one's turn to become a department chief. As the age factor decreases in importance, only those who steadily improve their performance on the job will rise to key positions and be rewarded accordingly. Performance will be judged by three elements of business acumen: foresight, decisiveness and dynamism. The self-sacrifice demanded of salaried workers in the past will no longer be needed; the test will be the ability to devise new lines of business and make them profitable.

Source: Taichi Sakaiya (1986) New role models, for the work force. *Economic Views from Japan: Selections from Economic Eye* (Keizai Toho Center, Tokyo), pp. 166–73. Mr Sakaiya's article originally appeared in the March 1984 issue of *Chuo Koron*. As quoted in David J. Lu (1997) *Japan: A Documentary History*, Vol. II (M. E. Sharpe, Armonk, NY), pp. 547–50.

Document 33   INFORMATION DISCLOSURE

The Information Clearinghouse Japan is a non-profit organization working to promote transparency and freedom of information, a popular agenda in a nation where government secrecy has frequently come at the expense of the public's interests. In 2010 it sent a public letter to the Hatoyama government advocating comprehensive reforms aimed at promoting transparency by mandating fuller and more timely disclosure, improving remedies, expanding proactive information disclosure and ensuring proper management of public records.

In the past, information disclosure was dependent on administrative agencies for implementation; in pursuing the ideal of a shift from leadership by bureaucrats to leadership by politicians, imposing transparency in politics is also an important topic.

Further, as the judiciary becomes more familiar to the people through introduction of the lay judge system, increased transparency of the judiciary is also needed.

The 'open government' we demand from the Hatoyama Administration is a drastic revision of several existing legal systems and a change from a government characterized by secrecy to one of openness . . . because the current law has so many defects . . . secrecy in government has grown out of control.

Source: Open letter to Prime Minister Hatoyama from Information Clearing House, 4 January 2010 (translated by Lawrence Repeta).

--------------◄●►--------------

LAW SCHOOLS   **Document 34**

The establishment of law schools in 2004 raised hopes for judicial reform that remain unrealized.

With its first crop of graduates just entering the legal profession, Japan's new law school system is in trouble. The schools, most of which opened their doors in 2004, are already struggling with the mismatch between the number of law students, which is unregulated, and the number of people who are allowed to pass the bar exam, which is set by the government at an artificially low number. As a result, the most recent pass rate was about 40 percent, a figure that will continue to drop as more graduates and repeat takers compete for a fixed number of slots – an unattractive situation for both existing and prospective students alike.

[A] principal concern seems to be that more lawyers will mean more lawsuits and that Japan will become a 'litigation society' like the United States. . . . [Critics] raise valid issues about the very premise behind the law school system – that Japan even needs more lawyers – and the almost mindless process by which the current target of 3,000 new lawyers per year was arrived at . . .

One fascinating aspect of the whole debate over the number of lawyers in Japan is that it misses a simple, basic fact – that the average Japanese person may not regard the legal system as a useful tool for solving problems. If you are arrested and prosecuted for a crime you will be found guilty over 99 percent of the time. If you get divorced and lose contact with your children, going to court probably won't change a thing. Lawsuits against the national government are shown to be losing propositions almost daily in the news. Small wonder then that Japanese people are averse to litigation, when it is so often proven to be futile.

Law in Japan probably continues to exist first and foremost as something that is imposed from above as a means of preserving and enhancing authority, rather than being a democratically ratified set of rules intended to benefit individual citizens.

Source: Colin P. A. Jones. Law schools come under friendly fire. *Japan Times*, 28 January 2008.

Document 35   PARADIGM SHIFT

Ozawa is a conservative politician who was once a protégé of Prime Minister Tanaka. Coming from this milieu of shady deals and money politics, he is an unlikely champion of reform and the progressive ideas he expresses in this book. While acknowledging that Japan enjoys wealth and stability, Ozawa is an outspoken critic of what he terms an anachronistic system that does not serve the interests of the people.

Japan has become a society dedicated solely to its corporations. The people have become mere cogs in the Japanese corporate wheel.

Japanese people work long hours and are almost completely subject to the will of their companies. Companies retain most of the fruits of economic growth; the portion left to individuals is small by comparison. We may have nominally attained the world's highest income, but we continue to struggle with small residences, lengthy commutes, and extreme urban concentration.

I would like to see Japan strive toward the goal of 'five freedoms'.

- *Freedom from Tokyo* requires reversing the extreme concentration of population and resources in Tokyo and making the transition from urban overcrowding and rural depopulation to a more balanced development policy.
- *Freedom from companies* means placing the individual rather than the company at the center of the social and economic framework, so that each citizen can approach his or her work more freely and place greater value on his or her own individual life.

- *Freedom from overwork* requires steps that will aggressively reduce work hours so that people may work with greater ease and plan their own futures. We must also alter the excessively competitive examination system.
- *Freedom from ageism and sexism* means enabling the growing number of senior citizens to participate more fully in society, and building a society in which women can play more active and varied roles.
- *Freedom from regulation* entails abolishing anachronistic and meaningless rules. It also means allowing individuals and companies more freedom.

Source: Ichiro Ozawa (1994) *Blueprint for a New Japan: The Rethinking of a Nation* (Kodansha International, Tokyo), pp. 156–9.

Bibliography

REFERENCE WORKS

Allinson, G. D. (1999) *The Columbia Guide to Modern Japanese History*. Columbia University Press: New York.

Coulmas, F., Conrad, H., Schad-Seifert, A. and Vogt, G. (2008) *The Demographic Challenge: A Handbook About Japan*. Brill: Leiden.

Dower, J. (1986a) *Japanese History and Culture from Ancient to Modern Times, Vol. 7. Basic Bibliographies*. Markus Weiner Publishing: New York.

Duus, P., ed. (1988) *The Cambridge History of Japan, Vol. 6. The Twentieth Century*. Cambridge University Press: Cambridge.

International Society for Understanding Japan (1989) *Japanese Chronology*. International Society for Educational Information: Tokyo.

Kodansha Encyclopedia of Japan, 9 vols. (1983) Kodansha International: Tokyo.

Livingston, J., Moore, J. and Oldfather, F., eds. (1973) *Postwar Japan: 1945 to the Present*. Pantheon Books: New York.

Lu, D. J. (1997) *Japan: A Documentary History: The Late Tokugawa Period to the Present*. M. E. Sharpe: Armonk, NY.

Starr, D., ed. (2000) *Japan: A Cultural and Historical Dictionary*. Curzon Press: Richmond, UK.

GENERAL WORKS

Allinson, G. D. (1997) *Japan's Postwar History*. Cornell University Press: Ithaca, NY.

Buckley, R. (1999) *Japan Today* (3rd edn). Cambridge University Press: Cambridge.

Chapman, W. (1991) *Inventing Japan*. Prentice-Hall: New York.

Dower, J. (1993) *Japan in War and Peace*. New Press: New York.

Duus, P. (1998) *Modern Japan* (2nd edn). Houghton Mifflin: Boston, MA.

Field, N. (1993) *In the Realm of the Dying Emperor: Japan at Century's End*. Vintage: New York.

Gluck, C. and Graubard, S., eds. (1992) *Showa: The Japan of Hirohito*. W. W. Norton: New York.

Gordon, A., ed. (1993) *Postwar Japan as History*. University of California Press: Berkeley, CA.

Hane, M. (1996) *Eastern Phoenix: Japan since 1945*. Westview Press: Boulder, CO.

Kingston, J. (2004a) *Japan's Quiet Transformation*. Routledge: London.

Kingston, J. (2004b) Downsizing the construction state. *The Japanese Economy*, 32:4 (Dec.), 36–95.

McCormack, G. (1996) *The Emptiness of Japanese Affluence*. M. E. Sharpe: Armonk, NY.

Naff, C. (1994) *About Face: How I Stumbled onto Japan's Social Revolution*. Kodansha International: Tokyo.

Reischauer, E. (1977) *The Japanese*. Harvard University Press: Cambridge, MA.

Smith, P. (1997) *Japan: A Reinterpretation*. Pantheon Books: New York.

AGEING

Campbell, J. (1992) *How Policies Change: The Japanese Government and the Aging Society*. Princeton University Press, Princeton, NJ.

Campbell, J. and Ikegami, N. (1998) *The Art of Balance in Health Policy*. Cambridge University Press: Cambridge.

Coulmas, F. (2008) *Population Decline and Aging in Japan*. Routledge: London.

Harris, P. B. and Long, S. O. (1999) Husbands and sons in the US and Japan: Cultural expectations and caregiving experiences. *Journal of Aging Studies*, 13:3 (Fall), 241–67.

Hurd, M. and Yashiro, N., eds. (1997) *The Economic Effects of Aging and the US and Japan*. University of Chicago Press: Chicago, IL.

Long, S. O., ed. (2000) *Caring for the Elderly in Japan and the US*. Routledge: London.

Noguchi, Y. and Wise, D., eds. (1994) *Aging in the United States and Japan*. University of Chicago Press: Chicago, IL.

Ohtake, F. (1999) Aging society and inequality. *Japan Labor Bulletin*, 38:9 (July), 5–11.

Yamamoto, N. (1997) The continuation of family caregiving in Japan. *Journal of Health and Social Behaviour*, 38:2 (June), 164–76.

ECONOMY

Amyx, J. (2004) *Japan's Financial Crisis*. Princeton University Press: Princeton, NJ.

Chalmers, N. (1989) *Industrial Relations in Japan: The Peripheral Workforce*. Routledge: London.

Cole, R. (1971) *Japanese Blue-Collar*. University of California Press: Berkeley, CA.

Dore, R. (1973) *British Factory, Japanese Factory: The Origins of Diversity in Industrial Relations*. University of California Press: Berkeley, CA.

Emmott, B. (1989) *The Sun Also Sets: Why Japan Will Not Be Number One*. Simon & Schuster: New York.

Fallows, J. (1994) *Looking at the Sun: The Rise of the New East Asian Economic and Political System*. Pantheon Books: New York.

Fingelton, E. (1995) *Blindside: Why Japan is Still on Track to Overtake the US by the Year 2000*. Simon & Schuster: New York.

Garon, S. (1987) *The State and Labor in Modern Japan*. University of California Press: Berkeley, CA.

Genda, Y. (2005) *A Nagging Sense of Job Insecurity*. LTCB Library Trust/ International House: Tokyo.

Gordon, A. (1998) *The Wages of Affluence: Labor and Management in Postwar Japan*. Harvard University Press: Cambridge, MA.

Hein, L. (1990) *Fueling Growth: The Energy Revolution and Economic Policy in Postwar Japan*. Harvard University Press: Cambridge, MA.

Johnson, C. (1982) *MITI and the Japanese Miracle: The Growth of Industrial Policy, 1925–1975*. Stanford University Press: Stanford, CA.

Katz, R. (1998) *Japan: The System that Soured: The Rise and Fall of the Japanese Miracle*. M. E. Sharpe: Armonk, NY.

Krugman, P. (1994) The myth of the Asian miracle. *Foreign Affairs*, (Nov–Dec), 62–78.

Lincoln, E. (1990) *Japan's Unequal Trade*. Brookings: Washington, DC.

Murphy, R. (1996) *The Weight of the Yen*. W. W. Norton: New York.

Murphy, R. (2000) Japan's economic crisis. *New Left Review*, (Jan–Feb), 25–52.

Nakamura, T. (1981) *The Postwar Japanese Economy: Its Development and Structure*. University of Tokyo Press: Tokyo.

Okimoto, D. (1989) *Between MITI and the Market: Japanese Industrial Policy for High Technology*. Stanford University Press: Stanford, CA.

Okita, S. (1992) *Postwar Reconstruction of the Japanese Economy*. University of Tokyo Press: Tokyo.

Prestowitz, C. (1990) *Trading Places*. Basic Books: New York.

Ries, P. (2000) *The Asian Storm: The Economic Crisis Examined*. Charles Tuttle: Tokyo.

Sato, K., ed. (1999) *The Transformation of the Japanese Economy*. M. E. Sharpe: Armonk, NY.

Saxonhouse, G. and Stern, R., eds. (2004) *Japan's Lost Decade*. Blackwell: Oxford.

Tachibanaki, T. (1996) *Wage Determination and Distribution in Japan*. Clarendon Press: Oxford.

Tachibanaki, T. (2005) *Confronting Income Inequality in Japan*. MIT Press: Boston, MA.

Uriu, R. (1998) *Troubled Industries: The Political Economy of Industrial Adjustment in Japan*. Cornell University Press: Ithaca, NY.

Wood, C. (1993) *The Bubble Economy: The Japanese Economic Collapse*. Charles Tuttle: Tokyo.

Yamamura, K. and Yasuba, Y., eds. (1987) *The Political Economy of Japan*, Vol. 1. Stanford University Press: Stanford, CA.

FOREIGN POLICY

Arase, D. (1995) *Buying Power: The Political Economy of Japan's Foreign Aid*. Lynne Reinner: Boulder, CO.

Buckley, R. (1992) *US–Japan Alliance Diplomacy 1945–1990*. Cambridge University Press: Cambridge.

Calder, K. (1997) *Asia's Deadly Triangle: How Arms, Energy and Growth Threaten to Destabilize the Asia-Pacific*. Nicholas Brealey: London.

Curtis, G., ed. (1993) *Japan's Foreign Policy after the Cold War: Coping with Change*. M. E. Sharpe: Armonk, NY.

Dore, R. (1997) *Japan, Internationalism and the UN*. Routledge: London.

Green, M. J. (1995) *Arming Japan: Defense Production, Alliance Politics and the Postwar Search for Autonomy*. Columbia University Press: New York.

Inoguchi, T. (1993) *Japan's Foreign Policy in an Era of Global Change*. Pinter: London.

Johnson, C., ed. (1999) *Okinawa: Cold War Island*. Japan Policy Research Institute: Cardiff, CA.

Johnston, E. (2004) The North Korea abduction issue and its effect on Japanese domestic politics. Japan Policy Research Institute (JPRI). JPRI Working Paper No. 101 (June).

Koppel, B. M. and Orr, R. M., Jr., eds. (1993) *Japan's Foreign Aid: Power and Policy in a New Era*. Westview Press: Boulder, CO.

Matthews, R. and Matsuyama, K., eds. (1993) *Japan's Military Renaissance?* Macmillan: London.

McCormack, G. (2004) *Target North Korea*. Nation Books: New York.

McCormack, G. (2007) *Client State*. Verso: New York.

McCormack, G. and Wada, H. (2005) The strange record of 15 Years of Japan–North Korean negotiations. *Japan Focus*, 1894, 2 September.

Oros, A. (2008) *Normalizing Japan*. Stanford University Press: Stanford, CA.

Orr, R. (1990) *The Emergence of Japan's Foreign Aid Power*. Columbia University Press: New York.

Rix, A. (1993) *Japan's Foreign Aid Challenge*. Routledge: London.

Samuels, R. (2008) *Securing Japan*. Cornell University Press: Ithaca, NY.

JAPAN AND ASIA

Brook, T., ed. (1999) *Documents on the Rape of Nanking*. University of Michigan Press: Ann Arbor, MI.

Buruma, I. (1994) *The Wages of Guilt: Memories of War in Germany and Japan*. Farrar Strauss Giroux: New York.

Chang, Iris. (1997) *The Rape of Nanking: The Forgotten Holocaust of World War II*. Basic Books: New York.

Curtis, G., ed. (1994) *The United States, Japan and Asia: Challenges for US Policy*. W. W. Norton: New York.

Dudden, A. (2006) *Japan's Colonization of Korea*. University of Hawaii Press: Honolulu.

Dudden, A. (2008) *Troubled Apologies*. Columbia University Press: New York.

Fogel, J. (2000) *The Nanjing Massacre in History and Historiography*. University of California Press: Berkeley, CA.

Goto, K. (1997) *Returning to Asia*. Ryukei Shyosha: Tokyo.

Goto, K. (2003) *Tensions of Empire*. Ohio University Press: Athens, OH.

Harris, S. (1995) *Factories of Death: Japanese Biological Warfare, 1932–45, and the American Cover-up*. Routledge: London.

Hasegawa, T. and Togo, K. (2008) *East Asia's Haunted Present*. Greenwood: Santa Barbara, CA.

Hatch, W. and Yamamura, K. (1996) *Asia in Japan's Embrace: Building a Regional Production Alliance*. Cambridge University Press: Cambridge.

Havens, T. (1987) *Fire Across the Sea: The Vietnam War and Japan*. Princeton University Press: Princeton, NJ.

Hein, L. and Selden, M., eds. (2000) *Censoring History: Citizenship and Memory in Japan, Germany and the United States*. M. E. Sharpe: Armonk, NY.

Hicks, G. (1995) *The Comfort Women*. Yen Books: Tokyo.

Honda, K. (1999) *The Nanjing Massacre*. M. E. Sharpe: Armonk, NY.

International Public Hearing Report (1993) *War Victimization and Japan*. Toho Shuppan: Osaka.

Kang, J., Arimitsu, K. and Underwood, W. (2009) Assessing the Nishimatsu Corporate approach to redressing Chinese forced labor in wartime Japan. *Asia-Pacific Journal*, (Nov 23), Vol. 47-1-09.

Katzenstein, P. and Shiraishi, T., eds. (1997) *Network Power: Japan and Asia*. Cornell University Press: Ithaca, NY.

Kingston, J. (2008) Nanjing's Massacre Memorial: renovating war memory in Nanjing and Tokyo. *Japan Focus*, (August 2008), 2859.

Kitamura, M. (2007) *The Politics of Nanjing*. University Press of America: Lanham, MD.

Kratoska, P. (2005) *Asian Labor in the Wartime Japanese Empire*. M. E. Sharpe: Armonk, NY.

Marshall, J. (1995) *To Have and Have Not: Southeast Asia's Raw Materials and the Origins of the Pacific War*. University of California Press: Berkeley, CA.

McNeill, D. (2005) History Redux: Japan's Textbook Battle Reignites. Japan Policy Research Institute (JPRI). JPRI Working Paper No. 107 (June).

Reader, I. and Soderberg, M., eds. (2000) *Japanese Influences and Presences in Asia*. Curzon Press: Richmond, UK.

Saaler, S. (2005) *Politics, Memory and Public Opinion*. German Institute for Japanese Studies: Munich.

Sato, S. (1997) *War, Nationalism and Peasants: Java under the Japanese Occupation, 1942–45*. M. E. Sharpe: Armonk, NY.

Seaton, P. (2007) *Japan's Contested War Memories*. Routledge: London.

Seraphim, F. (2006) *War Memory and Social Politics, 1945–2005*. Harvard University Press: Cambridge, MA.

Soh, C. (2009) *The Comfort Women*. University of Chicago Press: Chicago, IL.

Tanaka, Y. (2001) *Japan's Comfort Women*. Routledge: London.

Toer, P. (1999) *The Mute's Soliloquy*. Hyperion East: New York.

Togo, K. (2005) *Japan's Foreign Policy*. Brill: Leiden.

Togo, K. (2006) A moratorium on Yasukuni. *Far Eastern Economic Review*, (June), 5–15.

Underwood, W. (2008) New era for Japan-Korea history issues. *Japan Focus*, 2689.

Wakabayashi, B. (2007) *The Nanking Atrocity, 1937–38: Complicating the Picture*. Berghahn Books: New York.

Wakamiya, Y. (1999) *The Postwar Conservative View of Asia*. LTCB International Library Foundation: Tokyo.

Yamazaki, J. (2005) *Japanese Apologies for WWII*. Routledge: London.

Yoshida, T. (2006) *The Making of the Rape of Nanking*. Columbia University Press: New York.

Yoshimi, Y. (2001) *Comfort Women*. Columbia University Press: NY.

Young, L. (1998) *Japan's Total Empire: Manchuria and the Culture of Wartime Imperialism*. University of California Press: Berkeley, CA.

POLITICS

Bowen, R. (2003) *Japan's Dysfunctional Democracy*. M. E. Sharpe: Armonk, NY.

Broadbent, J. (1998) *Environmental Politics in Japan: Networks of Power and Protest*. Cambridge University Press: Cambridge.

Calder, K. (1991) *Crisis and Compensation: Public Policy and Political Stability in Japan, 1949–1986*. Princeton University Press: Princeton, NJ.

Curtis, G. (1988) *The Japanese Way of Politics*. Columbia University Press: New York.

Curtis, G. (1999) *The Logic of Japanese Politics: Leaders, Institutions and the Limits of Change*. Columbia University Press: New York.

Estevez-Abe, M. (2008) *Welfare and Capitalism in Postwar Japan*. Cambridge University Press: Cambridge.

Hartcher, P. (1997) *The Ministry: The Inside Story of Japan's Ministry of Finance*. Harper Collins: London.

Leheny, D. (2006) *Think Global, Fear Local*. Cornell University Press: Ithaca, NY.

Maclachlan, P. (2002) *Consumer Politics in Japan*. Columbia University Press: New York.

Neary, I. (2002) *The State and Politics in Japan*. Polity: Cambridge.

Otake, H. (2000) *Power Shuffles and Policy Processes: Coalition Government in Japan in the 1990s*. Japan Center for International Exchange: Tokyo.

Ozawa, I. (1994) *Blueprint for a New Japan: The Rethinking of a Nation*. Kodansha International: Tokyo.

Packard, G. (1966) *Protest in Tokyo*. Princeton University Press: Princeton, NJ.

Pempel, T., ed. (1990) *Uncommon Democracies*. Cornell University Press: Ithaca, NY.

Pempel, T. (1998) *Regime Shift: Comparative Dynamics of the Japanese Political Economy*. Cornell University Press: Ithaca, NY.

Ramsayer, M. and Rosenbluth, F. (1993) *Japan's Political Marketplace*. Harvard University Press: Cambridge, MA.

Richardson, B. (1997) *Japanese Democracy: Power, Coordination and Performance*. Yale University Press: New Haven, CT.

Samuels, R. (2005) *Machiavelli's Children*. Cornell University Press: Ithaca, NY.

Scheiner, E. (2005) *Democracy Without Competition in Japan*. Cambridge University Press: Cambridge.

Schlesinger, J. (1997) *Shadow Shoguns: The Rise and Fall of Japan's Postwar Political Machine*. Simon & Schuster: New York.

Schoppa, L. (1997) *Bargaining with Japan: What American Pressure Can and Can Not Do*. Columbia University Press: New York.

Schoppa, L. (2006) *Racing for the Exits*. Cornell University Press: Ithaca, NY.

Stockwin, J. (1998) *Governing Japan: Divided Politics in a Major Economy*. Blackwell: London.

Vogel, S. (2006) *Japan Remodeled*. Cornell University Press: Ithaca, NY.

von Wolferen, K. (1989) *The Enigma of Japanese Power*. Macmillan: London.

SOCIETY

Adelstein, J. (2009) *Tokyo Vice*. Pantheon: New York.

Arudou, D. (2004) *Japanese Only*. Akashi Shoten: Tokyo.

Bornoff, N. (1991) *Pink Samurai*. Grafton: London.

Cummings, W. (1980) *Education and Equality in Japan*. Princeton University Press: Princeton, NJ.

Dale, P. (1986) *The Myth of Japanese Uniqueness*. Routledge: London.

Davis, W. (1992) *Japanese Religion and Society*. SUNY Press: Albany, NY.

DeVos, G., et al. (1983) *Japan's Minorities*. Minority Rights Group: London.

Doi, T. (1973) *The Anatomy of Dependence*. Kodansha International: Tokyo.

Douglass, M. and Roberts, G., eds. (2000) *Japan and Global Migration*. Routledge, London.

Feldman, E. (2000) *The Ritual of Rights in Japan*. Cambridge University Press: Cambridge.

Freeman, L. (2000) *Closing the Shop: Information Cartels and Japan's Mass Media*. Princeton University Press: Princeton, NJ.

Fuess, H. (2004) *Divorce in Japan*. Stanford University Press: Stanford, CA.

Goodman, R. (2000) *Children of the Japanese State*. Oxford University Press: Oxford.

Goodman, R., ed. (2002) *Family and Social Policy in Japan*. Cambridge University Press: Cambridge.

Greenfield, T. (1994) *Speed Tribes: Days and Nights with Japan's Next Generation*. Harper Collins: New York.

Hall, I. (1997) *Cartels of the Mind*. W. W. Norton: New York.

Ishida, H. (1993) *Social Mobility in Contemporary Japan*. Stanford University Press: Stanford, CA.

Ishida, H. and Slater, D. (2009) *Social Class in Contemporary Japan*. Routledge: London.

Kaplan, D. and Dubro, A. (1986) *Yakuza*. Addison-Wesley: Reading, MA.

Kitaguchi, S. and McLauchlan, A. (2000) *An Introduction to the Buraku Issue*. Japan Library: Richmond, UK.

Lebra, T., ed. (1992) *Japanese Social Organization*. University Press of Hawaii: Honolulu.

Lee, C. and DeVos, G. (1981) *Koreans in Japan*. University of California Press: Berkeley, CA.

Lifton, R. (1999) *Destroying the World to Save It: Aum Shinrikyo, Apocalyptic Violence and the New Global Terrorism*. Metropolitan Books: New York.

Mouer, R. and Sugimoto, Y. (1986) *Images of Japanese Society*. KPI: London.

Murakami, H. (2001) Underground: The Tokyo Gas Attack and the Japanese Psyche. Vintage: NY.

Nakane, C. (1970) *Japanese Society*. University of California Press: Berkeley, CA.

Pekkanen, R. (2006) *Japan's Dual Civil Society*. Stanford University Press: Stanford, CA.

Rauch, J. (1992) *The Outnation: A Search for the Soul of Japan*. Harvard Business School Press: Cambridge, MA.

Reader, I. (1991) *Religion in Contemporary Japan*. Macmillan: Basingstoke.

Reader, I. (1996) *A Poisonous Cocktail? Aum Shinrikyo's Path to Violence*. Nordic Institute of Asian Studies: Copenhagen.

Richie, D. (1971) *The Inland Sea*. Weatherhill: Tokyo.

Richie, D. (1992) *A Lateral View: Essays on Culture and Style in Contemporary Japan*. Stonebridge Press: Berkeley, CA.

Rohlen, T. (1983) *Japan's High Schools*. University of California Press: Berkeley, CA.

Schwartz, F. and Pharr, S. (2003) *The State of Civil Society in Japan*. Cambridge University Press: Cambridge.

Shimada, H. (1994) *Japan's 'Guest Workers': Issues and Public Policies*. University of Tokyo Press: Tokyo.

Shinoda, T. (2009) Which side are you on? Hakenmura and the working poor as a tipping point in Japanese labor politics. *Asia-Pacific Journal*, (April 4), Vol. 14-3-09.

Upham, F. (1987) *Law and Social Change in Postwar Japan*. Harvard University Press: Cambridge, MA.

Vogel, E. (1980) *Japan as Number One*. Charles Tuttle: Tokyo.

Weiner, M., ed. (1997, revised 2009) *Japan's Minorities: Illusions of Homogeneity*. Routledge: London.

Whiting, R. (1999) *Tokyo Underworld*. Pantheon Books: New York.

WAR AND OCCUPATION

Barnhardt, M. (1988) *Japan Prepares for Total War*. Cornell University Press: Ithaca, NY.

Bix, H. (2000) *Hirohito and the Making of Modern Japan*. HarperCollins: New York.

Cohen, T. (1987) *Remaking Japan: The American Occupation as New Deal*. Free Press: New York.

Davis, G. (1997) *An Occupation Without Troops*. Charles Tuttle: Tokyo.

Dower, J. (1986b) *War Without Mercy: Race and Power in the Pacific War*. Pantheon: New York.

Dower, J. (1999) *Embracing Defeat: Japan in the Wake of World War II*. W. W. Norton: New York.

Finn, R. (1992) *Winners in Peace: MacArthur, Yoshida and Postwar Japan*. University of California Press: Berkeley, CA.

Forsberg, A. (2000) *America and the Japanese Miracle: The Cold War Context of Japan's Postwar Economic Revival 1950–1960*. University of North Carolina Press: Chapel Hill, NC.

Frank, R. (1999) *Downfall: The End of the Imperial Japanese Empire*. Random House: New York.

Gold, H. (1996) *Unit 731: Japan's Wartime Human Experimentation Program*. Yen Books: Tokyo.

Harvey, R. (1994) *The Undefeated: The Rise, Fall and Rise of Greater Japan*. Macmillan: London.

Hein, L. and Selden, M., eds. (1997) *Living with the Bomb: American and Japanese Cultural Conflicts in the Nuclear Age*. M. E. Sharpe: Armonk, NY.

Norris, R., *et al.* (2000) "Where They Were: How Much Did Japan Know?" *The Bulletin of Atomic Scientists*, Jan.–Feb. (www.thebulletin.org), 27–35.

Schaller, M. (1985) *The American Occupation of Japan: The Origins of the Cold War in Asia*. Oxford University Press: Oxford.

Takemae, E. (2002) *Inside GHQ: Allied Occupation of Japan and its Legacy*. Continuum: London.

Tanaka, Y. (1998) *Hidden Horrors: Japanese War Crimes in World War II*. Westview: Boulder, CO.

WOMEN

Barraclough, R. and Faison, E., eds. (2009) *Gender and Labor in Korea and Japan*. Routledge: London.

Bernstein, G. (1983) *Haruko's World: A Japanese Farm Woman and Her Community*. Stanford University Press: Stanford, CA.

Brinton, M. (1993) *Women and the Economic Miracle: Gender and Work in Postwar Japan*. University of California Press: Berkeley, CA.

Chambers, V. (2007) *Kickboxing Geisha*. Free Press: New York.

Condon, J. (1985) *A Half Step Behind: Japanese Women of the 1980s*. Dodd, Mead: New York.

Cook, A. and Hayashi, H. (1980) *Working Women in Japan: Discrimination, Resistance and Reform*. New York State School of Industrial and Labor Relations: Ithaca, NY.

Dalby, L. (1983) *Geisha*. Vintage Books: New York.

Dales, L. (2009) *Feminist Movements in Contemporary Japan*. Routledge: London.

Flowers, P. (2009) *Refugees, Women and Weapons: International Norm Adoption and Compliance in Japan*. Stanford University Press: Stanford, CA.

Gelb, J. (2003) *Gender Policies in Japan and the US*. Palgrave Macmillan: New York.

Hertog, E. (2009) *Tough Choices: Bearing an Illegitimate Child in Japan*. Stanford University Press: Stanford, CA.

Imamura, A. (1987) *Urban Japanese Housewives: At Home and in the Community*. University of Hawaii Press: Honolulu.

Iwai, S. (1993) *The Japanese Woman: Traditional Image and Changing Reality*. Free Press: New York.

Jolivet, M. (1997) *Japan: The Childless Society?* Routledge: London.

Kato, M. (2009) *Women's Rights? The Politics of Eugenic Abortion in Modern Japan*. Amsterdam University Press: Amsterdam.

Kawakami, S. (2007) *Goodbye Madame Butterfly: Sex Marriage and Modern Japanese Women*. Chin Music Press: Seattle, WA.

Kondo, D. (1990) *Crafting Selves: Power, Gender and Discourses of Identity in a Japanese Workplace*. University of Chicago Press: Chicago, IL.

Lam, A. (1992) *Women and Japanese Management*. Routledge: London.

Lebra, J. (1976) *Women in Changing Japan*. Westview Press: Boulder, CO.

Mackie, V. (2003) *Feminism in Modern Japan*. Cambridge University Press: Cambridge.

Mercier, R. (1999) Power, not sex, behind pornography. *Japan Times*, (12 July), 16.

Norgren, T. (2001) *Abortion Before Birth Control: The Politics of Reproduction in Postwar Japan*. Princeton University Press: Princeton, NJ.

Ogasawara, Y. (1998) *Office Ladies and Salaried Men*. University of California Press: Berkeley, CA.

Okano, K. (2009) *Young Women in Japan*. Routledge: London.

Osawa, M. (1988) Working mothers: Changing patterns of employment and fertility in Japan. *Economic Development and Cultural Change*, 36:4, 623–50.

Rebick, M. and Takenaka, A. (2008) *The Changing Japanese Family*. Routledge: London.

Roberts, G. (1994) *Staying on the Line: Blue Collar Women in Contemporary Japan*. University of Hawaii Press: Honolulu.

Saso, M. (1990) *Women in the Japanese Workplace*. Shipman: London.

Smith, R. (1987) Gender inequality in contemporary Japan. *Journal of Japanese Studies*, 13:1, 1–25.

Smith, R. and Wiswell, E. (1982) *The Women of Suye Mura*. University of Chicago Press: Chicago, IL.

Summerhawk, B. and Hughes, K., eds. (2008) *Sparkling Rain: And Other Fiction from Japan of Women who Love Women*. New Victoria Publishers: Chicago, IL.

Tachibanaki, T. (2010) *The New Paradox for Japanese Women: Greater Choice, Greater Inequality*. I-House Press: Toyko.

Tendo, S. (2008) *Yakuza Moon: Memoirs of a Gangster's Daughter*. Kodansha: Tokyo.

Yu, W. (2009) *Gendered Trajectories: Women, Work and Social Change in Japan and Taiwan*. Stanford University Press: Stanford, CA.

LITERATURE

(Date of publication in Japanese in parentheses.)

Abe, K. (1962) *The Woman in the Dunes*. Vintage: New York, 1991.

Ariyoshi, S. (1972) *The Twilight Years*. Kodansha International: Tokyo, 1984.

Birnbaum, A. *Monkey Brain Sushi: New Tastes in Japanese Fiction*. Kodansha International: Tokyo, 1991.

Dazai, O. (1956) *The Setting Sun*. Charles Tuttle: Tokyo, 1981.

Endo, S. (1957) *The Sea and Poison*. New Directions: New York, 1992.

Gessel, V. and Matsumoto, T., eds. *The Showa Anthology: Modern Japanese Short Stories* (2 vols). Kodansha International: Tokyo, 1985.

Kaiko, T. (1972) *Darkness in Summer*. Charles Tuttle: Tokyo, 1974.

Kawabata, Y. (1961) *Beauty and Sadness*. Vintage Books: New York, 1996.

Kirino, N. *Grotesque*. Knopf: New York, 2003.

Mishima, Y. (1968) *Forbidden Colors*. Charles Tuttle: Tokyo, 1969.

Mitsios, H., ed. *New Japanese Voices: The Best Contemporary Fiction from Japan*. Atlantic Monthly Press: New York, 1991.

Miyabe, M. (1992) *For All She is Worth*. Kodansha International: Tokyo, 1996.

Murakami, H. (1987) *Norwegian Wood*. Kodansha International: Tokyo, 1989.

Murakami, H. (1997–98) *Underground: The Tokyo Gas Attack and the Japanese Psyche*. Vintage: New York, 2001.

Murakami, R. (1976) *Almost Transparent Blue*. Kodansha International: Tokyo, 1992.

Murakami, R. (1980) *Coin Locker Babies*. Kodansha International: Tokyo, 1995.

Oe, K. (1964) *A Personal Matter*. Grove Press: New York, 1969.

Shimazaki, T. (1906) *The Broken Commandment*. Columbia University Press: New York, 1987.

Sumii, S. *The River With No Bridge*. Charles Tuttle: Tokyo, 1961–73.

Tanizaki, J. (1955) *Some Prefer Nettles*. Perigree: New York, 1981.

Yamasaki, T. (1976) *The Barren Zone*. Kodansha International: Tokyo, 1987.

VIDEOS

(Available with English subtitles; * = original in English.)

Harada, M. (1999) *Jubaku: Archipelago of Rotten Money*.<director's name to follow, then put in alphabetical order>

Capra, F. (1945) *Know Your Enemy: Japan*.*

Center For New American Media (1991) *The Japanese Version*.*

Choy & Tong (Filmmakers Library) (1995) *In the Name of the Emperor*.*

Hatta, K. (1996) *Picture Bride*.*

Higashi, Y. (1996) *Village of Dreams*.

Ichikawa, K. (1959) *Fires on the Plain*.

Imamura, S. (1963) *The Insect Woman*.

Imamura, S. (1983) *The Ballad of Narayama*.

Itami, J. (1987) *The Funeral*.

Itami, J. (1987) *Tampopo*.

Itami, J. (1987) *The Taxing Woman*.

Itami, J. (1992) *Minbo No Onna*.

Kobayashi, M. (1958–61) *The Human Condition* (3 parts).

Kumai, K. (1974) *Sandakan 8*.

Kurosawa, A. (1946) *No Regrets for Our Youth*.

Kurosawa, A. (1949) *Stray Dog*.

Kurosawa, A. (1952) *Ikiru (To Live)*.

Kurosawa, A. (1960) *The Bad Sleep Well*.

Kurosawa, A. (1963) *High and Low*.

Logan, J. (1957) *Sayonara*.*

Mann, D. (1956) *Teahouse of the August Moon*.*

Morita, Y. (1983) *Family Game*.

Okada, E. (1964) *Woman in the Dunes*.

Oshima, N. (1960) *Cruel Story of Youth*.

Ozu, Y. (1953) *Tokyo Story*.
Pacific Century Series (1992) Vol. 5: *Reinventing Japan*; Vol. 6: *Inside Japan, Inc.**
PBS–Oregon (1996) *Occupied Japan: An Experiment in Democracy.**
Suo, M. (1996) *Shall We Dance?*
Tsukamoto, S. (1988) *Tetsuo: The Iron Man*.
Yanagimachi, M. (1985) *Fire Festival*.
http://www.homefilmfestival.com/foreign.html
http://www.facets.org/

INTERNET LINKS

http://www.japanfocus.org/ (Japan Focus)
http://www.japanesestudies.org.uk/ (Electronic Journal of Contemporary Japanese Studies)
http://www.jstor.org/ (JSTOR-database academic articles on Japan)
http://www.japantoday.com/ (Japan Today)
http://www.japanechoweb.jp/ (Japan Echo)
http://www.elibrary.com/ (On-line Searchable Library of Articles)
http://www.bijapan.com/ (Business Insights Japan)
http://www.jinjapan.org/ (Japan Information Network)
http://www.criticalasianstudies.org/ (Critical Asian Studies)
http://jin.jcic.or.jp/stat/index.html (Government Statistics)
http://www.newsonjapan.com/ (Current news on Japan culled from various sources)
http://www.jcer.or.jp/eng/index.html (Japan Center for Economic Research)
http://www.asahi.com/english/english.html (Asahi Newspaper)
http://www.bridgetojapan.org/ (Daiwa Foundation (UK) Information Resources)
http://fuji.stanford.edu/jguide/ (Stanford University Jguide – Info clearing house)
http://coombs.anu.edu.au/asia-www-monitor.html (Australian Asian Info Resources)
http://www.ndl.go.jp/e/index.html (National Diet Library)?
http://www.jpri.org/ (Japan Policy Research Institute)
http://www.yomiuri.co.jp/dy/ (Yomiuri Newspaper)
http://mdn.mainichi.jp/ (Mainichi Newspaper)
http://nias.ku.dk (Nordic Institute of Asian Studies)

PRINTED PUBLICATIONS

AMPO Japan-American Quarterly
Asian Survey
Asia Human Rights Watch
Economist
Far Eastern Economic Review (1946–2009)
Japan Echo
Japan Economic Institute Reports
Japan Policy Research Institute Reports
Japan Quarterly
Journal of Asian Studies
Journal of Japanese Studies
Oriental Economist
Pacific Affairs
Social Science Japan Journal

Index

Notes: Japanese names are indexed with the family name first as is custom in Japan; Pl. = Plate

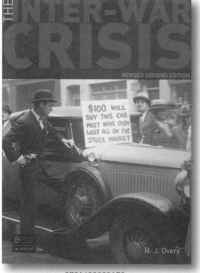

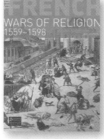